Health Informatics

This series is directed to healthcare professionals leading the transformation of healthcare by using information and knowledge. For over 20 years, Health Informatics has offered a broad range of titles: some address specific professions such as nursing, medicine, and health administration; others cover special areas of practice such as trauma and radiology; still other books in the series focus on interdisciplinary issues, such as the computer based patient record, electronic health records, and networked healthcare systems. Editors and authors, eminent experts in their fields, offer their accounts of innovations in health informatics. Increasingly, these accounts go beyond hardware and software to address the role of information in influencing the transformation of healthcare delivery systems around the world. The series also increasingly focuses on the users of the information and systems: the organizational, behavioral, and societal changes that accompany the diffusion of information technology in health services environments.

Developments in healthcare delivery are constant; in recent years, bioinformatics has emerged as a new field in health informatics to support emerging and ongoing developments in molecular biology. At the same time, further evolution of the field of health informatics is reflected in the introduction of concepts at the macro or health systems delivery level with major national initiatives related to electronic health records (EHR), data standards, and public health informatics.

These changes will continue to shape health services in the twenty-first century. By making full and creative use of the technology to tame data and to transform information, Health Informatics will foster the development and use of new knowledge in healthcare.

Arlen Meyers
Editor

Digital Health Entrepreneurship

Second Edition

 Springer

Editor
Arlen Meyers
School of Medicine
University of Colorado Denver, Anschutz Medical Campus
Denver, CO, USA

ISSN 1431-1917   ISSN 2197-3741   (electronic)
Health Informatics
ISBN 978-3-031-33901-1   ISBN 978-3-031-33902-8   (eBook)
https://doi.org/10.1007/978-3-031-33902-8

This Springer imprint is published by the registered company Springer Nature Switzerland AG
The registered company address is: Gewerbestrasse 11, 6330 Cham, Switzerland

Contents

Chapter 1
Introduction to Digital Health Entrepreneurship

Sharon Wulfovich and Arlen Meyers

Overview and Importance of Digital Health Entrepreneurship

Digital health entrepreneurship is the pursuit of opportunity under conditions of uncertainty with the goal of creating user defined value through the deployment of digital health innovations. It is the pursuit of information and communication technologies (including telemedicine, wearables, mobile health and data analytics) to transform the medical field with the goal of improving patient outcomes, increasing quality of health care, improving the health professional experience and reducing costs. Using this quadruple aim framework, we will discuss how digital health entrepreneurship has the potential and opportunity to greatly improve the U.S. health care system.

In terms of improving patient outcomes, there is always room for improvement. Digital health technologies have the potential to not only measure patient outcomes in in more diverse and complete ways but also simultaneously improve patient outcomes. There are many current examples that illustrate this potential including multiple studies on the impact of telehealth on chronic conditions. For example, multiple studies have shown that telehealth can improve outcomes in patients with congestive heart failure [1–4]. A systematic review that analyzed 14 randomized controlled trials with a total of 4264 patients found that remote monitoring systems decreased hospital readmission rates by 21% and all-cause mortality by 20% [5]. This provides evidence for the use of telehealth on improving patient outcomes. Additional telemonitoring technology and other telehealth technologies need to be created, accepted and used in order to continue improving patient outcomes.

S. Wulfovich
UC San Diego, School of Medicine, La Jolla, CA, USA

A. Meyers (✉)
University of Colorado School of Medicine, Society of Physician Entrepreneurs, Denver, CO, USA
e-mail: Arlen.Meyers@ucdenver.edu

© The Author(s), under exclusive license to Springer Nature Switzerland AG 2023
A. Meyers (ed.), *Digital Health Entrepreneurship*, Health Informatics,
https://doi.org/10.1007/978-3-031-33902-8_1

There are many factors that influence the quality of health care. The growing physician shortage greatly impacts access and as a result the current and future quality of health care. According to the 2018 report by the Association of American Medical Colleges (AAMC), there may be a shortage of up to 120,000 physicians in the United States by 2030 [6]. Digital health entrepreneurship has the potential to lower the effect of this shortage on health care. For example, the application My GI Health (My Total Health) (https://mygi.health) is a digital health platform that systematically compiles patient reported gastrointestinal symptom data and turns it into a report for the physician to read before seeing the patient. This allows the clinic visit to become more focused on addressing the problem versus collecting patient information [7]. A cross-sectional study compared the identification of risk factors by the My GI Health algorithm to those of physicians and found that the algorithm was able to identify a greater quantity of risk factors [8]. This shows that there can be great value in using digital health platforms and checklists. It could reduce the time needed for each patient and allow physicians to focus on doctor-patient communication while seeing more patients in a given day. This idea could be scaled to many specialties and used to maximize and improve doctor-patient communication and interactions, increasing the quality of care provided.

Similarly, the growing physician shortage results in an increased burden on all health professionals. Health professionals are overworked and have a high rate of burn out. Digital health entrepreneurship has the potential to improve the health professional experience. The application discussed above, My GI Health (My Total Health), can not only increase the quality of care but also greatly improve the health professional experience. In reducing the amount of time that health professional collect data from patients specifically data that could be accurately and efficiently be located by applications, health professionals can reduce the time needed for each patient. This could allow health professionals to feel less overworked and focus on providing quality care. This is just one example of how new digital health technology could greatly improve the health professional experience.

Healthcare costs are continuing to rise—in 2016 U.S. healthcare expenditures made up 18% of the total GDP or $3.4 trillion [9]. According to the National Health Expenditure Data from the U.S. Centers for Medicare and Medicaid Services (CMS), healthcare spending is projected to increase at an average rate of 5.5% per year (2017–2026), reaching a projected $5.7 trillion by 2026 [10]. Digital health could help lower these increasing costs. For example, the Veterans Health Administration (VHA) initiated a national home telehealth program entitled "Care Coordination/Home Telehealth" (CCHT) [11]. vThis program used health informatics, telehealth, and disease management technologies to allow veterans with chronic conditions to live at home and delay the need for long-term residential care [11]. The data collected over a 4 year period from 17,025 participants demonstrated a 25% decrease in total bed days of care and a 19% decrease in total hospital admissions [11]. The continued growth of this program (over 380,000 enrolled veterans) has resulted in significant financial savings with an average yearly saving ranging from $1238 to $1999 per patient in 2011 [12]. This impact is continuing to grow and illustrates the potential of digital health in lowering health care costs while continuing to provide quality care.

This quadruple aim does not fully illustrate the benefits and importance of digital health entrepreneurship. Digital health entrepreneurship provides other benefits to healthcare industry and population health including bringing new perspectives, empowering individuals, increasing use of preventative medicine, and increasing access to care. Digital health entrepreneurs are not just healthcare providers, cooperation with non-healthcare related is highly common (and sometimes even needed). The increase in communication and collaboration between a diversity of disciplines brings new perspectives and solutions. Digital health empowers individuals with the rise of the do-it-yourself applications and devices. Individuals can now take greater control over their health, by using applications that are convenient and accurate to control or track the progression of an illnesses or simply monitor health. Additionally, these devices may even have an innovative new approach to treatment. It is through these applications and devices, that digital health plays an increasing role in preventative medicine. It can help detect and intervene promptly as well as be used as a tool to improve health. Lastly, digital health is also enabling an increase in access to healthcare for rural and remote communities. Communities where hospitals or clinics are not conveniently accessible can now use telemedicine to get access to care more conveniently.

Recent Trends

Recent trends in digital health entrepreneurship highlight the growing acceptance of digital health as well as areas of improvement. They include:

1. **Stable levels of investment and new investment vehicles**—Investors are becoming more confident in the digital health sector, Quarter 1 of 2018, marked the largest Quarter 1 for digital health with $1.62 Billion invested in 77 digital health deals [13].
2. **Technologies are being applied to medicine**—Social media, blockchain, artificial intelligence, internet of things
3. **Policy and regulatory changes**—Regulations and policies are being changed to hamper or adapt to the dissemination and implementation of digital health innovation. For example, the FDA recently issued the Digital Health Innovation Action Plan [14] and the twenty-first Century Cures Act (Cures Act) [15]. These improved policies allow products to get to patients in a more efficient and timely manner.
4. **Large companies are getting involved**—Apple, Amazon, Google, Facebook, Microsoft
5. **More health IT education**—Education programs are offering more degrees and interdisciplinary courses in digital health entrepreneurship and data science [16]. These programs are being offered both at undergraduate and graduate levels.
6. **Academic medical centers, innovation centers, accelerators, incubators and generators are increasingly emphasizing digital health development and implementation**

7. **The rise of physician entrepreneurs**—Physicians are becoming more involved in early stage start-ups and many medical students are forgoing residency for startup involvement [16].
8. **Digital health clinical trials**—Entrepreneurs are starting to collect evidence of the effectiveness and necessity of their products and services [16, 17]
9. **Increased medical and non-medical collaboration**—Entrepreneurs in the healthcare field are bringing non-healthcare related entrepreneurs to help. Additionally, the complexity of the healthcare industry creates the need for team members with healthcare experience. The vast amount of regulations including HIPAA, FCC, FTC and FDA create many barriers to success. Additionally, the intricate healthcare delivery system contains reimbursement models coupled with various stakeholders. This makes it very challenging to create a functional, compliant and profitable product and especially challenging if there is not a team member with relevant healthcare related experience. The fact that medical and non-medical entrepreneurs are starting to work together has enabled an evolution of regional digital health ecosystems.
10. **Increased comfort in using digital health technologies**—Patients, healthcare providers and individuals are becoming more comfortable using digital health technologies as part of their daily practice.

Barriers and Possible Solutions

Although digital health entrepreneurship has picked up in the past couple of years and continues to grow at a high rate. There are many barriers that digital health entrepreneurship faces. Here are some highlights and possible solutions:

1. **Physicians as Entrepreneurs**—There are many persistent barriers for physicians to become entrepreneurs including: lack of an entrepreneurial mindset; lack of courage to persist with an entrepreneurial venture; lack of knowledge (intellectual property, business development, funding, recruiting team members, FDA clearance etc.); poor innovation culture; lack of recognition; anti-entrepreneurial culture of education and training; high opportunity costs and risk management [18].

   Possible Solutions: developing social support and mentorship networks, increasing early-on education about entrepreneurship and innovation

2. **Targeting multiple stakeholders**—the healthcare industry is constantly dependent and intertwined with multiple stakeholders (patients, providers, payers, partners etc.). Therefore, it is very challenging to simple target one stakeholder without making sure that the other stakeholders also see value for the given product or service.

Possible Solutions: create fully integrated solutions that fulfill the needs of multiple stakeholders; understand every stakeholders point of view

3. **Security and privacy**—Privacy and security are very important concerns for the healthcare industry. A recent national survey, the eighth Annual Industry Pulse Survey from Change Healthcare and HealthCare Executive Group, found that for about half of the organizations surveyed, privacy and security concerns were the leading factor on why adoption of these technologies was not more extensive [19].

    Possible Solutions: make it a priority, lots of trials

4. **Risk adverse nature of the health industry**—In order to ensure quality patient care, the health industry is naturally very risk adverse. This results in a lot of oversight and the hurdles that come with it. Entrepreneurs need to worry about satisfying the FDA, FCC, HIPPA, FTC etc.

    Possible Solutions: Consider the risks early on in product development; clinical trials and evidence go a long way

5. **Successful Implementation into Clinical Practice**—Healthcare Providers May Not Have all the Information that they Require to Know whether to Recommend or Use a Given Digital Health technology in a Given Scenario

    Possible Solution: Communication with healthcare providers on the scenarios when to recommend or use a given digital health technology, create better knowledge exchange programs

The New Era of Medicine

We are entering the new digital era of medicine where telemedicine, virtual reality, robotics, smart phones, and other technological advancements are slowly becoming part of regular healthcare practices. Digital health technology offers a way to change many of the current issues that the U.S. healthcare system faces. However, there is an urgent need for entrepreneurs, both in the healthcare field and non-related fields, to challenge the status quo, work together and forge ahead. As discussed, digital health entrepreneurship has many benefits. It has the potential to transform the medical field by improving patient outcomes, increasing quality of health care and reducing costs (specifically long-term costs).

This book provides an overview of a large variety of topics ranging from artificial intelligence to regulatory affairs in digital health with the aim of helping digital health technologists, entrepreneurs, health care providers, investors, service providers and other stakeholders transform the healthcare system.

References

1. Antonicelli R, Testarmata P, Spazzafumo L, Gagliardi C, Bilo G, Valentini M, et al. Impact of telemonitoring at home on the management of elderly patients with congestive heart failure. J Telemed Telecare. 2008;14:300–5.
2. Dang S, Dimmick S, Kelkar G. Evaluating the evidence base for the use of home telehealth remote monitoring in elderly with heart failure. Telemed J E Health. 2009;15:783–96.
3. Kvedar J, Coye MJ, Everett W. Connected health: a review of technologies and strategies to improve patient care with telemedicine and telehealth. Health Aff (Millwood). 2014;33:194–9.
4. Polisena J, Tran K, Cimon K, Hutton B, McGill S, Palmer K, Scott RE. Home telemonitoring for congestive heart failure: a systematic review and meta-analysis. J Telemed Telecare. 2010;16:68–76.
5. Clark RA, Inglis SC, McAlister FA, Cleland JGF, Stewart S. Telemonitoring or structured telephone support programmes for patients with chronic heart failure: systematic review and meta-analysis. Br Med J. 2007;334:942–5.
6. Association of American Medical Colleges. The complexities of physician supply and demand: projections from 2016 to 2030. 2018. https://aamc-black.global.ssl.fastly.net/production/media/filer_public/85/d7/85d7b689-f417-4ef0-97fb-ecc129836829/aamc_2018_workforce_projections_update_april_11_2018.pdf.
7. Almario CV. The effect of digital health technology on patient care and research. Gastroenterol Hepatol (N Y). 2017;13:437–9.
8. Almario CV, Chey WD, Iriana S, Dailey F, Robbins K, Patel AV, et al. Computer versus physician identification of gastrointestinal alarm features. Int J Med Inform. 2015;84:1111–7.
9. Reid TR. How we spend $3,400,000,000,000. The Atlantic. 2017; https://www.theatlantic.com/health/archive/2017/06/how-we-spend-3400000000000/530355/
10. Centers for Medicare and Medicaid Services. NHE Fact Sheet. 2018. https://www.cms.gov/research-statistics-data-and-systems/statistics-trends-and-reports/nationalhealthexpenddata/nhe-fact-sheet.html. Accessed 27 July 2018.
11. Darkins A, Ryan P, Kobb R, Foster L, Edmonson E, Wakefield B, Lancaster AE. Care coordination/home telehealth: the systematic implementation of health informatics, home telehealth, and disease management to support the care of veteran patients with chronic conditions. Telemed J E Health. 2008;14:1118–26.
12. Darkins A. Experience of the VA and IHS. In: The role of telehealth in an evolving health care environment: workshop summary; 2012. p. 99–113.
13. Zweig M, Tran D. Q1 2018: funding keeps climbing as digital health startups double down on validation. 2018. https://rockhealth.com/reports/q1-2018-funding-keeps-climbing-as-digital-health-startups-double-down-on-validation/. Accessed 6 Aug 2018.
14. U.S. Food and Drug Administration. Digital health innovation action plan. 2017. https://www.fda.gov/downloads/MedicalDevices/DigitalHealth/UCM568735.pdf.
15. U.S. Food and Drug Administration. 21st Century Cures Act. 2016.
16. Zajicek H, Meyers A. Digital health entrepreneurship. In: Rivas H, Wac K, editors. Digital health: scaling healthcare to the world. Berlin: Springer; 2018. p. 271–88.
17. Meyers A. Recent trends in digital health entrepreneurship. 2017a. https://www.linkedin.com/pulse/recent-trends-digital-health-entrepreneurship-arlen-meyers-md-mba. Accessed 6 Aug 2018.
18. Meyers A. Barriers to physician entrepreneurship. 2017b. https://www.linkedin.com/pulse/barriers-physician-entrepreneurship-arlen-meyers-md-mba/. Accessed 6 Aug 2018.
19. Change Healthcare. Change healthcare releases 8th annual industry pulse report. 2018. https://www.prnewswire.com/news-releases/change-healthcare-releases-8th-annual-industry-pulse-report-300596765.html. Accessed 6 Aug 2018.

Chapter 2
Driving Outcomes-Digital Health Business Model Innovation

Jeffrey M. Nathanson

Driving Outcomes-Digital Health Business Model Innovation

This is a unique time for healthcare and digital health entrepreneurs. New demands have been layered on top of long standing system challenges to deliver cost effective quality healthcare.

Various healthcare components are seeking internally or externally developed innovations to achieve this valued outcome. New interventions and new business models are required to deliver these new value propositions sustainably.

Our society has been threatened by one of the most pervasive, painful health emergencies of our lifetimes. We are years past the initial discovery of COVID-19. Along with the immediate catastrophic health impacts, the global pandemic wrought dramatic and widespread tsunamis of change, testing the healthcare status quo, our health priorities and values. Our definition of what constitutes physical and mental health, how our system delivers care, are all being questioned and are ripe for disruption through innovation.

Simultaneously, we are attempting to withstand the pandemic's almost knock-out blow to the world's economic health. We are wrestling with numerous complex challenges stemming from inflation and recession. We are grappling with a complex adaptive system (CAS).

These attributes are layered on top of existing fundamental intrinsic challenges for the current system. Throughout these experiences, we have recognized, though we have not yet built a comprehensive and resilient health information and delivery system.

The problems digital health entrepreneurs might solve are enormous and urgent.

J. M. Nathanson (✉)
Strategic Catalysts, LLC, Denver, CO, USA

© The Author(s), under exclusive license to Springer Nature Switzerland AG 2023   7
A. Meyers (ed.), *Digital Health Entrepreneurship*, Health Informatics,
https://doi.org/10.1007/978-3-031-33902-8_2

Pandemic Challenges

The COVID-19 pandemic battered and stress tested the delivery of positive outcomes for physical and mental health. The care system components-networks, workforces and other stakeholders have been challenged in ways never experienced nor anticipated previously. The response to COVID-19 has changed the way consumers and clinicians seek and provide healthcare services. We have learned the value of real time health information systems that inform the delivery of care.

Whole person care, care access, care quality, data driven decision making and value based outcomes are all being re-evaluated and redefined from our recent lived experience with the pandemic. We felt the overwhelming pain and frustration of overworked healthcare staff and burnout. We witnessed grieving family members saying goodbye to failing loved ones through video chat apps. We witnessed end of life rituals postponed or held virtually. We experienced the challenges of insufficient materials and inefficient supply chains. Scheduling, testing and implementing new health innovations like at-home testing in the middle of the siege were novel and challenging. Access to new care protocols, accurate real time public health information and new guidelines were difficult to find even though there has been an increase in the use of electronic health records. The battles against misinformation about the pandemic and therapeutic interventions were daunting. Contact tracing and tracking were unfamiliar terms, yet they were new processes to engage the public to join the fight. Collecting incidence data was complex, rigorous and vexing. Analyzing out of date data to inform real time interventions was frustrating and painful.

These hurdles for delivering care stressed the system for stakeholders and patients during the siege. Now, there is an accelerated quest to deliver new care modalities and build new efficiencies. The pandemic's strains and frustrating experiences have provided insights on the processes and resources needed to reduce the pains of the future. Necessity drives innovation. What have we learned from the experience?

Equitable Whole Person Care

Traversing these health gauntlets was difficult enough, yet, an additional cold hard truth revealed itself. A disproportionate incidence rate of COVID-19 was discovered in low income and specific racial and ethnic groups. Data showed chronic co-morbidities of overweight, diabetes and heart conditions also had high correlation with the incidence of COVID-19. These chronic conditions were more prevalent among lower income groups and people of color-African American and Latino. These factors contributed to greater COVID-19 hospitalization rates and eventually disproportionate death rates.

Unfortunately, these results were not surprising. Disparities and gaps in our economic and health delivery systems have been apparent for years, though insufficiently acknowledged or resolved.

The impacts of chronic disease disparities rendered or exacerbated by the social determinants of health (SDoH) have been tested and confirmed in numerous published research studies. These health disparity drivers include the increased burden of disease, injury, violence or opportunities to achieve optimal health that are experienced by socially disadvantaged populations as defined by race or ethnicity, sex, geographic location, socio-economic status [1]. The conclusions have alarmed some for years. Wrestling these complex issues has not been sufficiently publicized, accepted, pursued, nor resolved. The epic COVID-19 health emergency though, has intensified and amplified the shrill alarm.

Inclusive, whole person public health interventions that improve clinical (physical and behavioral) and social health outcomes is a new goal.

A Digital Divide

These health disparities including digital inequities added to the widely permeating distrust from previous healthcare experiences for communities of color. The lack of access to broadband services, limited digital device ownership, and low computer literacy all constrain the inclusive delivery of digitally enabled whole person continuum of care. Health delivery enhanced through digital transformation (digital health) for some, may further exacerbate existing gaps for patients left behind.

Despite these challenges, consumer's overall acceptance and demand for digital-first health solutions has increased dramatically. We have seen increased adoption rates for digital products and services. Dr. Estaban Lopez, Google HCLS Market Lead America, shared in a personal conversation July 2022, searches on Google reached 1 billion per day during the height of the pandemic. We saw an increase in the utilization of digital health contact tracing aps and the apps supporting at home testing for COVID-19.

COVID-19 created the necessity for real time digital information, mobile contact and communications processes, community engagement, digital health passports. non-contact, efficient ways to access care remotely enhancing the adoption of virtual care like Telehealth.

Mental Health-The Next Pandemic

Strong emotions generated by the pandemic-uncertainty, fear, isolation and loneliness have all rendered another pandemic in the offing, stressed societal and personal mental health. The broader healthcare system is working toward delivering sustainable care at scale to targeted and mass markets. To achieve goals for behavioral health delivery system segments though, efficiencies from digital tools will be needed. Many reports indicate aggregated behavioral health resources, referral processes, and scheduling assistance will be enhanced by digital resources scaling telehealth audio, video or combined services. Even before the pandemic, mental health support smart phone apps including wellbeing and meditation facilitation were marketed and downloaded. We are now seeing more and more behavioral health platforms and marketplaces that aggregate provider panels to assist patients gain access to the care they need in an efficient and cost effective process.

Who is going to develop these solutions? Government sets policy though will not, by itself, solve these care delivery challenges. Larger industry components may recognize these opportunities, but will they disrupt themselves? Will they strive for lower costs while attempting to maintain profit? Research institutions will not bring solutions to these problems to market. A new perspective is required to resolve many challenges. This is a unique time for entrepreneurs.

New Care Delivery Modalities

Telehealth[2, 3]

Prior to COVID-19, virtual visits had far less market penetration compared to in-person medical interventions. There were concerns about the quality of virtual health visits. Was there sufficient patient doctor connection for a diagnosis? Was there reimbursement for the encounter at sufficient parity?

Concern over viral disease transmission and contactless care options during the apex of the pandemic in 2020 increased consumer and physician adoption of live virtual telemedicine substantially. Of physicians surveyed in 2020, 64% viewed telehealth more favorably than before COVID-19 [2].

Vaccines and therapeutics have reduced disease severity. The pandemic is moving to an endemic stage of disease management. In person visits are being encouraged. Virtual visits subsequently have decreased, though the volume remains substantially higher than before COVID-19. In 2021, only 58% of surveyed physicians viewed telehealth more favorably than before COVID-19. Two thirds of consumer survey participants reported accessing live telemedicine through their clinicians as opposed to insurance, employer or other service [2].

Several studies recognized the value of telehealth for personal care and overcoming the divide in equitable delivery of care. There are now enhanced criteria including health equity metrics for qualifying and adopting digital health tools and interventions. Overall health outcomes coupled with social determinant outcomes are now key considerations. Equitable design processes aiding digital health tools development are an increased focus. More than ever design, development and integration into the healthcare work environment and standard workflows are now all product considerations.

Health efficacy and reduced disparities are the new goals for demonstrating health equity for socially disadvantaged patient populations.

According to the U.S Centers for Disease Control (CDC),

Health equity is achieved when every person has the opportunity to "attain his or her full health potential" and no one is "disadvantaged from achieving this potential because of social position or other socially determined circumstances." Health inequities are reflected in differences in length of life; quality of life; rates of disease, disability, and death; severity of disease; and access to treatment [4].

Two prestigious reports, "The Future of Telehealth Roundtable" from the National Committee for Quality Assurance (NCQA) and the Harvard Business Review (HBR)'s "The Telehealth Era Is Just Beginning" promoted equitable access to telehealth resources in a post-pandemic world.

The Telehealth Roundtable identified three key strategies to promote equitable access in telehealth delivery:

- Tailoring telehealth services that cater to personal patient preferences and needs, as some individuals face struggles due to their primary language and socioeconomic status
- Addressing regulatory, policy and infrastructure barriers to access and changing regulations to allow fair telehealth access and expanded provider eligibility for licensure
- Leveraging Telehealth and Digital Technologies to Promote Equitable Care Delivery [5].

The HBR article explored the post COVID-19 telehealth marketplace based on health improvements delivered previously at reduced costs within two preeminent healthcare systems, Kaiser Permanente and Intermountain Health Systems. The authors projected use cases for telehealth and remote patient monitoring deploying value propositions generated recently for their two organizations. Combined with policy suggestions, they projected the substantial value the entire Healthcare Delivery system might capture if virtual care were adopted and deployed throughout.

The article presents five substantial market opportunities that wider telehealth utilization could generate:

- A reduction in expensive, unnecessary ER visits through greater disease management focus.
- An improvement in timeliness and efficiency of specialty care
- Access to the best doctors
- A reversal of America's chronic-disease crisis
- Mitigation of health care disparities [3].

Telehealth Reimbursement

The rapid adoption of these new care modalities has also included changing reimbursement regulations for virtual visits. The U.S. House of Representatives Bill 4040 to extend reimbursement passed in July 2022. The bill will allow beneficiaries to receive telehealth services at any site regardless of type. If passed by the

U.S. Senate this would extend services through January 2025. Through the pandemic, CMS reimbursed for digital, video and audio only services [6]. Entrepreneurs, new market entrants, retail giants, select incumbents and tech players like Amazon and Google are offering various telehealth products in all 50 states.

Federal Requirement Drivers-Key to Enhancing Digital Health

There are several other key drivers promoted by the federal government that are enhancing the adoption of digital health products. The Interoperability and Patient Access final rule (CMS-9115-F) gives patients access to their health information when they need it most and in a way, they can best use it. The MyHealthEData initiative, focused on driving interoperability and patient access to health information by liberating patient data using CMS authority to regulate Medicare Advantage (MA), Medicaid, CHIP, and Qualified Health Plan (QHP) issuers on the Federally-facilitated Exchanges (FFEs) [7].

Lack of seamless data exchange in healthcare has historically detracted from patient care, leading to poor health outcomes, and higher costs. The CMS Interoperability and Patient Access final rule establishes policies that break down barriers in the nation's health system to enable better patient access to their health information, improve interoperability and unleash innovation, while reducing burden on payers and providers. Patients and their healthcare providers will have the opportunity to be more informed, which can lead to better care and improved patient outcomes, while at the same time reducing burden. In a future where data flows freely and securely between payers, providers, and patients, we can achieve truly coordinated care, improved health outcomes, and reduced costs [8].

> *CMS has also mandated a new Patient Access API*: CMS-regulated payers, specifically MA organizations, Medicaid Fee-for-Service (FFS) programs, Medicaid managed care plans, CHIP FFS programs, CHIP managed care entities, and QHP issuers on the FFEs, excluding issuers offering only Stand-alone dental plans (SADPs) and QHP issuers offering coverage in the Federally-facilitated Small Business Health Options Program (FF-SHOP), are required to implement and maintain a secure, standards-based (HL7 FHIR Release 4.0.1) API that allows patients to easily access their claims and encounter information, including cost, as well as a defined sub-set of their clinical information through third-party applications of their choice [8].

The purpose of the new CMS Rule is to support seamless and secure access, exchange, and use of electronic health information. More specifically, hospitals, including psychiatric hospitals and Critical Access Hospitals (CAHs), are required to send electronic patient event notifications of a patient's admission, discharge, and/or transfer (ADT) to care coordination by empowering providers to proactively reach out to their patients to ensure proper follow-up care after a medical emergency [8].

Venture Capital Investment in Digital Health 2020, 2021

If investment in an entrepreneurial segment is an indication of opportunity, digital health continues to acquire funding at record pace for a new market segment. Year over year investment funding continues to increase. This funding growth demonstrates a maturing market and stability. Investors continue to see value created and product adoption.

According to Rock Health's annual year-end report, digital health funding among US-based startups soared to a record $29.1 billion across 729 deals in 2021.With an average deal size of $39.9 million, 2021 also saw 88 digital health deals over $100 million. Although biopharma and medtech R&D held the top funding slot, mental health and diabetes interventions had increases in funding. Two new sectors emerged with financing, digital health infrastructure and interoperability startups had increases in acquired capital, securing $2.2 billion across 40 deals. Overall the healthcare marketplace experienced a 3.2X year-over-year funding growth in 2021 according to Rock Health's analysis [9, 10]. StartUp Health in their assessment of investment during the first half of 2022, tracked $16 B in investment [11].

This figure is in line with previous investment trends for healthcare marketplaces and more broadly multi-sided health platforms. The pandemic reinforced the power of digital marketplaces, their ability to connect and match previously disparate parties and facilitate timely transactions-for example matching clinical talent with facilities in need [10].

Given this level of venture investment digital health is one of the fastest growing segments in the VC universe. There is an acceleration in scale, income growth and acquisitions. There is an engagement in the broader consumer and enterprise software offerings. Nationwide scale in years not decades, is the new timeline for tech companies.

> …Companies that take in Capital without investing in infrastructure, business model innovation, or talent and leadership are headed for tough future quarters to meet the expectations that come with high valuations [9].

Growing Direct to Consumer Market

Community members and patients were anxious to have readily available at home remote testing. The government, payers and healthcare delivery providers accepted and promoted direct to consumer COVID-19 sampling and testing channel to overcome congestion at public mass testing and vaccination centers. The intent was to enhance convenience and greater vaccine adoption rates. Often these tests were administered with a smartphone app. The public's health literacy was tested though enhanced. New bio-medical science concepts like antigen and anti-body testing, therapeutics and contact tracing were introduced to a broader public understanding.

Our experience with this pandemic, has provided greater awareness of the steps to researching and adopting new therapeutic interventions. Through our experience, we have learned more about vaccine research, monoclonal antibodies, RNA vaccines and boosters, clinical trials, disease variants and rapid digital enabled, home based testing.

According to a recent reported study "Policy changes, aging patients and coverage cutbacks are the primary culprits driving a roughly 10% continual annual growth rate in out-of-pocket healthcare payments, according to recent market projections." The study by Kalorama Information reported nearly $500B in consumer out-of-pocket healthcare expenditures. Consumers have become a major payor of sorts [12, 13].

Even before COVID-19, with shrinking profit margins, employers have been unwilling to support increasing employee health plan costs. Just less than half of our population is covered under employer sponsored health insurance, and this percentage is declining. More employers are considering providing employees fixed yearly health stipends to allow them to purchase their own benefit packages. Consumers, whether part of an employee health plan or an individual purchased plan, are challenged with greater responsibility for their health and payment for any cost increases.

Study after study has determined, regardless of whether the costs are insurance premiums, copayments, deductibles for employer, direct consumer purchased health plans or self-pay, consumers are shouldering increased costs. All varieties of "health system" components are shifting this increased healthcare cost burden and the responsibility for health to the patient [14–17]. For the first time, consumers, the users of health services, are responsible and increasingly engaged with how they use health services as they become patients. It has been difficult to gain the benefit of behavioral economics when someone else pays for the costs of healthcare, like employers or insurance companies. A change to the payment formula is needed. Is opportunity hiding?

Most healthcare experts acknowledge unhealthy behaviors are healthcare cost drivers for upwards to 80% of all healthcare costs from a variety of chronic medical conditions like diabetes, hypertension, cardiovascular disease and the impact of overweight or smoking. Considering the variety of healthcare service components requiring increased participation from consumers, patients are key targets for greater engagement. A key question remains, are consumers willing to pay for the value of maintaining their health? Are they willing to have a more proactive role in maintaining healthy behaviors as the data points to potential increased reduction in costs?

Healthcare System Needs

Data analytics, and AI have taken center stage combing through troves of data and organizing supply chains of personal protective equipment (PPE) or ventilators. AI systems were placed in overdrive to identify, analyze, monitor and screen COVID-19 data and facilitate drug and vaccine targeting.

Digital transformation has delivered cost reductions, productivity enhancements and efficiency improvements to other industries, like online retail. We have seen engaged consumers driving incredible profitability. Similar improvement gains have been promised for healthcare though the comparable outcomes have not yet been fully realized.

Despite the pandemic, the healthcare system was economically challenged as long term healthcare costs in the United States continue to rise while national health outcomes woefully lag most industrialized nations. The United States has a lower average life expectancy and higher avoidable mortality than other middle and high income countries [18].

Some healthcare delivery systems have profited during the pandemic, others have been stressed financially. Regardless, many can agree that the entire healthcare delivery system is searching for resiliency and sustainability. Demonstrable ROI and efficiency gains are key building block for the adoption of digital resource interventions.

Financial distress partly emanating out of COVID-19 has become a real and medium term threat to many hospital systems nationwide. As of mid 2022, most U.S. hospitals and health systems have survived financially, though under stress. Expenses have remained high from supply chain challenges, inflation and labor shortage pressures. Operating margins are in the red, significantly lower than pre-pandemic levels [19].

Overcoming Staffing Shortages

Hospital systems are feeling the pain of competing for workers in the aftermath of the pandemic. Housekeeping and food service staff are in great demand by the hospitality sector-hotels and restaurants. At the center of the workforce challenge though is the shortage of clinical staff, particularly nurses. Nurses are the back-bone of the healthcare system. Through the pandemic, they were the tip of the spear caring for patients. Through the siege of COVID-19 they were stressed to burnout.

Although for years, a staffing shortfall has been predicted, the pandemic exacerbated this stark reality. There is now a real nurse staffing crisis. Many nurses battled through exhaustion, despair and fear out of a sense of duty and faith that medical researchers would find ways to combat the disease. Throughout COVID-19 nurses were fatigued, weakened and frustrated and then confronted by the disease's latest resurgence. More and more nurses are leaving healthcare-rapidly.

Nurses, many of the baby boomer generation, left their positions and entered retirement. Some left nursing for a while to spend time with their families. Others sought out less stressful jobs other than acute care. Others have been enticed to accept contracts with temporary and traveling nursing agencies at two to four times their rate of pay and cost to the hospitals. These and other clinical staff member vacancies leave hospitals strained to deliver high quality care [20].

New approaches are needed to overcome these labor shortage challenges. New technology applications and digital solutions are being sought. Can artificial intelligence and machine learning aid in some of the more mundane administrative nursing tasks?

Many hospitals have developed innovation centers and business development units to identify, develop and deploy disruptive and creative innovations that emanate or are tested at their organization. They are exploring how technology can support clinicians and other clinical components to serve at the top of their licensure and relieve more administrative duties. Are there technologies to aid in diagnoses? Can scribes or voice based technologies relieve some of the burden of documentation for these clinicians? [20]

Children's Hospital, Los Angeles (CHLA) has targeted a set of pediatric care problems and challenges they wish to solve using innovative digital solutions. They have engaged and recruited a global ecosystem of pediatric innovators, entrepreneurs and investors to facilitate their multifaceted strategy to develop, test and adopt internally and externally generated innovations. A personal conversation August 30, 2022 with Omkar Kulkarni, MPH, Chief Digital Transformation Officer and Chief Innovation Officer for CHLA revealed some key components. KidsX accelerator works with a consortium of over 40 children's hospitals to support, test early stage digital health products and mentor a cohort of company leaders to achieve product and business model validation. CTIP, the West Coast Consortium for Technology and Innovation in Pediatrics is focused on accelerating medical device product/market fit-assessments, development and adoption.

Geisinger Health System in Pennsylvania, although not an "early adopter" of innovations, established a tele ICU monitoring system prior to COVID-19. Serving patients remotely from a command center, additional health professionals provide monitoring and alert functions, reducing the burden for on-site doctors and nurses. The tele ICU technology analyzes patient data continuously fed from monitors, life support systems, electronic health records and other sources of information.

In the mid 2000's, Geisinger experienced full capacity at Intensive Care Units for several of their hospitals. It was very difficult to hire enough Intensivists and to retain them due to the physician shortage at the time. In response, they deployed tele ICU to remote ICUs that were both in network and outside of the network to ensure all ICU beds were utilized. The original goal was to improve patient safety and the efficiency of delivering care. The initial outcomes achieved have been significant. Published data showed between 29-64% decrease in mortality and a 50 percent decrease in patient length of stay" [21]. After the tele ICU was in place, other uses for telemedicine were developed including inpatient consultation and clinic office visits. The HIPAA compliant telehealth solution provides a two way, audio/video system offered in either a mobile app or technically outfitted clinics.

During the surge of the pandemic, outpatient clinics saw a surge of effort to care for patients remotely. This allowed patient needs and their plan of care to be followed during a period when patients and physicians were trying to care for people who could not or did not want to, come in for a face to face clinic visit.

Susan Fetterman, R.N., MSN, MBA FACHE, former Chief Administrative Officer and Director of Business Strategy for Geisinger Clinic was instrumental in developing the tele ICU program and is a leader in the telehealth innovation field.

Queried on the fervent search for post COVID-19 innovations, she observed in a personal conversation August 17, 2022, "the pandemic drove the *'why'* and the *'how'* to implement digital health products…The innovation space is very busy right now."

Finance leaders in hospitals, medical practices and health systems are now leveraging the best technologies they can acquire to optimize their operations, facilities management, patient communications and revenue cycle management systems. There is an emphasis on increasing efficiency and overcoming the waste in the system. Are there technologies to improve coding? Are there bots and assistant systems that can help automate phone calls prior to a nurse intervention. Are there technologies to support patient self-scheduling and service? [20]

Throughout the industry, there is a search for alternative sources of revenue and above all a readjustment of perspective on resiliency planning. There is a search for technologies to overcome manual functions better served digitally. With rote functions managed through digital resources, staff team members can focus on other attributes of instability and unpredictability going forward into the future.

Longstanding National Market Conditions

On top of the acute economic impact the pandemic has leveled for U.S. healthcare, costs have continued to rise despite our recognition that most activities supporting health happen outside of the clinic and hospital walls. Numerous researchers have estimated the relative impact on healthcare from health behaviors, social, and environmental factors on health outcomes. The pandemic has demonstrated the weightiness of these factors. While these researchers have used different methodologies to estimate the relative weight of these factors, health (clinical care) is estimated to account for anywhere from 10 to 27 percent of health outcomes, while health behaviors and socio-economic factors are estimated to account for 60 to 85 percent of health outcomes.

Despite the pandemic, year after year, healthcare costs in the United States have increased while our health outcomes are worse than most industrialized nations. We spend close to $4.3 trillion annually [22], or $12,530 per person in 2020, accounting for over 19.6% of our National Gross Domestic Product (GDP) [23]. The percentage of the population with health insurance peaked at 91.1% in 2022 [24].

According to the Kaiser Family Foundation roughly 49% of the U.S population have health insurance through their employers [25]. Employers originally provided healthcare to attract and retain employees-enhancing their productivity and health as a benefit for their families. As a result, the consumers of healthcare services did not fully pay for it. Without cost considerations, consumers used their health services. Concurrently, providers of health services could sell them at reasonable margins. We have now reached a tipping point. Cost increases are no longer sustainable for consumers, employers, payers, providers or healthcare delivery systems.

With the endemic, the cost containment imperative has never been more pronounced. Engaged healthcare players for the last several years including state and federal government have all sought cost saving measures. The National Academy of Sciences, Institute of Medicine in 2012 recommended adopting new efficiency measures and information technologies to reduce costs by upwards to one third [26]. A few years earlier the Institute for Healthcare Improvement developed and promoted the *"triple aim"-high patient satisfaction, quality; improved health outcomes and reduced costs* as an assessment tool to measure the value of new health interventions [27].

Electronic Health Records (EHRs) originally funded by the 2009 HITECH Act were a parallel attempt to improve health delivery efficiency and lower costs. Actual use though, added new administrative burdens for physicians and nurses dramatically decreasing provider satisfaction. Along with nurses, physicians are retiring at a rapid pace. The greying provider workforce, private practice consolidation throughout the industry and decreased patient interaction while using these electronic tools have revealed *a fourth required aim in addition to the other three-the quadruple aim- provider satisfaction.*

Now, along with customer design and development, integration into the healthcare work environment and standard workflows are all now considerations. Not only are impacts on overall health considered but also social determinant outcomes. *A fifth goal is demonstrating health efficacy and reduced health disparities for socially disadvantaged patient populations.*

Entrenched healthcare market incumbents have little incentive to disrupt the system. They are aware of the market requirements for cost reduction. Without incentives, though, these current "system" members have no reason to help "decrease the cost curve." Will a passionate digital health entrepreneur find a solution that delivers the desired *quintuple aim*?

This is a unique time for healthcare solutions. COVID-19 and market indicators point to an increased need for new approaches that deliver these *multifaceted aims*. Digital interventions have clearly impacted other industries, through cost reductions, productivity enhancements and efficiency improvements. Mobile phones, texting, facetiming, streaming and social media have all seen significant ubiquitous adoption and engagement.

These same processes and systems might positively impact the delivery of healthcare services in a sustainable fashion. Now with the experience of COVID-19, digital entrepreneurs have significant opportunities to intervene with demonstrable virtual care cost efficiency, high consumer satisfaction; improved equitable quality and improved health outcomes across the entire population base with more data analysis informing decisions.

Healthcare Is Ripe for Disruption. It Is Hard, Not Impossible. Yet, Where Do We Start?

Generally, the costs for starting a business have decreased, aided by digital products and systems. With more and more startups, there is increased competition for financing and market share. Speed to market and lower customer acquisition costs are all key elements for startup competitive advantage. There are now tested tools and systems to better target the "pain" of potential customers and determine if a proposed solution has traction. There are new methodologies to assess customer personas and analyze the specific sub tasks and processes needing improvement within a system like healthcare. If we use the National Academy of Sciences study as a benchmark there is a close to a trillion dollars of wasted expenditures in healthcare to finance these new approaches.

Although still striving for significant market penetration, we have seen all the major tech companies, Amazon, Google, Apple, Oracle, SAP and even Uber introduce products and services to disrupt the delivery of health. They are focused on transforming healthcare taking advantage of their relentless focus on consumer experience to create new solutions for the greater market. To be sure, whoever enters the digital health marketplace will use many of the tools and processes highlighted below.

Healthcare-A Complex Adaptive System

Understanding the Healthcare (Health) marketplace landscape is difficult, though not impossible. Healthcare is a complex adaptive system (CAS). With its unique properties, it generates wicked problems like childhood obesity, toxic stress, the need for integrated mental health, data liquidity, affordable housing and other social determinants. Government has tried to understand the system and wrestle some of these wicked problems. We have learned though, it is complicated. Government sets policy. Incumbents and other large industry components may identify these opportunities, but will they disrupt themselves? They are geared to grow. Will they strive for lower costs while attempting to increase margins to grow profit? Research institutions will not bring solutions for these problems to market. A new perspective is required. This is a unique time for entrepreneurs.

For an entrepreneur seeking opportunity within the system, understanding the complex system of health is required. What are the components of the complex adaptive system? What are the wicked problems? How are these wicked problems generated? How are they wrestled to efficiency?

Complex Adaptive Systems (CAS) are dynamic and non-linear. There are a wide variety of elements in the system. There are independent agents each with their own goals and behaviors. These behaviors are likely to change, evolve and conflict. One agent's action, process or function can change the context for the others. The agents respond in unpredictable ways, either innovatively, creatively or in error. They are part of a living system. The whole is not the sum of the parts. A key trait of a CAS is they lack a single system point of control. There is no single actor in charge. The individual components are not always linked in a system. Sometimes, the components are self-organizing into a collection of individual strands of value generation delivering health with the constraints of the components within the adjacency of the rest of the system. The healthcare CAS as a result is unpredictable. Throughout the CAS, various segments create value throughout the created supply chain. Yet, each of the components are usually dependent on health and cost outcomes generated by other individual component performances rather than operating as an integrated whole.

As a result, wicked problems arise and are entrenched in complex adaptive systems. A problem doesn't achieve wicked status just because it's large or difficult though. Building a skyscraper is a huge and complicated problem. Deriving the field equations for Einstein's Theory of General Relativity is extraordinarily hard to do. But neither of these problems are wicked problems. "Wickedness" is not merely a matter of degree of difficulty. First outlined by two University of California, Berkeley professors in 1973, wicked problems elude description and defy solution [28]. Wicked problems stem from numerous causes, spread in every direction and tend to become entangled with other wicked problems. What's worse, conventional approaches usually just make things worse. They can be a societal scourge, such as poverty, or a seemingly more specific problem, like health data liquidity, homelessness or Alzheimer's disease.

Discovering Opportunity Within Healthcare Wicked Problems

How would an entrepreneur start? Where would you begin to address this unique need for disruption of a strand or an entire huge health system while gaining a defensible market opportunity? Entrepreneurs have the potential to turn their products into great opportunities yet, it often takes process, methodology and focus.

Gaining insight on the components by mapping the complex adaptive system and the customer problems are key steps in the process. How would an entrepreneur whiteboard map the system? What are the associations between actors? What are the constellation of actors and their various interactions? What are the various enablers or inhibitors for each of the segments? Where are the various points of greatest pain or friction that customers wish to resolve?

While mapping the healthcare CAS, the entrepreneur must identify the key stakeholders (see Fig. 2.1). Who are the customers experiencing the pain and how will they pay for the solution? Are there feedback loops that influence the actors? Once the CAS components and relationships are mapped, there are specific tools, processes, and powerful communities needed to turn the identified healthcare problems into large opportunities for impact and ROI. A systems approach to solutions is necessary.

Fig. 2.1 Mapping health

Start with the Problem

If we compare the various highlighted processes, wicked problems will most likely be more difficult to analyze and map than individual jobs to be done. They tend to require a systematic approach to finding a path to solution, ROI and impact-delivering the *quintuple aim*.

Tom Higley, another successful serial entrepreneur and angel investor founded 10.10.10. The organization was built on the premise that entrepreneurs can change the world for the better by focusing exclusively on turning wicked problems into entrepreneurial opportunities.

To be effective, Higley argues that startup founders and teams need to gain deeper understanding of the requirements for solutions and potential value creation they might develop and control. With his team, Higley developed a 10-day program for 10 recruited and vetted serial entrepreneurs, to unpack 10 wicked problems in a vertical segment by developing market based solutions.

Higley advises startup founders to begin with a problem they care about. He suggests entrepreneurs start with a customer they care about with a problem they care about. Higley recently tweeted all customers have problems; all problems have solutions. Yet, not all solutions have problems, and not all problems have customers (Higley 2017) [29–31]. This may become a mantra for digital health entrepreneurs.

Jan Ground PT, MBA and retired Director of Virtual Care at Kaiser Permanente Colorado, shared in an August 21, 2022 phone call, "I always focus on the quantifiable problem the company is trying to solve internally or externally. A critical factor for effective digital implementation is the interoperability with the EMR in a single click."

Innovating Business Models

Startup tools and systems are available to help determine potential customers' pain, test and validate the viability of a proposed solution. There are tools for customer discovery and development, and resolving lean and business model canvases to create new business models.

"Designing toward the North Star of improved outcomes at reduced costs will allow entrepreneurs to embrace business model innovation-and specifically value based care models-regardless of the specific reimbursement codes that may or may not include specific provider-patient care interactions" [9].

Gaining Marketplace Insight

Steve Blank and Eric Ries introduced a new standard process for bringing entrepreneurial opportunities to market [32–35]. First, they recognized startups were not miniature enterprises. Their shared experience and insight as serial entrepreneurs revealed startups were not really, yet in business. They recognized from their own experience with startup failure and success, that most-startups didn't always have a clear understanding of true market needs or customer wants before they spent all their investment funds. Startups, they recognized, were in fact unique search organizations seeking a repeatable and scalable business model. They began to work with Alexander Osterwalder to easily display a business model in a short template [36].

Together with Blank and Ries's insights with Lean Startup methodology, Osterwalder recruited and led a team effort to invent, describe, design, challenge and pivot a business model through the Business Model Canvas. The team recognized a single page broken into nine key components would effectively describe a business model. (see Fig. 2.2 below).

Blank and Ries urged entrepreneurs and eventually investors to forget business plans. They realized that business plans made assumptions about customers that were not correct. Instead they recognized, tested and demonstrated a methodology that increases speed to market focusing on delivering paying customers. They coined the term "lean startup" methodology with unique shortened, iterative product development cycles.

Their goal was to quickly discover and determine market insights regarding the "pain" a prospective customer experiences, first through customer discovery and then a process called customer development. The processes enhanced an entrepreneur's recognition and determination of the (customer's) market pain, the depth of the pain and their willingness to resolve the pain through a purchased or created solution. The methodology includes a design process, hypothesizing a solution, testing the hypotheses, iterating toward the development of an initial product offering and quantifiably testing the startup solution with prospective customers. The

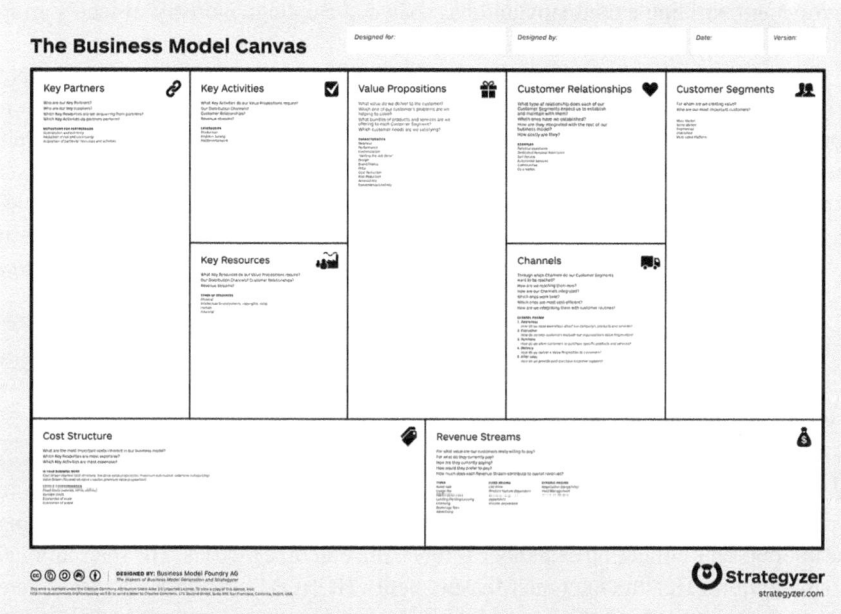

Fig. 2.2 The business model canvas was designed by Strategyzer, AG, https://www.strategyzer.com, Creative Commons Attribution-Share Alike 4.0 Unported License

process focused on iterative product releases validated through data driven learning continuously improving the product/solution offering.

Their process demonstrated finding market interest was best done through a minimum viable product (MVP) a far more agile and effective iterative approach than building a costly prototype to beta test a product. It is a way to fail fast and learn. They urged entrepreneurs to "get out of the building" to speak to prospective customers. Their efforts focused on finding "**product/market fit**" [32–35]. Entrepreneurs and investors have grown to see product/market fit as the match between the customer's needs and the solution the entrepreneur's company is providing.

- Product/market fit is the sought-after prize for early stage startups. When there is alignment with customer needs and the developed solution, customers are so eager to ease their job to be done, they jump at the chance to open their wallets to use what is developed.
- Product/market fit is the magic for digital health startups as well, like Omada, Cirrus MD, Rx Revue, Dispatch Health, Burst IQ and Concert Health.

Blank and Ries shared the Lean Startup Methodology through multiple distribution channels-universities, federal agencies, venture and angel investors, and business accelerators. Steve Blank developed *iCorps* in 2011 with funding from the U.S. National Science Foundation (NSF) to train scientists and engineers in how to commercialize their discoveries. Their process now is a dominant method for starting and building a company and has spawned a cottage industry of lean startup books, workshops and websites.

Testing and validating product/market fit or testing digital health products, there is really no difference. There are other elements determining healthcare fit in addition to the standard consumer requirements. There are heightened expectation levels for product features in healthcare including user interfaces or the quality of user experience, the UI/UX. Healthcare purchase decisions also, have additional elements for purchase and adoption-does it work and is it HIPAA compliant? Does it get the job done, particularly in clinical settings? Does it deliver the *quintuple aim* and can the company deliver those results and document validated outcomes?

Measuring Outcomes

We are experiencing the next wave of electronic health records use. Better and more complete data is being collected to help inform health decisions. We are even seeing the international collection of standards for health outcome metrics. The International Consortium for Health Outcome Measurements, (ICHOM), has created a set of care standards for various conditions and the expected data driven outcomes that matter to patients. All the while they promote tracking the costs per institution required to achieve those expected outcomes. The leaders and founders are the Harvard Business School, Boston Consulting Group and the Karolinska Institutet. They formed after the publishing of Harvard Professor Michael Porter's Book that outlined the argument for using health outcomes data to redefine the nature of competition in health care [37]. Might we see the compensation formula change to one that compensates for value instead of volume?

Digital health provides a key enhancement to increased focus on data collection and data analysis. Huge challenges persist with health data liquidity and the interoperability of health data systems. We are still challenged to secure data and ensure it is tied to a specific identity.

As the digital health market matures there are twinkles of bright shining stars delivering solutions. There is an increased need to go further, to understand the key elements needed to seize more substantial entrepreneurial opportunity in healthcare.

Product Development Innovation

The insights from Blank and Ries added to a product development process that evolved around Stanford University. In the early 1990s a new company IDEO, was formed by a group of designers and product development professionals bringing a key ingredient to many new products developed in Silicon Valley. Design thinking was created, focused on the needs of the customer. A new process for rapid product development and a new cottage industry was created, filled with whiteboards, individual brainstorming, sticky pads, dot voting and filling out templated "artifacts".

With their early success, the IDEO founders brought the idea of a customer centered design training institute to Stanford University. The non-degree oriented Stanford d. School was formed. Customer insight gained from customer interviews informed the customer centered "design thinking" practiced in the new design efforts of IDEO, the Stanford d. School and their minions.

New systems for product development propagated within the Silicon Valley area surrounding the Stanford campus. One of the area spin-out corporate unicorns was Google. The founders, Larry Page and Sergey Brin fostered the development of additional internal design and product development processes, they called them design sprints. Their goal was to build and test prototypes for a product in just five days. They too wanted to fail quickly. They focused on small teams challenged to rapidly progress from problem to tested solution using a proven repeatable step by step process. They cleared participating staff schedules for an entire week to determine how customers react to a product design prior to the investment of time and expense for a completed product.

Testing the process within various Google divisions, Jake Knapp of Google Ventures wrote a step by step cookbook for these sprints [38]. Over the five days, each day there is a targeted sprint process uniquely focused on one of five key steps **Map, Sketch, Decide, Prototype** and **Test**.

Customer Development Innovation

Accurately determining customer pain proved to be challenging though. Sometimes the customers true pain was elusive to the assessment process. How could an entrepreneur ensure they learned candidly from prospective customers their truthful feelings about a product hypothesis or MVP? This became known as the "mom test"-recognizing a mother would often tell you what you wanted to hear rather than a candid, truthful review of your product idea? [39]

Understanding the customer assessment process became a passion for Tony Ulwick, the key product manager for the IBM PC Jr. a computer system-developed and launched with great market acclaim only to be ultimately deemed a market failure, as it missed solving the markets' key needs. Ulwick created the "job to be done" theory to decrease the customer's reporting bias in describing their pain [40].

Together with Harvard University Professor Clayton Christensen, Ulwick postulated innovation was borne on understanding the "job to be done" methodology to discover ways to improve systems and processes for customers. Ulwick hypothesized the assessment of the "job to be done" would uncover key insight within a market segment. Without these prospectives, customer interviews he postulated, were little more than hopeful wandering with unsystematic inquiry that may occasionally turn up interesting tidbits of information. These intellectual wanderings rarely uncover the best ideas or an exhaustive set of opportunities for growth. To aid the process, he developed an outcome driven innovation process.

Ulwick developed a simple system called "job mapping" breaking down the tasks the customer wants completed into a series of discrete process steps. The methodology provided a complete view of the constraints or points of friction a customer might want help in overcoming.

With this process and the insight gained, entrepreneurs can assess the features and benefits most significant and helpful to the customer. Ulwick's methodology provides a comprehensive framework with identified metrics customers themselves use to measure success in executing a task. *This approach would be most appropriate to map the jobs to be done in certain healthcare processes and condition management settings.*

The Business Model Innovation Process Detailed

Capturing Value

Instead of describing a new product or service, business model innovation delineates the innovative processes and rationale for how a business creates, delivers and captures value.

Business model innovation is built on a key first step. How does your business create, deliver and capture value for customers?

Through these design processes, and quantifiable testing the hypothesized solution with prospective customers, the startup entrepreneur gains a clear understanding of their needs and job to be done. The startup aligns its key resources, processes and profit formula toward crafting and delivering their new value proposition. Customer value is the customer's perception of the worth of your product or service. Worth can mean several things: the benefit these products or services provide to the target market, or the value in money they offer for purchase.

The Lean Canvas

Ash Maurya, another entrepreneur and author in pursuit of even greater speed in product development, created another enhanced, yet compatible methodology for raising the odds for success-the Lean Startup [41].

Through insight from his predecessors in Lean Startup methodology and customer development processes, Maurya determined that Osterwalder's Business Model Canvas might be more appropriate for the enterprise than the startup.

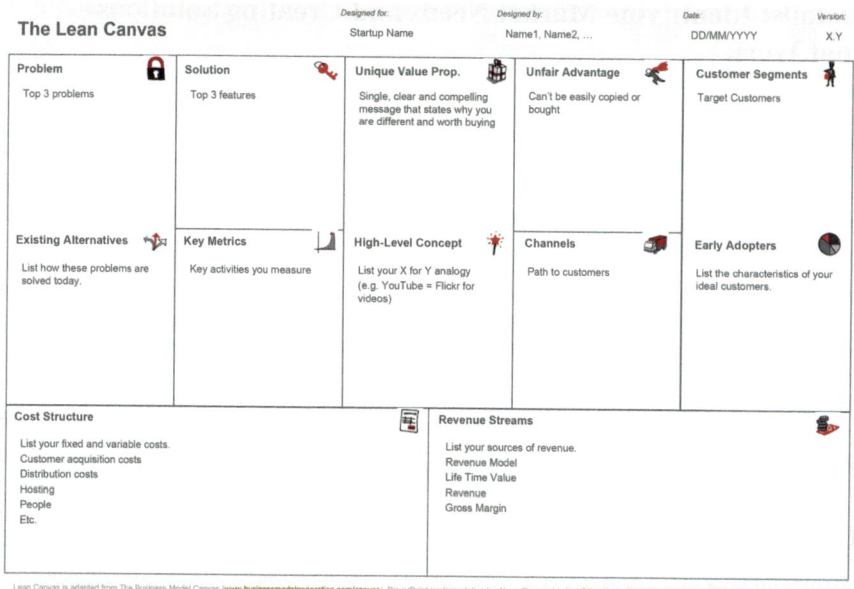

Fig. 2.3 Lean canvas is adapted from the Business Model Canvas, by Ash Maurya of LeanStack, https://blog.leanstack.com/why-lean-canvas-vs-business-model-canvas/ Image implementation by Neos Chronos Limited (https://neoschronos.com). Creative Commons Attribution 4.0 International License

Following Ulwick and Christiansen, he determined that to better understand the customer value creation process, an entrepreneur must better understand customer problems. He developed a modified process to map those problems.

Maurya created a new template to change the emphasis of the business model canvas to include the segments of problem, solution and unfair advantage (see Fig. 2.3).

These same processes and methodologies can significantly aid a digital health entrepreneur in finding opportunities in helping resolve the pain in the Health marketplace highlighted throughout this chapter. We have indications opportunity resides in a variety of use cases in terms of cost reduction strategies for example. Recent studies have found that the costs for major procedures continue to escalate. The key medical specialties with the highest out-of-pocket cost estimates year over year for patients, include: Orthopedics Plastic Surgery, Urology and Neurology all of which are significantly higher than average across all specialties. These represent marketplace pain. Are there business opportunities present in delivering care through digital means that will cut the cost of delivering care into these segments? To be sure.

Details: Identifying Market Needs and Creating Solutions that Work

The methodology that these business model thought leaders have built and are constantly improving on is a Customer Discovery and Development Process. This is focused on-identifying prospective customers and their needs through an iterative interviewing process. Once prospects are identified, they are interviewed to determine key points of "pain" in their health job to be done workflow. Once there is a determination of the company's solution hypothesis, product or service hypotheses and product concepts are tested through a proffered minimum viable product (MVP) that are hypothesized to resolve the customer pain.

The Discovery Process of Customer Development

Customer Search Stages

Development of product hypotheses based on perceived market problem:

Customer Discovery-identify customers and needs your product may be able to resolve. Product specifications are identified. Initial testing of product hypotheses through prospect interviewing.

Customer validation-Product concepts are validated and tested with prospective customers in follow up interviews to determine if there is product/market fit. Solution hypotheses are tested to determine a minimum viable product offering.

Customer creation-generating demand through product presentations

Customer Sales/Scale-Spending time and money to build and scale sales process

Customer Development Process Participants?

Several team members should be involved in gaining, building products for and keeping customers.

Speaking directly to customers, understanding their inputs and formulation of marketing requirements is the domain of product management, business development and sales. Key team members in these roles should participate in prospective customer interviews. Understanding the comprehensive impact of the voice of the customer is also important to senior executives and finance.

Customer Search Stages Detailed

Customer Discovery

Product hypotheses are formulated based on defining the customer's work flow problems and the potential solution to resolve the problem. The goal is to gain information about the prospective customers- the health information "pain" they face and the overall market for potential products. The goal is to *Identify* the prospective customers (who will buy our products) what are their "jobs to be done" and how will the product resolve their "pain". This stage of the process *identifies the prominent points of friction*, headache or "pain" as well as the amount they are willing to pay to solve the problem. The intent is to determine whether the MVP product or service can resolve the pain and if the customers believe our concept resolves their problem. The greater the "pain" the larger the interest in "buying" your product offering.

Customer Validation

In this stage, a product concept or aggregation of products is developed that is expected to satisfy the customer's needs. This phase, testing our solution hypothesis, is referred to as finding product/market fit. It is time to prepare to sell the product. This is also when we are striving to develop a repeatable sales process that can be replicated and scaled to sell to early stage customers.

This phase draws on the information gleaned in the customer discovery phase. The information aids in the development of a business model canvas, sales collateral, value propositions and product positioning. Customer types (existing and new) are significant in impacting sales, marketing and business development.

According to Steve Blank, one of the principal creators of the customer development process, this is the step when you determine if the designed product is viable. If the feedback suggests product modification, returning to the first stage to determine a better solution.

Value Propositions

Your goal is to determine the depth of the pain prospective customers are feeling and the price they would pay for resolving their pain. You want to develop and test a group of value propositions. A value proposition is a short statement that communicates why buyers should choose your products or services. More than a product or service description-it's the specific solution your products provide and the promise of value that a customer can expect you to deliver. The validated value propositions will be tested in a variety of marketing materials and channels presented to a variety of respondents. Once tested these value propositions will be used to continue your sales processes in the next phase.

Customer Creation

During this phase, you work toward creating demand for the validated product in the marketplace. The focus of this phase is on getting more customers trying the initially validated product or products. During this phase, you figure out how to scale or function well with growth.

Listening to prospective customers, understanding their needs and their reaction to the minimum viable product is essential at this stage. The goal is to offer the best solution to customers and retain them in the long run by delivering a sustainable product offering.

Customer Sales/Scale

The last stage of the customer development process is building a sustainable, repeatable sales process at scale. Here the focus is on specific roles for marketing, product development and finance to assure the fulfillment of customer interest.

Customer Development Interviews

Customer development interviews are designed to be simple and easy to manage. You want to gain insight into the "pain" respondents are experiencing regarding whole person health. We want to develop a survey instrument that can allow open ended responses to product oriented questions. As interviews are conducted the goal is to understand targeted customer types and identify "customer personas" to ensure you are assessing the needs of specific types of individuals with targeted jobs to be done. Once you target those individuals, you want to contact them for an interview.

Through your customer development you are trying to identify the customers (who will buy your products) and what are their "jobs to be done"? How will your product solve their "pain"? The first stage of the process identifies the prominent points of friction, headache or "pain" [42].

Customer Development Interview Questions Defined

As we develop our iterative interviewing with prospective customers we want to gain insights and reactions to our various hypotheses through a variety of questions.

- **Problem Hypothesis**: A hypothesis that addresses the problem you are looking to solve. Is it an actual problem people have? What's the scope of the problem? Why does the problem exist?

- **Solution Hypothesis**: A hypothesis that addresses the proposed solution to a problem you have identified. Does your solution solve the problem in the customer's eyes?
- **Price Hypothesis**: A hypothesis that addresses the feasibility of our solution. Can it generate revenue? Are customers willing to purchase at our price to alleviate their pain?
- **Go-to-Market Hypothesis**: A hypothesis that addresses how we will get our solution in the hands of the customer. Is our MVP (minimum viable product) able to be distributed? How will they find our product? How will they purchase our product?
- Tell me how you currently do ___ (Job to be done) _____.
- How is that process working for you?
- If you could do anything to improve your experience with _____, what would it be?
- What's the hardest part about _____?
- What do you like/dislike about _____?

Can you tell me a story about a time you struggled with [issue related to your product idea]?

Why is that [hard, frustrating, etc.]?

What was the hardest part about this problem you faced?

Why was this the hardest part?

How did you solve this problem at the time?

How did you find t h a t solution? What frustrates you about this solution? Are you actively searching for/ trying out other solution? [41]

Go to Market Strategies

Go-To-Market strategies are critical for market adoption of digital health companies. Julie Yoo, of the Andreessen Horowitz investment firm writes about them in an article, "The New Go-To-Market Playbook for Digital Startups". She describes the digital health market overall as slow to mature. She observes, multiple healthcare technology products have struggled to gain traction. The slow adoption of these products, she postulates, was their inability to find an "executable path for sustainable distribution and value capture." Distribution was "historically a very steep hill to climb." Market maturity was stifled by integration, absorption and payment hurdles for new technology-based products. Budgets and care plans were fixed without room for new approaches. As a result, there were long enterprise sales cycles for initial paths to market. Without sufficient capitalization, few companies could withstand the cash flow challenge [43].

The current growth of the digital health marketplace, Ms. Yoo suggests, has been driven by the unique revisioning of Go-To-Market (GTM) strategies. She observes since 2010, the primary market and distribution channel for digital health products was through incumbent providers, payers, life sciences companies and self-insured employers.

She identifies several new key go-to-market strategies she is tracking in her work. As a leading investor in digital health, her focus is on a sustainable distribution and value capture with key customer segments [43].

The first GTM is a business to consumer to enterprise model of product marketing-she calls **B2C2B**. The company gains traction with consumers. Once aggregated, they are a valuable resource for enterprise customers.

The second GTM Yoo describes is a business to small business model (**B2SMB**). Digital health companies for example, have become a market for infrastructure services.

Yoo observes a third GTM opportunity for digital health companies is the adoption of **Risk Based** contracting. She believes this payment strategy is a key to digital health startups as they take responsibility for the comprehensive care for a patient. Value based reimbursement has gained increased emphasis throughout healthcare. Nimble digital health companies with their customer engagement capabilities are uniquely able to successfully navigate this emerging reimbursement approach [43].

The most successful digital health market leaders are built on evidence-based product validation. One leader, Omada Health, has 10 peer-reviewed studies demonstrating their product efficacy. They also demonstrated to the U.S. Centers for Disease Control how their virtual program could deliver the Diabetes Prevention Program cost effectively with higher outcomes. The company demonstrated how their program was delivered digitally, privately and securely. They also showed how the long-standing program could be scaled cost effectively. So convinced of their outcomes and metrics, they have become a leader in Risk Based contracting managing cohorts of patients with their disease management system.

Revenue-Value Based Reimbursement

For years, the Centers for Medicare and Medicaid Services (CMS) and other policy organizations have promoted value-based care models to reimburse for quality care. The models include the Accountable Care Organization, Medicare Shared Savings and the Next Generation ACO Model. Additionally, six common value-based care models are developing as alternatives to the standard fee for service reimbursement model. digital health companies would do well to monitor and keep abreast of these revenue models.

- **Bundled payments** focused on an entire episode of care.

Patient-centered Medical Homes (PCMH), a primary care physician coordinates a centralized care setting providing a more personalized care approach.

Accountable care organizations (ACOs) are patient centered networks designed to improve quality and delivery of patientcare through a group of physicians and healthcare providers working together to leverage health information technology to gather data and improve patient care at reduced costs.

Shared Savings is passed on to providers by payers through reimbursements based on quality and spending targets.

Shared Risk also known as downside risk models hold the provider accountable to the ACO to have their costs stay at or below the target rates set for delivery of targeted outcomes.

Global Capitation requires the provider assume 100% of the risk in a value-based care model. This model designates a specific amount for each patient served and allows the provider to keep any savings [44].

Another set of GTMs Yoo observed is a trend first identified by Rock Health in an article on multi-sided virtual care platforms or marketplaces [45].

The article identifies a variety of new platform value strands emerging in the maturing digital health marketplace-infrastructure and service/product offerings:

- Care management platforms-condition management
- Convenience care-common condition management
- Remote pharmacy infrastructure
- Unified virtual platforms
- Retail platforms
- Integrated digital and physical care platform
- Tech infrastructure platforms
- Data integration-Links to EMRs
- Biomarker tracking

Companies building these platforms have crafted unique business models based on determination of their customer and path to payment. They strive to build competitive advantage through technical assets, hard assets, human capital and intellectual property [45].

Significantly, Rock Health's 2021 year-end digital health funding study identified $3.2B in funding for healthcare marketplaces in 2021 [9]. digital health platforms or marketplaces include two sided or multi-sided networks and platforms.

Two-sided networks—This go-to-market approach builds a product or service that is valuable to one market constituent, and then leverages that network of users, and/or the data generated by those users, into a sale to a second market constituent [43].

Multi-sided platform—The multisided platform business model is, basically, a service or product that connects two or more participant groups, playing a kind of intermediation role. Its value proposition is to enable this connection, making it easier for them to find and relate to each other [46].

These business models typically engender network effects and have mutually reinforcing dynamics based from the two complementary customer sets. A two-sided marketplace works well when its design allows it to add increasing numbers of users to create a network effect-when a product (like delivering a health outcome) or a service (like a network of social service providers) becomes more valuable as more people use it.

Building Customer Value

- Time saved to find the service brokered by the marketplace
- Hassle and friction reduced in finding services
- Increased trust in marketplace system vs. the alternative

Highlighting distribution strategies, Yoo identifies another GTM, **Distribution partnerships through aggregators**. She cites the growing number of single digital health solutions as a cause for vendor fatigue and a drive to streamline the aggregation and purchase of digital health products through aggregators or already existing incumbent channels for enterprises [43].

The marketplace for hybrid products is evolving. Companies offering new combined care delivery products with advanced analytics are finding renewed go-to market traction with payers. McKinsey & Co identified this adoption trend to better serve individuals with increasing complex healthcare needs [47].

They observe continuous provider interventions for chronic disease and long-term condition management supported by payers. Acquisitons and adoption of "next-generation" managed care models by nine of the top ten payers are key indicators of a growing trend in care delivery. From their assessment these models foretell a payor reorientation focused away from operational concern targeting financing and pricing risk toward a more integrated managed care model to better align incentives to provide higher-quality, beter experience, lower-cost and more accessible care [47].

The authors also observe a shifting market with growing investments in alternative sites of care and pursuit of diversified business models for health systems encompassing a greater range of care delivery assets (physician practices, ambulatory surgery centers and urgent care centers) that are generating returns above expectations. These lowered costs are generated by enhanced coordination, improved patient experience and enhanced quality of provided services. They sense indications of greater emphasis toward innovative tech-enabled care that "unlocks value by integrating digital and non-acute settings into a comprehensive, coordinated and lower-cost offering" [47].

The healthcare services market is shifting, with technology enhancing all segments of the healthcare ecosystem. Payers and providers are better enabled to link actions and outcomes. Consumers are engaged with real-time and convenient access to health information. There is an increased integration of data analytics, utilization management and clinical information systems. Areas such as behavioral health and social determinants of healthare are driving innovation. Patient engagement and population health management are enhancing innovation

Regardless of the initial strategy to market, successful health innovators resolve identified market pains for specific customer segments. They deliver tested value propositions through new distribution channels, funded by new revenue models

Additional Business Model Considerations

Healthcare requires innovation. Despite the pandemic, healthcare costs continue to increase while health outcomes are worse than most industrialized nations. Remember over $4 trillion is spent on healthcare annually, over $12,500 per person and rising, accounting for almost 20% of our National Gross Domestic Product. \\If one-third of the market is waste, then there is a $1.3 trillion-dollar market for efficient, engaging digital health products that deliver on their value propositions.

Startup founders and teams seek to gain a deeper understanding of the requirements for solutions and potential value creation they might develop and control. The quest for digital health entrepreneurs is an "executable path for sustainable distribution and value capture". The market has improved in terms of system integration, absorption and payment [43].

The first step is assessing how your business creates, delivers and captures value for customers.

Then, your business is fundamentally envisioned around this clear, new customer need. Your challenge is to align your key resources, processes and profit formula around your new value propositions.

There are many new players in the field. We have seen the entry of Apple, Google, Salesforce and Microsoft. Each of these have their own distribution networks and value propositions.

Amazon is still trying to find its optimal path to impact the healthcare industry. Recent acquisitions indicated a major new thrust. One Medical, a membership-based, technology enabled concierge primary care network offering digital and in-office care and PillPack, an on-line drug by mail provider were acquired. The combination seemed to foretell a vertical integration of healthcare services. Though, recently it was announced that the internal virtual Amazon Care offering was going to be closed.

We expect that despite their size and product development expertise they will all use similar variations of the design methodologies to bring their products to market. Yet, will they truly disrupt healthcare? Or, is this a great time for passionate aligned entrepreneurs?

References

1. Artiga S, Hinton E. Beyond Health Care: The Role of Social Determinants in Promoting Health and Health Equity, Kaiser Family Foundation website, May 10, 2018. www.kff.org/racial-equity-and-health-policy/issue-brief/beyond-health-care-the-role-of-social-determinants-in-promoting-health-and-health-equity/
2. DeSilva J, Dell'Aquilio G, Zweig M. Consumer Adoption of telemedicine in 2021, December 15, 2021, Rock Health website. www.rockhealth.com/insights/consumer-adoption-of-telemedicine-in-2021/

3. Pearl R, Wayling B The Telehealth Era Is Just Beginning, Harvard Business Review Magazine, May-June 2022, https://hbr.org/2022/05/the-telehealth-era-is-just-beginning
4. Centers for Disease Control and Prevention website, Health Equity, https://www.cdc.gov/chronicdisease/healthequity/index.htm
5. The National Committee for Quality Assurance (NCQA)The Future of Telehealth Roundtable, May 2022, page 5. https://www.ncqa.org/wp-content/uploads/2022/05/NCQA-TelehealthAndEquity-Whitepaper-Draft5.pdf
6. Text: H.R. 4040-117th Congress (2021-2022), July 28, 2022, https://www.congress.gov/bill/117th-congress/house-bill/4040/text
7. Interoperability and Patient Access Final Rule. CMS.gov website. https://www.cms.gov/files/document/cms-9115-f.pdf
8. Interoperability and Patient Access Fact sheet. CMS.gov website. https://www.cms.gov/newsroom/fact-sheets/interoperability-and-patient-access-fact-sheet
9. Evans B, Krasiniansky A, Zweig M. Year-end digital health funding: Seismic shifts beneath the surface. Rock Health website; 2021. https://rockhealth.com/insights/2021-year-end-digital-health-funding-seismic-shifts-beneath-the-surface/
10. What Bubble? Digital Health Funding Year in Review 2021, Seth Joseph, Forbes.com website January 11, 2022
11. Plaster L. StartUp Health, Global Health Innovation Funding Hits $16B Despite Market Recalibration, July 2022 https://healthtransformer.co/global-health-innovation-funding-drops-yoy-yet-continues-10-year-growth-curve-2dcb8dc387b0
12. Out-of-Pocket Healthcare Expenditures in the United States, 5th Edition. Kalorama Information. https://kaloramainformation.com/product/out-of-pocket-healthcare-expenditures-in-the-united-states-5th-edition/
13. Muoio D. August 3, 2021, Nationwide out-of-pocket spending jumped 10% in 2021 Fierce Healthcare website. https://www.fiercehealthcare.com/payer/nationwide-out-pocket-spending-grew-10-to-1-650-per-person-2021-expect-to-continue-through
14. PwC's Health Research Institute (HRI). Medical cost trend: behind the numbers 2019. 2018. www.pwc/us/medicalcosttrends.
15. Wiik J. Healthcare revolution: the patient is the new payer. 2017. https://www.wellsteps.com/blog/2018/01/03/benefits-of-wellness-lower-health-care-costs/.
16. Mercer. https://www.mercer.com/newsroom/mercer-survey-shows-employers-face-increase-in-health-benefit-cost-in-2018.html.
17. Mercer. National survey of employer sponsored health plans. In: Health insurance coverage in the United States. 2021. https://www.mercer.us/what-we-do/health-and-benefits/strategy-and-transformation/mercer-national-survey-benefit-trends.html
18. Williams R, Gunja M, Bumgartner J, Gumas E. Americans, no matter the state they live in, die younger than people in many other countries. The Commonwealth Fund. https://www.commonwealthfund.org/blog/2022/americans-no-matter-state-they-live-die-younger-people-many-other-countries
19. Swanson E. National Hospital Flash Report: July 2022, Kaufman Hall website. https://www.kaufmanhall.com/sites/default/files/2022-07/KH-NHFR-July-2022.pdf
20. Doyle P. Hospitals innovate amid dire nursing shortages, American Association of Medical Colleges website. https://www.aamc.org/news-insights/hospitals-innovate-amid-dire-nursing-shortages
21. Newswise.com "Geisinger to roll out eICU program", December, 3, 2009. https://www.news-wise.com/articles/geisinger-to-roll-out-eicu-program
22. National Health Expenditure Projections 2021-2030-CMS. https://www.cms.gov/files/document/nhe-projections-forecast-summary.pdf
23. Research Trends in health care spending. American Medical Association. websit: https://www.ama-assn.org/about/research/trends-health-care-spending
24. National Health Expenditure Projections 2021-2030 Forecast Summary Major Findings. https://www.cms.gov/files/document/nhe-projections-forecast-summary.pdf
25. Kaiser Family Foundation website, State Health Facts, Health Insurance Coverage of the Total Population, 2019 https://www.kff.org/other/state-indicator/total population/?dataView=0&cu

rrentTimeframe=0&selectedDistributions=employer&sortModel=%7B%22colId%22:%22Lo
cation%22,%22sort%22:%22asc%22%7D

26. Institute of Medicine of the National Academies, Recommendations. Best of care at lower cost. Washington, DC: National Academies Press; 2012.
27. Institute for Healthcare Improvement website https://www.ihi.org/Engage/Initiatives/ TripleAim/Pages/default.aspx
28. Rittel H, Webber M. Dilemmas in a general theory of planning. Policy Sciences. 1973;4(2):155–69.
29. Higley T. Process? I don't need no stinkin' process, a serial entrepreneur's guide to opportunity and risk. 25 May 2017. 2017.
30. Higley T. Creating a model for successful generation of new ventures (Part Two); 2017.
31. @TomHigley, @101010.net, July 22, 2018, [Twitter Post] Advice for founders from our CEO @tomhigley Start with a problem you care about. Or start with a customer you care about who has a problem you care about. All customers have problems, All problems have solutions, Not all solutions have problems Not all problems have customers.
32. Blank S. The four steps to the epiphany. Pescadero, CA: K&S Ranch Inc.; 2003.
33. Blank S, Dorf B. The startup owner's manual, vol. 1. Pescadero, CA: K&S Ranch Inc.; 2012.
34. Blank S. Harvard business review. In: Why the Lean startup changes everything; 2013.
35. Ries E. The Lean Startup: how today's entrepreneurs use continuous innovation to create radically successful businesses. New York: Crown Business, Random House; 2011.
36. Osterwalder A, Pigneur Y. Business model generation: a handbook for visionaries, game changers, and challengers. Hoboken: Wiley; 2010.
37. Porter ME, Teisberg EO. Redefining health care: creating value-based competition on results. Boston: Harvard Business School Publishing; 2006.
38. Knapp J, Zeratsky J, Kowitz B. Sprint: how to solve big problems and test new ideas in just five days. New York: Simon and Schuster; 2016.
39. Fitzpatrick R. The mom test: how to talk to customers & learn if your business is a good idea when everyone is lying to you. New York: Founder Centric Press; 2013.
40. Ulwick AW. Jobs to be done: theory to practice. Idea Brite Press; 2016.
41. Maurya A. Running lean, iterate from plan A to a plan that works. Sebastopol, CA: O'Reilly Media Inc; 2011/2012.
42. Garbugli E, Lean B. Leanpub.com. https://leanpub.com/ lean-b2b-build-products-businesses-want-customer-development
43. Yoo J. The new go-to market playbook for digital health startups. https://a16z.com/2021/10/19/ the-new-go-to-market-playbooks-for-digital-health-startups/
44. Willcox-Lee C. Value-based reimbursement: an overview, health recovery solutions, April 27, 2022 https://www.healthrecoverysolutions.com/blog/value-based-reimbursement-an-overview
45. Kaganoff S. The starter pistol for the virtual care platforms race, https://rockhealth.com/ the-starter-pistol-for-the-virtual-care-platforms-race/
46. Pereira, D. The Business Model Analyst, March 19, 2022, https://businessmodelanalyst.com/ multisided-platform-business-model/
47. Clark E,Singhai S, Weber K. The future of healthcare: Value creation through next-generation business models, McKinsey & Company, January 4, 2021., https://www. mckinsey.com/industries/healthcare-systems-and-services/our-insights/the-future-of-healthcare-value-creation-through-next-generation-business-models

Chapter 3
Innovating with Health System Partners: Value Propositions and Business Models

Susan L. Moore

Health Care Innovation and Digital Health Opportunity

In 2001, as part of its historic in-depth analysis of health care in the United States, the National Academy of Medicine (NAM) found that information technology (IT) had the potential to promote the provision of health care that achieved the six key aims of being safe, effective, patient-centered, timely, efficient, and equitable [1]. In its report, the committee noted the potential for health IT to play a critical role in the transformation of the health system. Over the decade and a half since, technological advances in health care and otherwise have occurred at an extraordinary pace, resulting in a "digital revolution" as new, previously unimagined systems and solutions have come into being, together with the ability to capture near-unfathomable volumes of data that promise hidden answers to all of health care's problems [2].

A clear trend has emerged over the last few years with regard to the use of existing and emerging digital health technologies to identify and implement novel solutions, augmented by a perceived need for collaboration among industry partners, technology developers, health care leaders, clinicians, patients, community members, and public health practitioners. The passage of the twenty-first Century Cures Act reflected additional interest in this direction at the federal level by providing $4.8 billion to the National Institutes of Health over 10 years, dedicated to multiple initiatives that drive innovation in digital health [3]. Increasingly, these technologies are miniaturized and mobilized, taking advantage of ever-increasing computing power contained in smaller and smaller devices [4]. The pace of global market growth in mobile digital health alone clearly demonstrates the extensive landscape

S. L. Moore (✉)
Colorado School of Public Health, University of Colorado at Anschutz Medical Campus, Aurora, CO, USA
e-mail: Susan.L.Moore@cuanschutz.edu

© The Author(s), under exclusive license to Springer Nature Switzerland AG 2023
A. Meyers (ed.), *Digital Health Entrepreneurship*, Health Informatics,
https://doi.org/10.1007/978-3-031-33902-8_3

of opportunity in this sector, with a 47.6% compound annual growth rate and a projected market value of up to $59 billion by 2020 [5].

In 2015, the *New England Journal of Medicine* (NEJM) Group announced a new resource, NEJM Catalyst, targeted toward clinical decision makers and health care leaders who seek to drive transformative change in health care through innovation [6]. In a business context, the concept of innovation represents not only the new idea itself, but the application of the new idea as a solution to an existing problem or unmet need [7]. Considered from this perspective, innovation encompasses a range of activities designed to discover, develop, and improve solutions, processes, operations, functions, and outcomes. As a result, it seems only natural that the health care industry, with its commitment to continually improving aspects of health care such as quality, value, delivery, and overall population health, would be a welcoming environment for innovation, even disruptive innovation.

In a recent survey of health care leaders, Catalyst reported that hospitals and health systems, health care information technology (IT), and primary care were identified as the top three areas most in need of innovation [8]. Moreover, respondents overwhelmingly felt that not only was innovation essential to improve health care, but that the principal drivers of innovative change would come from outside health care organizations [8]. Health care executives, administrators, and clinicians all believed that crucial change for hospitals and delivery systems overall and in health IT in particular would come from focused startups rather than internal experts or existing organizations, which is good news for digital health entrepreneurs.

However, despite identified need and express willingness to innovate, health care is a complex adaptive system [9–11]. Such systems are non-linear, dynamic, and inherently chaotic, exhibiting emergent behaviors and unanticipated consequences [10]. As a result, innovation in one area of health care can cause unexpected problems in other areas. In *The Digital Doctor*, Robert Wachter describes in detail how a series of perfectly logical, automated, error-checked steps within a state-of-the-art computerized prescription order-and-dispensing system resulted in a 16-year-old patient being given an overdose of medication that was *39 times higher* than what he should have gotten [12]. Awareness of such risk leads to notable reluctance among health system stakeholders when it comes to adopting unproven solutions.

Resistance to change is also a factor that affects innovation adoption, driven in part by the complex adaptive system, but also by innovation fatigue among end users [13]. A 2016 study in the Annals of Internal Medicine found that for each hour health care providers spent providing direct clinical care to patients, they spent an additional 2–3 hours performing administrative work—the majority of it due to required interactions with electronic health records and similar systems [14]. No matter how impressive the technology, it's perhaps quite understandable why providers might be reluctant to further burden themselves without good reason. In short, without substantial evidence of impact and worth, innovative digital health solutions may never be adopted at all.

Making the Case for Digital Health Solutions: The Value Proposition

One way for digital health entrepreneurs to distinguish themselves and their products from the mass of competitors, promote adoption, and increase their chances of establishing advantageous relationships with health system partners is to develop a strong *value proposition*.

A value proposition is a clear, concise statement that convincingly articulates why a customer should purchase a particular product. A digital health company or product can have more than one value proposition, depending on how many different market sectors or unique customers are being targeted. At its core, the value proposition describes **what the product does** to solve a problem or meet a need, for **whom**, and **what benefit** can be expected as a result. An effective value proposition should address the following key elements [15]:

- Relevance
- Quantified value
- Unique differentiation

Relevance refers to the product's appropriateness and ability to meet the customer's needs or solve a problem that the customer has. Quantified value refers to the specific benefits that the product can provide to the customer. Finally, unique differentiation refers to the set of identifiable factors that enable a product to stand out from other similar products in the market in ways that make the product well-suited for the customer (the product's **fit**).

The Value Proposition Canvas, created by Alexander Osterwalder, is a diagram and visual tool set that digital health entrepreneurs can use to define and refine their products and offerings, understand and describe their customer and target market, and identify ways to achieve fit (Fig. 3.1) [16].

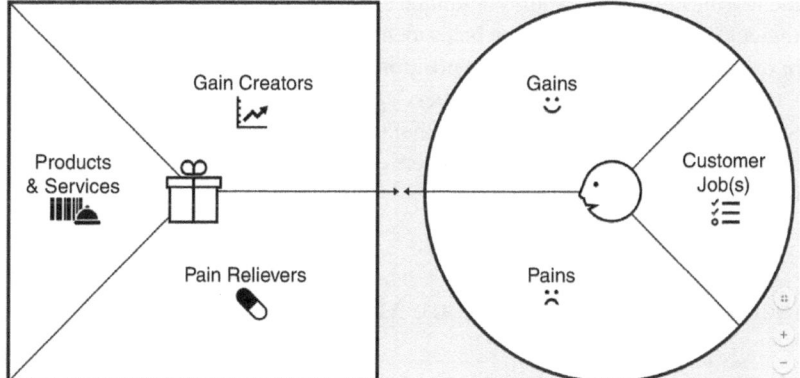

Fig. 3.1 The Value Proposition Canvas (©Strategyzer AG) Source: https://strategyzer.uservoice.com/knowledgebase/articles/506842-can-i-use-the-business-model-canvas-or-value-propo

On the left side of the Value Proposition Canvas is the Value Map (the square box). The Value Map is where the user defines the features and characteristics of their innovative, entrepreneurial solution. The more specific the definition, the better; vague and nebulous descriptions won't help promote clarity or understanding either for the entrepreneur or the customer. At the same time, it's best to keep things short and sweet, because the more detailed the explanation required, the less likely the customer is to be successfully engaged by what the entrepreneur is trying to do.

The three sections of the Value Map are:

- **Products and Services:** This section is where the user identifies the specific items or things that their solution is, does, and provides to the customer. The list created in this sector of the map comprises the central elements of a value proposition.
- **Gain Creators:** This section should be used to identify the ways in which a digital health solution can provide or create value for the client.
- **Pain Relievers:** This section should be used to match the needs that a customer has to the particular aspects of the digital health solution that will solve the customer's problems for them.

Both gain creators and pain relievers should ideally be written in such a way as to describe not only the *what*, but the *how.* The ideal statement should be explanatory, but succinct, with no more than one short sentence per gain creator or pain reliever.

The right side of the Value Proposition Canvas contains the Customer Segment Profile circle. The sections of this circle can be used to quantify and describe a customer in a detailed, structured fashion. This allows the entrepreneur to simplify the customer down to core components which comprise the central nature of a business relationship: namely, what does the customer do in their work (the customer's **jobs**), what needs or problems does the customer have (the customer's **pains**), and what precise advantages the entrepreneur's solution can provide (the customer's **gains**).

Rather than trying to use the circle to create a single profile that represents all things to all customers, separate profiles should be created for each customer market segment. This allows the capture of unique elements that might be different from one customer to another, which in turn helps identify a specific value proposition for each.

In order to craft a good value proposition, therefore, digital health entrepreneurs first need to understand their customers' profile characteristics and their overall target market. This includes the things that their customers need to do and the problems or the difficulties that their customers currently have which could be solved by a digital health product.

Understanding the Health Care Market

The health care market represents a significant opportunity for digital health business investment. National health expenditures in 2016 amounted to $3.3 trillion and accounted for 17.9% of total national gross domestic product [17]. Within those expenditures, hospital care accounted for 32%, physician and clinical services accounted for 20%, and prescription drugs accounted for a 10% share. Health care spending is expected to continue growth at a rapid pace, and is projected to increase overall by almost 75% to $5.7 trillion over a mere ten years [18]. As of March 2018, hospitals and health delivery systems in the United States accounted for $991 billion in market share, which alone represents a full 5% of national gross domestic product ($19.4 trillion, 2017) [19, 20].

According to the American Hospital Association, there are currently 5534 hospitals in the United States, including 4840 community hospitals, 209 federal government hospitals, 397 non-federal psychiatric hospitals, and 88 other hospital types including prison hospitals, long term care facilities, and school infirmaries [19]. Among community hospitals, the vast majority (n = 2849) are not-for-profit and non-governmental, with an additional 956 nonprofit hospitals supported by state and local government. The remaining 1035 community hospitals are classified as for-profit or investor owned. Geographically, 62% of community hospitals are located in cities and other metropolitan localities, with the remaining 38% located in rural areas.

Hospitals don't always operate as independent entities—in fact, just the opposite. Two-thirds (68%, n = 3321) of community hospitals are classified as members of health delivery systems, and 35% (n = 1689) are members of health care networks [19]. Health delivery systems are each owned or managed by a central organization. A system can be structured as multiple hospitals in association or as diversified, integrated delivery systems that include a single hospital combined with three or more other integrated health service organizations, such as primary care clinics, that represent at least 25% of the overall business makeup. In contrast, health care networks represent multiple organizations in collaboration to deliver coordinated services to their region. Membership in one does not preclude membership in the other, as an organization can be a member of both a system and a network.

When it comes to meeting health care needs and providing benefits to hospital, health system and practice partners, it's important to recall that the actual decision-making customer is not the organization itself, but one or more of the people within it. There are over 13 million people in the United States health care workforce in 2018, of whom just under one million (n = 968,743) are physicians [21]. According to the American Medical Association's Physician Practice Benchmark Survey, most physicians (68%) work in group practices, whether single-specialty (43%) or multi-specialty groups (25%), as opposed to other practice types, and under ten percent of health care providers are directly employed by hospitals [22]. Only 17% of physicians work in solo practices, and fewer than half of physicians (47%) own their own businesses.

Examples of hospital, health system, and health care practice influencers, key stakeholders and decision makers include:

- **C-suite executives.** Among the roles filled by these personnel are chief executive officer, chief financial officer, chief operating officer, and chief information or technology officer. These individuals hold high-level responsibility for organizational and operational performance, and often have the final say over budgets, discretionary spending, and other financial matters.

- **Health care administrators.** These personnel include various management and leadership roles, such as innovation managers, practice managers, and team leads.
- **Health care providers.** Providers include physicians, nurses, and advanced practice providers such as nurse practitioners and physician assistants [23, 24]. As targeted end users who often serve in leadership roles, providers often have particularly strong influence on digital health product decisions.
- **IT professionals.** Database and application administrators, security specialists, and technical support managers all have the potential to influence purchasing decisions for products that need to be integrated into existing information system architectures.
- **Patients and caregivers.** In addition to making purchasing decisions as consumers, patients and caregivers often serve in advisory capacities for hospitals, health systems, and practices, and provide their insight and expertise accordingly.

Hospital, Health Delivery System, and Health Care Practice Pains and Gains

As part of creating an entrepreneurial profile for targeted health care customers, it is essential to appreciate the work that potential health care clients are trying to do, the challenges that they are experiencing, and the sectors of the market that hold the greatest possibility of benefit. Digital health products and solutions that align with health care market needs are significantly more likely to be adopted. In short, what matters to the potential client must also matter to a digital health entrepreneur. While a comprehensive review of all current health care needs is beyond the scope of this chapter, several key concerns are presented below.

A Commonwealth Fund survey of 33 innovation centers affiliated with health care delivery systems across the United States found that nearly 90% of respondents were focused on care coordination, disease-specific outcomes, and access issues [25]. Additional areas of emphasis included patient engagement (84%), population health (77%), and clinical decision support (74%). These spheres of opportunity are closely aligned with critical needs identified by health system leaders [26, 27]. Such pains include but are not limited to providing value-based care, particularly in a rapidly-changing legislative environment with the potential to exert major impact on industry payment models and reimbursement approaches; providing care that is more patient-centered, consumer-focused, and personalized; and improving health outcomes and care management at the population level in addition to the individual level. Each of these broad topics can be further segmented, for instance into an interest in predictive analytics for chronic condition management or a desire to improve care across the continuum by addressing the social determinants of health. Being aware of these and other health care trends in developing and promoting solutions that are responsive to the market will contribute to entrepreneurial success.

In addition, while there is broad consensus that digital health holds great promise for addressing health care's critical pains, the context for implementing such solutions also matters. Over 98% of hospitals have implemented certified electronic health record (EHR) technology, manufactured by only 10 health IT developers and vendors [28]. More vendor diversity exists in the office-based ambulatory care practice market, where 684 developers supply solutions to over 350,000 providers who participate in federal EHR incentive programs, but the majority of the market share (60%) is still divided among just 5 vendor companies, with Epic alone supplying 30% of the market [29]. This is an important consideration when making a case for a digital health product, as solutions that interface easily with existing clinical information systems have lower barriers to adoption than solutions which need complex programming to achieve integration into the health care setting. Entrepreneurs who are familiar with clinical information system communications protocols and stan dards such as those curated by Health Level Seven (HL7) International will have an advantage over their competition [30]. HL7 is a standards-developing organization for health information exchange and management, accredited by the American National Standards Institute (ANSI).

Another consideration of critical importance for digital health entrepreneurs looking to establish client relationships with hospitals, health systems, and health care practice partners is the Health Insurance Portability and Accountability Act (HIPAA). HIPAA governs both health information privacy and the security of health information stored and exchanged in electronic form. The penalties for breaching HIPAA can be severe, from a minimum of $100 to $50,000 per violation up to annual maximums of $25,000 to $1.5 million [31]. As of 2013, business associates, such as digital health vendors, are legally held to the same HIPAA standards and subject to the same potential penalties as the health system partners that they work with, which makes information security, data storage, and data governance for digital health solutions even more important.

Finally, digital health entrepreneurs should consider whether or not their product is required to be approved by the U.S. Food and Drug Administration (FDA), which oversees authorization and regulation for medical drugs, devices vaccines, and certain digital health products [32]. Prior to introducing a digital health solution into the health care workflow, client stakeholders will want to know about its FDA approval status.

From Innovation to Infrastructure: Why Business Models Matter

Understanding the customer profile, creating a value map, and crafting a superior value proposition are only part of the path toward digital health innovation success. At the same time that the entrepreneur is working to learn and understand the potential customer, the customer is likewise evaluating the entrepreneur. Moreover, the strength of the value proposition and fit of the digital health product is necessary but often not sufficient for the potential client to make a purchase decision. The customer also needs to have confidence in the viability and stability of the company as well, including considerations such as the costs of continuance (e.g., technical support, licensing and maintenance fees, and upgrade fees) and vendor stability. After all, no matter how good a product may be, it can quickly become a futile investment if the business which provides it undergoes a collapse.

Developing a well-crafted **business model** is a fundamental process that entrepreneurs can use to demonstrate the viability and sustainability of their digital health products and solutions. A business model is a structured description of a company's plan for profit, and includes such aspects as the core customer base, essential infrastructure to support business operations, income sources and financial planning, and how the company's products or solutions can provide a return from the market. A good business model can serve as the basis for a detailed business plan. It can be used to inform strategic planning, as a roadmap for business development, and as a tool to guide response to customers' questions and concerns. Examples of questions that customers might ask when assessing a digital health product and company for potential fit which could be answered with the aid of a detailed business model include:

- What impact does the product have on existing workflows?
- Does the product require technical integration, or is it a stand-alone solution?
- How is training conducted, how long does it take, and how much does it cost?
- What personnel are required for product implementation and use?
- How is the product deployed? Are there access control, device management, security, and upgrade considerations that need to be cooperatively managed?
- What does available product inventory look like? What are the lead times for ordering, development, and delivery?
- What surety exists that the company will still be around in 5 years?

As with the value proposition, Alexander Osterwalder and Yves Pigneur have created a visual tool for business model development: the Business Model Canvas (Fig. 3.2) [33]. The Business Model Canvas encompasses nine foundational sections that can be assembled as building blocks to construct a comprehensive whole. Value propositions and customer segment profiles comprise two of the nine business modelsections, described further below.

1. **Key Partners.** This section is used to identify business relationships that are essential to or which strategically influence the function and performance of a company, such as suppliers, collaborators, and competitors.
2. **Key Activities.** These encompass the tasks and actions that must take place in order for the business to operate properly.
3. **Key Resources.** These are the assets necessary to support business operations. These resources not only include tangible things like supplies and equipment, but also include personnel resources, intellectual property, and operating cash (financial resources).

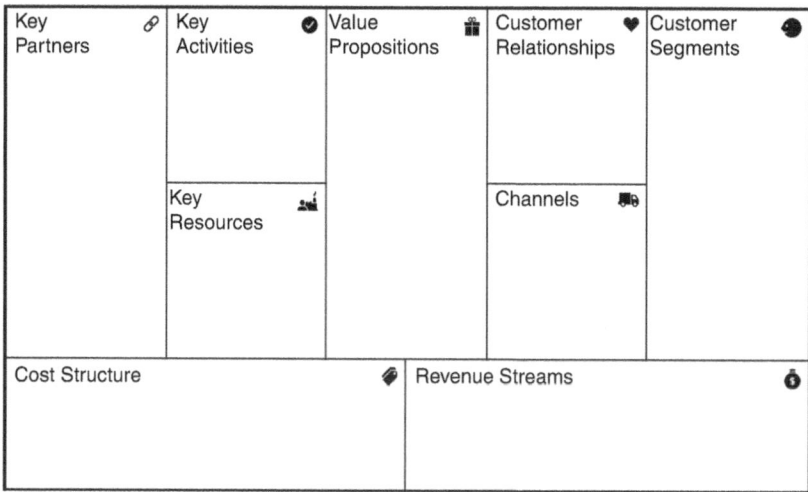

Fig. 3.2 The Business Model Canvas (©Strategyzer AG) Source: https://strategyzer.uservoice. com/knowledgebase/articles/506842-can-i-use-the-business-model-canvas-or-value-propo

4. **Value Propositions.** As described previously, a value proposition is a clear statement of why a customer should purchase a product, which includes a summary of what specific benefits the product provides and how the product meets customer needs.

5. **Customer Relationships.** These comprise the various types of relationships that can be established between the company and the customers identified in segment profiles. In addition to relatively straightforward provider-client associations, these can also refer to collaborative or co-creation relationships, support relationships, and referral relationships, among others.

6. **Channels.** Channels refer to the points and mechanisms for a company to use when communicating and engaging with customers. Channels can be used for disseminating information, distributing products, sales to support and everything in between.

7. **Customer Segments.** As discussed earlier, customer segments (or customer profiles) are structured descriptions of customer types and groups to be targeted and served by a company, based on their needs, the specific value the company's product can provide, and the goodness of fit between the company and the customer.

8. **Cost Structure.** This section is designed to include all of the costs associated with business operations. Production costs, office space and supply costs, personnel costs such as salaries and benefits, and materials costs are some of the more common elements to include in a detailed cost structure.

9. **Revenue Streams.** Sometimes described as lines of business, revenue streams refer to all the various sources of financial support attributable to a company

through its products, services, and investments. Product purchase prices, licensing or service fees, and advertising income are all examples of revenue streams. A company's net revenue comes from one or more streams after all costs have been accounted for.

Once a business model has been drafted, it's important to test its underlying premise and subsequent fit for the intended market – and not just once, but on a regular basis. Conducting a SWOT analysiscan provide great insight into whether a business is poised for success or must adapt to survive. As an acronym, SWOT stands for:

- **Strengths.** These are the elements of a business, solution, or strategy that position a company to address pains, provide value, and outperform its competitors. Examples of strengths might include the uniqueness of a product or established relationships with key clients that help secure market advantage.
- **Weaknesses.** The inverse of strengths, these are the vulnerabilities that place a company at risk. Lack of financial capital is but one example of a significant weakness.
- **Opportunities.** These represent prospects that can be leveraged to improve aspects of business success such as company performance or market share. For example, changes in health insurance reimbursement models for preventive care might create business opportunity for digital health entrepreneurs whose solutions address care coordination or population health management.
- **Threats.** The inverse of opportunities, threats signify challenges or pressures that could strain company resources or decrease market share. For example, the same changes in payment models that might benefit companies with population health products could reduce the client base for companies that focus on high-end fee-for-service solutions.

As the digital health business environment continues to develop, the savvy entrepreneur will reexamine their assumptions on a regular basis to ensure that they are able to pivot in response to market pressures and that they haven't been unexpectedly outmaneuvered by their competitors. Developing value propositions and business models are not one-off activities that can be completed and set aside after checking the appropriate box on the entrepreneurial success to-do list.

Final Thoughts

The field of digital health is highly competitive and rapidly evolving. New legislation continues to change the health care market, and new and emerging technologies constantly reshape the landscape of the possible. Health care stakeholders are inundated by multiple competing responsibilities which must be achieved within the constraints of complex systems and are subjected to a constant barrage of sales pitches in an exploding market. Understanding these customer needs and challenges is essential. Digital health entrepreneurs can position themselves for success through effective use of tools and strategies such as value propositions and business models to make their case for innovation.

Acknowledgements Thanks are due to the following people for their contributions to this work: M.E. Lasseter, MA, for reference checking, and Elaine Morrato, DrPH, Cathy Bodine, PhD, and Demetria McNeal, PhD, MBA, for providing leadership and education for emerging entrepreneurs through the iCorps program at the Colorado Clinical and Translational Sciences Institute, University of Colorado (Anschutz).

References

1. National Academy of Medicine (NAM). Crossing the quality chasm: a new health system for the 21st century. Washington, DC: National Academy Press; 2001.
2. Topol EJ. The creative destruction of medicine: how the digital revolution will create better health care. New York: Basic Books; 2012.
3. Mack H. 21st century cures act, ECHO Act both head to president's desk. MobiHealthNews, HIMSS Media; 2016. https://www.mobihealthnews.com/content/21st-century-cures-act-echo-act-both-head-presidents-desk
4. Moore GE. Cramming more components onto integrated circuits. Proc IEEE. 1998;86(1):82–5.
5. Heath S. mHealth App Market Sees $400 Million growth in five years. mHealth-Intelligence, Xtelligent Media; 2015. https://mhealthintelligence.com/news/mhealth-app-market-sees-400-million-growth-in-five-years
6. Lee TH, Campion EW, Morrissey S, Drazen JM. Leading the transformation of health care delivery—the launch of NEJM catalyst. N Engl J Med. 2015;373(25):2468–9.
7. Maranville S. Entrepreneurship in the business curriculum. J Educ Bus. 1992;68(1):27–31.
8. Dafny L, Mohta NS. New marketplace survey: the sources of health care innovation. NEJM Catal. 2017;16:2017.
9. Lipsitz LA. Understanding health care as a complex system: the foundation for unintended consequences. JAMA. 2012;308(3):243–4.
10. Rouse W. Health care as a complex adaptive system: implications for design and management. Bridges. 2008;38(1):17–25.
11. Plsek PE, Greenhalgh T. The challenge of complexity in health care. BMJ Br Med J. 2001;323(7313):625–8.
12. Wachter RM. The digital doctor: hope, hype, and harm at the dawn of medicine's computer age. xv, 330 p.
13. Christiansen C, Waldeck A, Fogg R. How disruptive innovation can finally revolutionize healthcare. Boston, MA: The Clayton Christensen Institute; 2017.
14. Sinsky C, Colligan L, Li L, Prgomet M, Reynolds S, Goeders L, et al. Allocation of physician time in ambulatory practice: a time and motion study in 4 specialties. Ann Intern Med. 2016;165(11):753–60.
15. Laja P. How to create a useful value proposition w/examples. https://conversionxl.com/blog/value-proposition-examples-how-to-create/. Accessed 16 Sep 2018.
16. Osterwalder A, Pigneur Y, Bernarda G, Smith A, Papadakos P. Value proposition design: how to create products and services customers want. Hoboken, NJ: Wiley; 2014.
17. Centers for Medicare and Medicaid Services (CMS). National health expenditures 2016 highlights. Baltimore; 2016.
18. Centers for Medicare and Medicaid Services (CMS). NHE Fact Sheet 17 April 2018.
19. American Hospital Association (AHA). Fast Facts on US Hospitals. 2018.
20. World Bank. GDP (current US$): World Bank national accounts data, and OECD National Accounts data files. 2018.

21. Kaiser Family Foundation (KFF). Professionally Active Physicians March 2018.
22. Kane CK. Policy research perspective: updated data on physician practice arrangements: physician ownership drops below 50 percent. American Medical Association; 2017. p. 15.
23. Corley J. Advanced-practice providers are key to America's healthcare future: Forbes. 2017. https://www.forbes.com/sites/realspin/2017/03/16/advanced-practice-providers-are-key-to-americas-healthcare-future/#5615b1da5998.
24. Morris J. Optimizing the value of advanced practice providers: Studer group. 2016. https://www.studergroup.com/resources/articles-and-industry-updates/insights/august-2016/optimizing-the-value-of-advanced-practice-provider.
25. Hostetter M, Klein S, McCarthy D, Hayes SL. Findings from a survey of health care delivery innovation centers. New York: The Commonwealth Fund; 2015.
26. Burrill S, Kane A. Deloitte 2017 survey of US health system CEOs: moving forward in an uncertain environment. Deloitte Center for Health Solutions; 2017.
27. Limited DTT. Global health care outlook the evolution of smart health care. 2018:2018.
28. Office of the National Coordinator for Health Information Technology. Hospital health IT developers: certified health IT developers and editions reported by hospitals participating in the Medicare EHR Incentive program. Department of Health and Human Services; 2017.
29. Office of the National Coordinator for Health Information Technology. Health care professional health IT developers: certified health IT developers and editions reported by ambulatory primary care physicians, medical and surgical specialists, podiatrists, optometrists. In: Dentists, and chiropractors participating in the Medicare EHR incentive program. Department of Health and Human Services; 2017.
30. Introduction to HL7 Standards: Health Level Seven International. http://www.hl7.org/implement/standards/index.cfm?ref=nav.
31. American Medical Association (AMA). HIPAA violations & enforcement. American Medical Association. https://www.ama-assn.org/practice-management/hipaa-violations-enforcement.
32. FDA. Digital health: U.S. Food and Drug Administration; 2017. https://www.fda.gov/medicaldevices/digitalhealth/
33. Osterwalder A, Pigneur Y, Clark T. Business model generation: a handbook for visionaries, game changers, and challengers. Hoboken, NJ: Wiley; 2010.

Chapter 4
Overcoming the Barriers to Dissemination and Implementation

Alan S. Young

The Age of the Electronic Medical Record

The rapid adoption of electronic medical records (EMRs) was catalyzed by government mandate and financial incentives to encourage healthcare practitioners, clinics, hospitals and systems to effectively transition the documentation within the electronic medical record from paper-based, manual processes to electronic and digital platforms. The rise of several electronic health record software companies eventually gave way to a handful of significant players who maintained dominance of the market for several years. While the survival of Epic, Cerner, Allscripts, Meditech and athenahealth promotes healthy competition, the implications on interoperability and data sharing are profoundly impactful. Today, the tight control each software vendor has maintained with their clients has limited the ability to share data in a meaningful way to find solutions to complex population health problems or gather relevant case studies for rare diseases. However, this tight control and corporate competition likely helped drive the adoption and utility of electronic medical records among the front-line users such as physicians and nurses. Despite the view that EMRs are costly, burdensome to physicians and interfere with the

A. S. Young (✉)
Everyoung Group, Everyoung Group, Arcadia, United States

doctor-patient relationship, wide spread adoption is continuing.[1] Epic Corporation was founded by the daughter of a physician who ultimately recognized the gross inefficiencies of hand-written medical charts and the inadequate use of historical charts to help patients.[2] As more and more entrepreneurs joined the race to create the ultimate electronic medical record, the adoption of the digital age in healthcare had begun.

Physicians who enjoyed creating detailed medical records for each patient encounter were a rare breed in comparison to those physicians who managed to capture the bare minimum amount of information in illegible notes. With the added pressure of productivity metrics such as RVU compensation or maximizing surgical caseloads, the volume of patient data was exceeding the ability of any individual to review and interpret on a regular basis. The added challenge was the variety of formats, hand-writing, abbreviations and clinical jargon that existed between different practice groups. Depending on your medical training in residency, fellowship and even medical school, the expectations for clinical documentation were not consistent across geographies. The concept of typing clinical notes or using a computer word processing software to capture this information was generally regarded as a distant dream that might happen in several decades. Leading healthcare organizations made initial investments to create their own proprietary medical record system or enlisted the help of these digital health entrepreneurs who offered a solution that could be used out of the box. Organizations like Kaiser Permanente chose a product from Epic[3] while other systems like Geisinger chose an alternate product from Cerner Corporation for population health.[4] During this time, there was no clear mandate to use electronic health records or penalties by way of government reimbursement to encourage wide adoption. The first movers who boldly took the risk by investing in the software soon faced the challenging task of achieving widespread stakeholder adoption and engagement.

Physicians are trained from an early age to excel at acquiring large volumes of scientific data and applying this information in a systematic way to help cure disease or alleviate suffering. The Hippocratic oath is usually taken at the end of medical school before a physician or surgeon embarks on another rigorous path of learning through an apprenticeship model. The focus on core sciences leaves physicians with very little bandwidth to explore other academic pursuits, such as music, literature or computer programming. Fast forward to the early years of electronic medical records and you have a population of extremely intelligent over achievers all able to perform procedures or deliver a differential diagnosis, but with limited computer or word processing skills. The newly introduced expectation of using computers during the practice of medicine was no doubt a challenging experience for many physicians young and old. Like any attempts at changing human behavior,

[1] https://www.mercatus.org/system/files/graboyes-electronic-health-records-mr-mercatus-v1.pdf.

[2] https://www.epic.com/about.

[3] https://ehrintelligence.com/news/10-biggest-epic-ehr-implementations-in-united-states.

[4] https://www.healthcarefinancenews.com/news/geisinger-taps-cerner-population-health.

there was a spectrum of responses ranging from angry rejection to joyful acceptance. Rebellion, outrage, burnout, cynicism and other emotional extremes could
have impeded the progress of the software implementations, but it is more likely
that physicians responded with cautious or reluctant acceptance. To those who
viewed the problems facing the healthcare industry with an astute perspective, the
transition to an electronic health record was inevitable, so why fight the change?
The proposed benefits of more efficient workflows, greater patient satisfaction and
access to information previously unavailable convinced many physicians to take on
the challenge and struggle through a clunky implementation project at the mercy of
the IT department. The results were mixed as some organizations reported immediate benefits from using the software while others struggled to regain productivity,
profitability and physician buy-in.

The surge in electronic medical record implementations followed closely behind
the introduction of the HITECH Act and Meaningful Use.[5] For the first time, the
U.S. government was in support of widespread adoption of some form of electronic
medical records and used a combination of legislation, policy, incentive payments
and reimbursement penalties to accelerate adoption of a software solution for paper
and hand-written medical records. The specific reasons why physicians started to
finally embrace the effort to move away from paper-based records could have been
one of many, but it is safe to assume that financial incentives coupled with financial
penalties for non-compliance were strong motivators for behavioral change. If clinical providers were salaried employees of larger health systems, the decision to
adopt an electronic medical record was usually made without any of their input or
agreement. This perceived oversight or lack of collaboration served as the basis for
many physicians and clinicians from fully engaging in the adoption and integration
process. There are several well documented examples of electronic medical record
implementation failures across the U.S. In one example, the medical group affiliated
with a large hospital in California felt neglected when they were not included in the
decision to purchase a specific software product. When it came time for the IT
implementation, the physician group remained detached. By the time the system
went live, the physicians reacted by refusing to use the system and instead reverted
to manual paper-based documentation processes while providing care. The hospital
leadership eventually succumbed to the demands of the medical group and had to
convert the current electronic medical record to another vendor solution that the
physicians preferred. There have been many organizations that have also switched
between software vendors such as Epic and Cerner due to early struggles following
implementation impacting operations or financial performance or because of merger
and acquisition activity.[6] The notion that consolidation and standardization leads to
cost savings and greater efficiency is carried over from the success of large health
systems such as Kaiser, Intermountain and Geisinger who used similar approaches
to manage hospital and ambulatory operations. Independent physicians and

---

[5] https://www.cdc.gov/ehrmeaningfuluse/introduction.html.

[6] https://ehrintelligence.com/news/ballad-health-swaps-cerner-ehr-for-epic-ehr-replacement.

free-standing community hospitals tended to delay spending to implement a new electronic health record and preferred to watch and learn as others went down the path towards the EMR first. Even then, sometimes the capital requirements to meet the demands of Meaningful Use or other legislation forced physicians or smaller hospitals to seek assistance in the form of an acquisition partner who would then invest to implement the needed technology.

The key lessons learned from observing the gradual adoption of electronic medical records over the past decade are as follows:

1. Adoption takes time—the complexity of healthcare systems and the personal nature of medicine make it unlikely that drastic changes will spread quickly and decisively
2. Healthcare stakeholders need incentives to drive change—Meaningful Use incentives and penalties created an irresistible pull for many organizations who viewed financial success as a critical part of their mission
3. There isn't a single magic bullet solution—the variation across software solutions and no single dominant player indicates that different organizations and patient populations require customized or localized solutions to meet their needs
4. Alignment from the executive office to the front lines will accelerate overall engagement but doesn't necessarily guarantee rapid adoption—stakeholder alignment is a pre-requisite for project success, but implementation plans still need to be systematic and dedicate enough time and resources to key components of the process such as change management and training

The Age of Big Data

The steady but persistent adoption of electronic medical records (EMRs) created growing databases of structured and unstructured clinical, financial and operational data. The promise of data-driven insights derived from the volume of collected information was one of the reasons EMR adoption gained momentum. Research studies benefitted from the easily accessible and categorized clinical charts compared to the previous experience of trying to collect and coordinate huge piles of paper charts with incomplete information in many cases. Revenue cycle departments gained access to more accurate and complete patient encounter records and clinical documentation to align with claims submissions and medical necessity reviews. The rising number of clinics, physicians and hospitals adopting EMR systems contributed to the data explosion that many organizations were not prepared to take advantage of. Those that did were able to apply business intelligence to the data and create clinical decision support tools, revenue cycle integrity practices and patient experience metrics as examples of successful implementation of analytics.

Having a repository of discrete data captured in the EMR gave physicians and other users the confidence they needed to accept the insights derived from any algorithms or analytics applied to the data sets. Reliability and reproducibility of data is a key factor in the eventual adoption and successful implementation of any dashboards or performance metrics used to support change. The use of evidence-based protocols and primary research sources have traditionally been used to convince stakeholders that a more proven methodology or process can be used instead of the current state. Even more powerful is the dissemination of peer-reviewed literature produced by authors that maintain some relationship with their colleagues in a selected sub-specialty or discipline in healthcare. Once the data has been blessed, it makes it easier to scale solutions to impact a larger number of stakeholders. The next hurdle to overcome is the wide range of applications that can be leveraged to manipulate data and to find the right solution for the problem at hand.

Scaling a concept to impact the greatest number of stakeholders is the dream of many entrepreneurs who have overcome adversity to achieve eventual success. Historically, the path to achieving this goal was well understood within the healthcare industry. New entrants into the healthcare space slowly developed their product or solution and gradually gained enough visibility to capture sufficient market share. The rise of new digital health companies continues to help push the envelop as to what is feasible for conservative, budget-conscious executives. However, many of the most promising start-up companies are facing cultural and logistical challenges that consume their time and resources. One approach to do is bring talented, like-minded high performing individuals to serve as champions for the adoption or change management process. A digital health startup may have the potential to solve very challenging and complex problems, but without advocates and champions across the various layers in a hospital or healthcare setting, the barriers to success are discouraging. A foundation of quality data is almost a prerequisite since many stakeholders evaluate novel ideas through objective measures and apply the same scrutiny previously reserved for research articles or journal publications. Merging reliable and reproducible data with strong champions across the organization has shown to accelerate the spread of entrepreneurial endeavors.

Big data by itself is not enough to win over all the relevant stakeholders to drive implementation of new ideas. The real value of the data comes from the insights or predictive models that can be derived from the aggregate information. It is important that gradual education and sharing of new ideas take place before any radical changes are introduced. Sometimes the culture and supporting infrastructure are not in a mature enough state to maintain the growth and development of new ideas. A carefully thought-out approach combined with effective execution of the strategic plan that includes big data as a component will likely be better positioned for success than forcing stakeholders to accept a new workflow without their early buy-in. The big ideas or "moonshots" tend to generate a lot of publicity, but it is the smaller, less glamorous projects that focus on solving relevant and practical problems that can generate positive early results when successful.[7] Learning from the challenges of adopting big data for practical applications in healthcare provides another

---

[7] http://fortune.com/2018/03/19/big-data-digital-health-tech/.

example of how to slowly disseminate a fundamental change in behavior and work-flows through the introduction of a new decision-making tool.

The key lessons learned from the rise of data repositories because of wide-spread electronic medical record implementation and usage over the past decade are as follow:

1. You can't engage downstream stakeholders and users without high quality, robust and accurate data to build credibility and eliminate one of the most common reasons for poor adoption and failed implementation of data tools
2. After establishing the data source is reliable and relative free of significant errors, the continued use of analytic tools is determined in large part by the driving force between the key performance indicators (KPIs). Be cautious of KPIs focused too heavily on financial or technical goals over clinical or quality ones.
3. Regular review and realignment of organizational goals and outside trends is needed to keep the performance targets of the data analytics consistent with the strategic objectives year after year.
4. The ability to scale and handle the exponential increase in data volume requires significant computing power and storage capabilities. A cloud migration strategy to integrate the data warehouse and the software applications needs to be carefully executed to avoid significant performance issues that could erode confidence in the data itself.

The Age of Value-Based Care

The increasing costs of delivering healthcare in the United States prompted the previous administration to enact several pieces of legislation that mandated the slow but inevitable migration of care delivery from fee for service to value-based care (VBC) models. Although the recent change in party leadership has threatened to undo several key features of the Affordable Care Act (ACA), otherwise referred to as Obamacare, the bipartisan support of value-based care initiatives reflects the stark reality that without significant intervention, the cost of healthcare in this country will outpace any attempts by politicians to control it.[8] The challenge lies in the incentives currently offered to healthcare organizations and physicians to generate revenue sometimes at the expense of the tax payers and the administrative expenses generated by health insurance companies and other non-essential parties that feed off the wasted dollars consumed and show no impact on health or outcomes. Value-based care is a noble aim and despite enormous effort and almost universal acknowledgement of the unsustainable course the healthcare system is on, the adoption of new policies, standards of care and well-intended technology have barely begun to make any change to the cost structure of the U.S. population.

---

[8] https://healthpayerintelligence.com/news/value-based-care-key-to-bipartisan-healthcare-system-reform.

Measuring the true impact of new healthcare policy at either the federal or state level down to the individual patient in a rural town requires the appropriate definition of what is the desired goal. There is no shortage of opinions around what the most important attributes are in our health system. Are we trying to extend the average life expectancy for all U.S. males and females? Do we want to lower the average per capita cost of delivering care? Is the elimination of certain chronic diseases or cancers an indication of how superior our healthcare system is compared to the rest of the world? A recent research article released by the World Health Organization (WHO) placed the United States at number 37 for overall health system performance. The Organization for Economic Cooperation and Development (OECD) in 2017 pointed out that the United States spends the most of any developed nation on healthcare but does not achieve better health outcomes for life expectancy at birth, infant mortality, management of asthma or diabetes or heart attack mortality.[9] How is this discrepancy explained between the amount of resources spent on healthcare in the U.S. (According to CMS, in 2016 17.9% of GDP was spent on healthcare which equals $3.3 trillion or $10,348 per person)[10] compared to measurements of performance? There is simply no easy answer but the move towards value-based care is an attempt to stop the bleeding before costs create a national budget crisis.

The single largest insurer in this country is expected to run out of funds needed to maintain Medicare, Medicaid and a whole host of other healthcare programs that millions of Americans depend on. A recent report released in June 2018 from key government program trustees revealed that Medicare will run out of money 3 years sooner than expected in 2026.[11] With this knowledge and the prospect of a failed system to care for the country's most vulnerable, there has been modest engagement across all levels of healthcare leadership to bend the cost curve and prolong the life of Medicare and other similar programs. While it is unlikely that solo or group practitioners will dramatically alter their current way of practicing medicine to save Medicare, larger organizations like Kaiser Permanente have strong leadership in place to implement value-based care programs that can impact the population on a grander scale. The recent increase in merger and acquisition activity across healthcare has folded many physician practices into health systems which move quickly to integrate new partners. Some view this activity as precautionary to prevent increased competition in a time of declining margins and reimbursements. Financial pressure on federal, state and local governments also put strain on the private non-profit health systems who care for a large percentage of the Medicare and Medicaid populations. The outcome of this stress produces long-lasting changes to workflows designed to lower the cost of caring for patient populations who do not generate profitable reimbursement.

---

[9] http://www.oecd.org/health/health-systems/health-at-a-glance-19991312.htm.

[10] https://www.cms.gov/Research-Statistics-Data-and-Systems/Statistics-Trends-and-Reports/NationalHealthExpendData/NationalHealthAccountsHistorical.html.

[11] https://www.cms.gov/Research-Statistics-Data-and-Systems/Statistics-Trends-and-Reports/ReportsTrustFunds/Downloads/TR2018.pdf.

Successful organizations have been able to adopt value-based care initiatives through internal projects or by bringing in outside expertise and leveraging recent wins. If there is no previous momentum around making the transition away from a fee-for-service model, the journey can be a long and arduous one. Early adopters of value-based care discovered that it was a difficult task to suddenly ask healthcare stakeholders to change the way they had been practicing medicine for decades if not generations. Physician champions or leaders were put in the middle of tense conversations between executives and clinicians. Even though the reasoning behind value-based care made sense, the reality was that financial contracts and incentives did not reward a more holistic approach to delivering cost-effective and outcomes-based care. Furthermore, some clinical departments lacked the project management experience to drive systematic process improvement with governance and change management. The result of these circumstances led to very slow incremental changes that did not significantly bend the cost curve or cause widespread behavioral change across clinical areas. Even today, many organizations still compensate physicians based on volume or RVUs and maximize financial returns without much thought given to better outcomes and lowering the cost of care burden. The success of some health systems to make significant progress in achieving the objectives of value-based care demonstrate that there is not a single uniform path to reach this goal. Rather, it is a pain-staking, complex journey that requires engagement and support from all areas of healthcare sharing the same goal of fixing a broken system for the benefit of the patients.

Value-based care resulted in a gradual movement that is still in the process of transforming the healthcare industry today. The focus on uncontrolled and unsustainable rising costs coupled with the misaligned incentives for hospital, doctors and executives led to legislative attempts to course-correct one of the most expensive and personal industries in the country. Some of the key drivers behind the expansion of value-based care include:

1. Financial and budget constraints at the level of federal, state and local government
2. Poor performance of the U.S. healthcare system when compared to the rest of the developed world and adjusting for average GDP expenditure per person
3. Shift towards quality performance and outcomes-based incentives for providers and payers
4. Consumerism in healthcare with changing population demographics and consumption patterns

The Age of Digital Health

The proliferation of digital health companies, applications and devices in healthcare has changed the way we think about innovation in medicine. The exponential growth in high speed internet service and wireless fidelity (Wi-Fi) access along with the ubiquitous nature of smart devices such as the iPhone, iPad and Apple Watch has created the foundation necessary for digital solutions to impact industries and business processes.[12] Some of the most profound examples of how a digital technology company has completed transformed the industry it evolved within include ride-sharing companies like Uber and Lyft, accommodation rental platforms like Airbnb, media and entertainment offerings like Netflix and Hulu and food delivery services like Postmates and Grubhub. The unifying theme of all these digital technology titans is the dramatic way they have transformed how normal business is conducted and the new standard that customers expect, while decimating competition that failed to adapt to the new norms of operating in a digital age. Healthcare has remained more resistant to dramatic industry disruption thanks in large part to the layers of regulation, compliance and regard for human safety. However, the demand is growing for digital health solutions and companies disrupting normal operating workflows to meet the consumer demand of growing populations of patients such as millennials and future generations of savvy buyers. The ideas of convenience, crowd-sourcing and virtual care have already created niche industries where patients can receive a telehealth consultation, order prescriptions and pay for services without leaving the comfort of their own home or other popular destinations. However, there are still significant challenges for these companies to enter the mainstream of healthcare delivery and convince established leaders to adopt digital health and accept the risks with any innovation. Digital health faces challenges to achieve widespread adoption and practical integration into the current healthcare landscape and infrastructure.

Healthcare providers are seeing a widening generational gap between themselves and their patients. A large segment of physicians, nurses and executives are considered traditionalists, baby-boomers or generation X. As the population ages, people born in generation Y, generation Z and the millennials are finding themselves in need of various healthcare services. Consumer behavior and expectations have shifted dramatically and in a short time coinciding with the proliferation of smart devices, internet access and technology applications. Instant communication and convenience are prevalent in multiple industries such as retail shopping, banking, dining and leisure travel. The ability to order food, make reservations, pay bills and communicate via text or emojis from a mobile device is transforming how companies engage their customers. Although healthcare is more than just a collection of simple transactions of goods and services, the growing sentiment among generation Z and millennials is to make healthcare as convenient and accessible as other necessities in life.[13] This dichotomy that exists between providers and patients has contributed to the slower adoption of digital health solutions and for many new entrants into the industry, caused their eventual demise. The demand for digital health solutions continues to grow, but the current supply of validated, compliant and evidence-based applications is limited and not enough to meet expectations. The result is a misalignment of priorities and a lack of empathy for each group's point of view. The

---

[12] https://www.ft.com/content/1efb95ba-d852-11e6-944b-e7eb37a6aa8e.

[13] http://blogs.deloitte.com/centerforhealthsolutions/bboomers-millennials-gen-z/.

acceptance of change and adoption of new care delivery models beginning with selected medical specialties or patient populations is starting to penetrate years of complacency and the reluctance to break from the traditional practice of medicine.

A major obstacle for digital health adoption is the ability of front-line staff and providers to become efficient users of a new technology or application. This challenge mirrors the difficulties faced by electronic medical record companies as they attempted to train thousands of providers to put down the pen and pad while turning to a computer keyboard regardless of their word processing or typing abilities. Frustration can be a long-term symptom of poorly integrated digital health solutions if the proper training, change management and elbow support is not in place. This frustration can easily turn to rejection of the solution or technology despite the positive benefits it may be able to demonstrate with continued usage. Careful planning and strategic mapping of key activities and milestones to engage stakeholders early is one approach to avoid poor adoption. Realistic expectations around how much training can be deployed and absorbed in relation to the group's baseline technical abilities can reduce friction when productivity and workflows do not return to baseline as quickly as planned. Applications can't be bolted on to existing tools without ensuring that workflows will be maintained and integration is achievable in a reasonable time frame. A one size fits all approach does not apply when you have a diverse and sophisticated work force that is accustomed to functioning at a high level at all times and understands the sensitivity of change when a patient's health is potentially at stake. Achieving the desired level of competency for a digital health tool requires a thoughtful and well-executed strategic plan that addresses the unique needs of the core users and bolsters their confidence with steady progression to a desired proficiency.

Another determining factor for digital health dissemination is the credibility and reproducibility of the underlying programming and data characteristics. During the rise of big data and analytics, physicians were quick to discredit algorithms or analyses that they did not fully understand or have visibility around the details. Some stakeholders can feel threatened when a new technology offers insights that seem to be generated from a non-medical or non-scientific formula. Despite the rigorous demands of computer engineering and data science programs that serve as the foundation for digital health solutions, medical professionals are slow to accept that a new idea originating from outside the industry can improve the current standard of care. A collaboration between clinicians and engineers or programmers in the form of a digital hackathon can create synergy and a deeper appreciation for each discipline. Transparency and sharing knowledge assist to drive support for digital health in organizations where multi-disciplinary teams work together to solve complex problems. This culture tends to be more receptive to outside contributors and can readily implement new technologies that have already been considered or discussed internally. When health organizations review data consistently and apply analytical tools to help mine for insights, it fosters an environment that values evidence-based approaches to clinical problems. This may result in higher standards for achieving recognition but is valuable to help identify quality initiatives that are sustainable and grounded in fundamental objective data to drive physician adoption.

Digital health implementation efforts also need to consider governance structure, data protection and cybersecurity along with current value-based care requirements. The volume of innovation and technology solutions can be overwhelming, and many organizations rely on the leadership of a Chief Information, Chief Innovation or Chief Intelligence Officer to help evaluate multiple options. Not all organizations have identified this leadership role and instead depend on seasoned executives who may not have the requisite background to fully evaluate the feasibility and applicability of new emerging technologies. The recent string of healthcare cybersecurity incidents has resulted in the loss of millions of personal health records containing sensitive information and increased scrutiny by organizations to identify their own vulnerabilities. New threats can distract leadership from considering substantial investments in unproven areas and instead increase their ongoing budgets for data security measures or infrastructure upgrades. Taking a conservative approach and being fiscally responsible is a comfortable approach for veteran hospital leadership, but this cultural preference makes it challenging for innovative digital health opportunities to gain traction and broad support. When an organization has achieved a robust data security infrastructure and has a forward-thinking governance and leadership in place, advancing projects in digital health is more achievable.

The challenges facing entrepreneurs in the digital health space can be daunting and may stifle creative ideas that require perseverance and patience to succeed in the healthcare industry. History suggests that the emergence of innovation in healthcare takes several years to reach a significant level of dissemination and adoption. The gradual implementation of electronic medical records was incentivized by government programs like the original Meaningful Use and HITECH Act that motivated physicians and healthcare organizations to invest in technology and change workflows. The rise of big data and analytics depended on high quality and reproducible data sets that withstood the scrutiny of skeptical physicians and other end users of the information. Slowly, stakeholders became comfortable with the tools and objectives of big data and started to see the benefits of continued adoption of analytics. The eventual realization of healthcare leaders that a volume driven or fee-for-service industry is unsustainable led to the introduction of more regulation by government to curb costs and shift to value-based care. The implementation of various quality reporting programs provided a combination of incentive payments or penalty avoidance along with the expected improvement to health outcomes. The overarching theme behind general adoption of new processes or solutions in healthcare is the alignment of not only incentives, but also the identification of what is most important to various stakeholders. Motivating people to change certain behaviors that pertain to an individual's health or personal values is a complicated and often time-consuming process. The momentum behind digital technologies across other industries may proceed at a break-neck speed, but in healthcare we are seeing a gradual adoption with pockets of hyper-activity depending on the specific demand or availability of a digital health innovation.[14]

---

[14] https://rockhealth.com/reports/digital-health-consumer-adoption-2015/.

Summary

The future of digital health is going to introduce even greater change to the health-care industry in the form of artificial intelligence, blockchain, wearable devices, virtual care and other technologies that will be applied to medicine in unique ways. One of the greatest barriers to adoption and knowledge sharing is the resistance of patients, providers and administrators to the unknown and untested. Scientific evidence has long been the gold standard against which new research and medical therapy is evaluated. However, the application of artificial intelligence in the form of computational decision making and cognitive learning using deep neural networks can greatly accelerate the time to bring novel ideas and therapies to the fore-front. The expectations and needs of each generation has shifted towards a more on-demand and convenience focused life-style where it is normal to have access to almost all aspects of a person's preferences through a smart device connected to the internet. Healthcare is facing the challenge of adapting to the needs of a younger patient population and an aging workforce that bring differing views on how to best deliver effective, compassionate and cost-effective care through current technology.

Chapter 5
Financing Your Digital Health Venture

Peter Adams

There has never been a better time to be raising capital for a digital health startup with the number and size of digital health deals increasing every year. The $100 million+ funding club continues to increase as companies grow and mature. Many digital health Digital Health companies are growing to become Unicorns worth $1 billion or more. Driven by an active M&Amergers and acquisitions environment, companies are able to raise capital, grow fast and provide liquidity for their investors. At the same time, with more and more digital health companies getting funded, it is getting harder to stand out from the crowd and digital health startups will have to show a strong awareness of activity in their space and present a clear differentiation from the rest. Understanding the early stage funding environment is a critical step towards success, and yet the process and language of venture capital are unfamiliar to many. In this chapter we'll cover some of the main points that lead to successful early stage digital health funding including the stages of funding and milestones, sources of funding, capital strategy, exit strategy, valuation and term sheets.

Sources of Funding for Digital Health Startups

Digital health startups are well poised to raise the funding they need for growth because of an active investor community in this space, great acquisition/exit environment and an industry that is hungry for innovation. We will review some of the most popular sources of capital for digital health companies at every stage of their growth.

P. Adams (✉)
Rockies Venture Club, Rockies Venture Fund, Denver, CO, USA
e-mail: peter@rockiesventureclub.org

© The Author(s), under exclusive license to Springer Nature Switzerland AG 2023   63
A. Meyers (ed.), *Digital Health Entrepreneurship*, Health Informatics,
https://doi.org/10.1007/978-3-031-33902-8_5

The earliest stage digital health startups still typically operate in bootstrap mode, raising money from friends, family and founders. While working towards development of a prototype or MVP (Minimum Viable Product) startup founders often keep their day jobs to pay the bills and work on their startup at nights or weekends. Additional cash resources may come from savings, credit cards or HELOC (Home Equity Line of Credit) from their bank. While the startup company itself will not qualify for funding, the founders themselves may have access to capital through these sources.

There is a caveat to using debt as an early stage funding source for the company. Angel and Venture Capital investors typically want their investments to go towards growing the company and will rarely allow founders to pay themselves back for the debt they may have incurred either from themselves or friends and relatives. An amortization schedule of 12–48 months is typically acceptable, so early debt investors should be prepared to be patient. Additionally, many founders are asked to convert their debt into equity, so it will be a long path to liquidity which should be considered before going down that path.

SBA (Small Business Administration) loan guarantees are another way for early stage companies to borrow money for their startup. The SBA effectively provides a loan guarantee to a local bank whose risk is significantly mitigated because of that. Many banks will still want to see your company as being close to positive cash flow before they will make the loan however, so that they know you will have the ability to pay off the loan. In addition to the caveat made earlier about investors not wanting to repay early debt, you should also be aware that SBA loans come with personal guarantee requirements, so you are personally on the hook in case of failure of the company and default. This additional risk to founders personally may make sense if they are the only owner of the company, but can be unfairly burdensome when stock is sold and others own the company and benefit from the use of the capital, but without their own personal risk.

Grants are a common source of early stage funding for digital health companies. SBIR (Small Business Innovation Research)grants are quite common. These grants range from $150,000 to over $1 million for different phases of research. The purpose of the grants is to outsource federal research and development expenses to companies with a strong likelihood of commercializing the technology. SBIR grants are issued through federal agencies such as the department of Health and Human Services, National Institute of Health, the National Science Foundation and others. STTR (Small business Technology TransfeR)grants provide funding for technology transfer from research institutions and can be a good source of early funding for projects coming out of U.S. research institutions.

The main things you need to do in order to be successful with grants is to become familiar with the granting agencies and develop relationships. Grant applications from parties unknown to the agencies are rarely granted. Additionally, grants work according to a strict calendar, so start early and get your ducks in a row. Finally, letters of support are crucial for success, so think through your reference strategy carefully.

In addition to federal grants you should also be looking at local economic development grants closer to home. These grants often require "matching funds", meaning that you need to match the grant dollars with dollars from other sources including revenue, investment or other grants. Some companies with strong grant strategies can create a domino effect when one grant is offered, two or three others may become activated.

Crowdfunding for either equity or "rewards" can work with some digital health companies, especially if the technology centers around some consumer oriented product such as wearables or fitness trackers. Rewards crowdfunding can be more effective in gauging consumer interest in a product than in actually raising capital. Being able to point to greater than expected consumer adoption is a great traction point that companies can use in their angel or venture capital pitch later on. The lure of crowdfunding can be great because it looks so easy from the outside. Be aware that it can cost tens of thousands of dollars to put together a crowdfunding campaign. Successful campaigns involve investors you already have in your network vs. investors who are registered on a platform. Additionally, if you are raising capital from an equity crowdfunding platform you should be aware of the dangers of taking on non-accredited investors or even large numbers of accredited investors. Both of those can be a red flag to VCs, many of whom will not want to join a capitalization table with so many other people. If you do use equity crowdfunding of any kind, be sure to have all the investors put their money into a Single Purpose Vehicle, an LLC that is a holding company for their investment, so that only one entity will show up on your capitalization table.

Accelerators can also be a source of funding for digital health startups. There are "horizontal" accelerators like TechStars that focus across technology in multiple industries. Other accelerators like Rock Health, Startup Health, Blueprint Health, Healthbox, TMCx, New York Digital Health Accelerator and many more are "vertically" oriented and focus just on digital health and/or healthcare oriented companies. Accelerators often contribute $25,000–$125,000 to their participants, usually from an accelerator fund, and also host a "demo day" for participants to pitch to the community of angel and VC investors for more capital.

Angel investors will typically look at a digital health startup when it is at the MVP or prototype stage. Angels will typically see their money used for putting finishing touches on technology and getting your company into some pilot projects with healthcare providers, or test your marketing channel strategies. When angels invest as individuals the typical investment range is between $25,000 and $100,000 per investor. When angels invest in groups, the typical range is $500,000–$1 million.

Many people confuse angel investors with the friends and family investors who invest early in the company. Angels think a lot more like venture capitalists than they do like your friends and family. While friends and family will invest primarily in you, the angels are investing primarily to make a profit. They will want to see a clear path to exit which provides them with at least ten times their money in return, with the possibility of up to one hundred times returned.

Angel investors present themselves in several ways, but one big distinction is that some angels are lone-eagles who invest on their own and others invest through angel groups. There are hundreds of angel groups across the U.S. Canada, Europe and Asia. You can find many of them on the Angel Capital Association website (www. angelcapitalassociation.org). The benefit of working through an angel group is that groups typically do their due diligence once all together and help angels make decisions to invest with having the entrepreneur go through "Groundhog Day" (as in the movie with Bill Murray) and having to go through diligence over and over for each investor. Additionally, many angel groups syndicate with other angel groups, so if you make the right connections, you can get your company funded by the collaboration of many groups investing together. Syndication is basically the process of one or more investors investing together on the same deal terms.

Family Offices are another source of capital. These act almost as a super-angel, doing their own due diligence and investing separately or through groups or syndicates. Family Offices have millions to invest, but often have only a small portion of their assets allocated for startup investments.

Venture capital is an option once you're well into revenue. Seed stage VCs may look at your deal in a pre-revenue stage, but getting to Series A, which is the first round of institutional venture capital, typically takes revenue in the $1 million–$2 million per year range. Series A investments can range anywhere from $5 million to $20 million dollars today.

You should begin developing relationships with venture capital funds up to a year or more before you actually need the money. VC is a relationship based transaction and they want to know you for a while and see how your company performs against its goals. If you meet with a VC and let them know your expected milestones for the next 6 months, it's a good strategy to over perform and come back 6 months later to show how you are able to execute. This extended relationship is actually a part of many VCs due diligence strategies. By watching your performance over time, they can get an idea of how well you'll execute once they have invested.

Corporate Venture Capital (CVC) has become a powerful player in the venture capital world and now accounts for over 25% of all venture capital investments. There is a particularly high amount of CVC action in the digital health space as institutions and healthcare companies are looking towards venture capital investments to keep their fingers on the pulse of the industry and to tap into new technologies. There is a saying that "M&A is the new R&D". This means that while research and development expenditures from major companies has been on the decline for many years, CVCs are investing in early stage companies to help fill their pipeline for mergers and acquisitions. It is easier, cheaper and faster for companies to bring on new products and revenue by acquiring companies rather than developing new technologies in house.

Keep in mind that working with CVCsis a two edged sword. On the one hand, having a "strategic" investor can provide you with faster growth, if your investors become customers, and on the other hand there can be a problem with "signaling" if they are on your cap table (a table showing all investors in your company) and they choose not to acquire you. When other companies are going through due diligence when looking to make an acquisition offer for your company, they will be wondering what the CVC knew after having sat on your board of directors for years and having decided not to acquire you. There may be perfectly good reasons why they did not choose to buy, but regardless it sends a signal to others that there may be something wrong with your company.

ICO or Initial Coin Offerings are a relatively new way for digital health companies to raise money, especially if their technology is in some way blockchain enabled. There have been many successful ICOs and the average ICO last year was about $44 million. There are many strategies for raising money using an ICO and the SEC (Securities Exchange Commission) is developing more transparent guidelines about whether "tokens" which are sold in the ICO are securities. ICOs have fallen out of popularity lately due to regulatory uncertainty and large swings in cryptocurrency markets. There is too much detail to go into here, but if you think this could be a good source of funding, do your research first!

Other sources of funding include factoring (accounts receivable finance), purchase order lending, other asset backed lending, revenue sharing (for companies with positive cash flow), and asking your customers to become investors—both by buying your product or service, and also by making a direct debt or equity investment in your company.

You may want to think about all of these funding choices as a suite of tools to serve your capital needs. You do not need to choose just one type or another. You can mix and match the most effective sources for capital for your stage of business and capital use needs.

A Tranching strategy is a good way to minimize your dilution as you raise capital. Regardless of the source of capital that you choose, you will want to think carefully about your capital tranching strategy. Tranching is basically the process of breaking up your total capital needs into phases. By raising only as much as you need to reach your next major milestones (and a little extra buffer since it will likely take you longer than you thought), you can minimize your dilution and make it easier to raise each round.

Most startup capital raises are enough to fund 12–24 months of runway. But it's not just about the amount of time you need to fund, you also need to be aware of the milestones you need to hit. For example, if you are raising a seed round which you hope will take you to a Series A venture capital round, then you should make sure that your raise will be sufficient for you to build your sales up to $1 million or more in annual revenue run rate.

Valuing Your Digital Health Startup

While valuing a pre-revenue startup may seem difficult or near impossible to many, this is something that is done every day and there are good tools to get you to a valuation number that will be satisfactory for both investors and entrepreneurs.

The first thing to realize when you're valuing your company is that the goal is not to come up with a number like $3,257,456.67. There is no process to get to a number that exact, and even if you could, negotiations for early stage equity are typically done more in round numbers. In fact, our goal is to come up with a satisfactory "negotiation range" in which there will be a fair deal for both founders and investors.

Many people think that you can't value early stage pre-revenue companies and that instead of doing a "priced round" in which the valuation is clearly negotiated and investors invest in stock in the company, some people think that you can escape valuation by using a simple agreement for future equity (SAFE) or "convertible debt" (a note payable that has a provision for conversion to equity at a set time or when a qualifying funding round occurs.) Just using a SAFE or convertible note does not get you out of having to value the company. One of the main terms of the SAFE and convertible note is the "valuation cap" or the value above which the conversion price will not go. So, if the valuation cap on a convertible note is $3.5 million, then the investor is likely to end up converting to stock at a later date at the $3.5 million price. So, obviously, if you use a SAFE or convertible note, you still need to go through the valuation exercise to determine the valuation cap. The simple formula for calculating the valuation cap and better understanding the difference between the company valuation cap and the company valuation is shown below. (Hint: they are the same.)

$$Valuation\ Cap = Equity\ Valuation$$

Valuation and negotiation in the venture capital world is not like it is in other types of commerce where the buyer wants the lowest price and the seller wants the highest price. In VC the best deal is the one that is most fair for both parties. If the price is too low, then there will not be enough dry powder equity available for future rounds of investment. If the price is too high then there is a risk of a "down round" where the share price in the next round is lower than the previous round, resulting in significant dilution for the founders.

The process of finding the negotiation range involves using multiple valuation methods. Think of this as an uncertainty reduction exercise in which your job is to start with great uncertainty and then, by applying several valuation methodologies, reducing uncertainty down to where you have a reasonable negotiating range.

The methodologies that you use are rarely satisfactory for coming up with a valuation on their own. Each has its own challenges and imperfections, but when used together, it actually works. Think of these as five drunks in an alley who can barely stand up on their own, but who, when working together manage to stand up. That's why we use multiple models. Another reason for using multiple models is that we are tackling the question of valuation from multiple viewpoints. It would not make sense to do five different DCF (Discounted Future Cash Flow) models, because they would all use the same inputs and would likely reproduce the outputs of each other. In our case we will recommend models that use DCF, models that use risk adjustment, models that are finance based, and models that are based on comps, much like a real-estate appraisal. By attacking the question of valuation from multiple angles, we get a fairly comprehensive view of what creates value in a startup company.

Here are a few samples of valuation methodologies at work. We don't have enough space to do them all, but these should give you a good idea of how you can get a good valuation even if the company is not in revenues yet. Note one benefit of using models like this is that when you are negotiating your deal you have supporting data to support your arguments. Investors and founders can negotiate on the assumptions vs. the Big Number all by itself.

The Venture Capital Method

The venture capital method comes to a valuation number by working from the exit and backing into a valuation number. This is a DCF (Discounted Future Cash Flow) method because we're going to model what a likely exit scenario is and then apply a venture capital discount to that to determine the value of the company today.

You can see in Table 5.1 that the Exit Year, Revenue at Year Five, Price to Revenues Ratio and the Exit Valuation are all working together to create the number from which we are going to be deriving our present day valuation. If the revenues are $ten million at year 5 and the standard exit valuation is 5 times top line revenues, then the exit valuation in our model is 5 times $ten million, or $50 million. Now we apply our discount rate of 60% IRR (Internal Rate of Return—IRR is effectively an interest rate that compounds over five years. One dollar invested at 60% IRR will yield about $10 dollars in 5 years). The discount multiple is based on the lack of liquidity for the investment, lack of control (since angel/vc investors are typically minority shareholders), and the extraordinary risk in investing in tech startups.

While coming up with the year five revenues in your proforma financial projections can be difficult, and researching the common price to revenues ratios can be difficult, doing the math for this method is easy. What number times ten equals our exit valuation? The number is $5 million. That is our post-money valuation (the valuation of the company including the investors capital contribution). Now we subtract our investment of $1 million and come up with the pre-money valuation of $4 million. You should always use the pre-money valuation when talking to investors.

Table 5.1 Venture capital valuation method

Investment amount	$1,000,000
Exit year (estimated)	Year 5
Revenue at year 5 (proforma)	$10,000,000
Price to revenues ratio for exits	5
Exit valuation	$50,000,000
Discount rate	60%
Discount multiple	10×
Post money valuation	$5,000,000
Pre-money valuation	$4,000,000

You will note that the Venture Capital Method only works on deals that have one round of funding. Other models will allow you to model valuations after Series A, Series B, etc. and will help you to calculate cumulative dilution for both founders and investors.

Dilution is not as bad as most entrepreneurs and investors think. If you mistakenly believe that owning 1,000,000 shares of founder stock and selling 25% of the company means that you have 750,000 shares after the transaction, then you would be justified in being worried about dilution. Instead, the founders will always have 1,000,000 shares of stock, and selling 25% of the company means that they are issuing 333,333 new shares of stock. Since 1,000,000 is 75% of 1,333,333 the founders keep their stock and dilution is not as bad as they thought. Additionally, any further rounds equally dilute first round investors and founders, so the dilution effect is shared. The average angel investment round in the U.S. is about 20–25%, but the investment range can vary widely from deal to deal.

The Scorecard Method

The scorecard method works like a real-estate appraisal. To do a real estate appraisal, the appraiser researches recent comparable transactions in the neighborhood. The appraiser then adjusts the prices up or down compared to the target house based on factors such as total square footage, number of bedrooms, number of bathrooms, granite countertops, etc. The scorecard method works much the same way. We start by researching the average startup value, then adjust the valuation up or down based on the key factors that impact startup valuation such as Team, Opportunity Size, Product, etc.

To use the Scorecard method shown in Table 5.2, you first need to research the average valuation for seed rounds in your industry. Last year the average was about $3.65 million nationwide. You can find this information from a variety of sources including the Angel Capital Association's Angel Funders Report, Crunchbase, Pitchbook or CB Insights among others.

Table 5.2 Scorecard valuation method

Average company valuation			$3,500,000
Value drivers	Weight	Score (0–400%)	Weight × score
Team	30%	200%	.60
Opportunity size	25%	200%	.50
Product/technology	15%	100%	.15
Competitive environment	10%	125%	.13
Marketing/sales partnerships	10%	200%	.20
Need for additional investment	5%	50%	−.03
Other factors	5%	150%	.08
			1.625
Scorecard adjusted valuation			$4,875,000

The Value Drivers and Weighting stay the same for every valuation. Team, for example, is always 30% of the value. It should be surprising to anyone that this is the most important driver.

The actual valuation exercise is in the Score column. If all of the rows were set to 100%, then the company would be average in all ways and the multiplier would be 1.0 and the valuation would then be $3.5 million (or whatever you used for your average for digital health startups). But companies are not all alike and this is where we score them. For the Team driver, 100% looks like three developers and a dog. If they have more people, then they would go up to 150% and even higher for a big team. It's not just about quantity of course but getting a lot of people to quit their day job to join your team is a significant validator of the quality of your company and demonstration of traction. On the other hand if you had only two people, then the score might be 50–75%. If you had a CEO with multiple $100 million exits under their belt, and a full team of highly qualified individuals, with all of the main areas covered (finance, strategy, marketing, technology, etc.) then it might get to 400%. Once you have entered all the scores, then you would multiply the score by the weighting and add it all up to get your valuation multiplier which you would apply to your baseline valuation to get your final valuation.

The Scorecard method is a good way to help you get through negotiation, but it takes a lot of experience and comparisons to other teams before you can do this one well. It does have a lot of subjectivity to it, but when used along with the other methods, it is quite valuable.

One last word on valuation. Now that you have an idea about how to calculate the valuation of a company, you should also know that the valuation of the company is not necessarily the same as the price for that company. One of the first digital health companies I ever invested in had a price that was easily $1 million less than the valuation that I got when I ran these models. I told the CEO that I had come up with a higher valuation and he told me that he knew the value was $4 million, but he was pricing it at $3 million because he had two pilots launching in 3 months and he needed the capital quickly to make sure that all the development work was done in time for the pilots. Indeed he raised the round in just a few weeks and the two pilots launched successfully and on time. The company is now worth more than $54 million and continues to grow very quickly. If he had priced it at the value of the company, it would have taken a few months and the opportunity window for the pilots would have closed.

Exit Strategies

Digital health startups are getting funded fairly easily today in part because there is such a robust M&A market for digital health companies. Established companies are buying up digital health companies for a variety of reasons and they are paying higher and higher multiples for them. Having a strong exit strategy is almost a necessity for raising capital today.

Just being a good digital health company is not enough to grab the interest of investors and then ultimately acquirers—you need to have a well-articulated exit strategy to maximize the value of your company. We've created the Exit Strategy Canvas to help you work through the exit value proposition and timing so that you can present the strongest story to your investors. Many investors will not admit it, but the exit strategy is the number one filter for whether they jump into a deal or not. It should be no surprise that having a well thought out strategy for returning the investor's money would be helpful in getting them to write a check.

Many people struggle to state their exit strategy and will resort to generalizations like "we're going to shoot for M&A or IPO". This is NOT a strategy and will do little to engage your investors. The six sections of the Exit Strategy Canvas will help you to find the elements of a strategy which can then be used to create your exit story.

Industry Vectors is the first segment to complete. A good CEO is also a good Futurist and should have a deep knowledge of his or her industry and the vectors that are impacting the future of the industry. Vectors could include "rising cost of healthcare", "problems with uninsured people," "changes in regulations", "competing technologies", "rapid growth of IoT", "blockchain", "DNA sequencing", etc. Another way to look at the Industry Vectors is to watch what the incumbents are doing and where their pain points are. What pain points now will be even bigger for them in the next three to 5 years. If you build your strategy by thinking about what the potential acquirers need rather than just the customer's needs, then you are a step ahead of your competition.

Values are the next thing to consider. If your goal is to be acquired, this is a relationship similar to getting married and you should make sure you understand the values of your organization and to find ways to ensure that your potential acquirers share those values. A significant amount of M&A transactions fail and a failure to match values is one of the biggest causes.

Recent Comparable Transactions are your next section to complete. Here you will report your research on acquisitions, showing who the acquiring company was, who got acquired, what the dollar amount of the transaction was, what the sales price was as a multiple of revenues and a summary of the acquisition strategy. Collecting this information tells you several important things. First, you learn about where the sweet spot is for acquisitions. You will find some outliers and digital health has certainly had a good number of unicorns (private companies valued at $1 billion or more) which are typically outliers. You will find that companies like yours will mostly be acquired within a certain zone like $100 million–$150 million. This helps you to develop your strategy and populate your proforma financial projections you give to investors. If, for example, you find that companies like yours are being bought for five times revenues and average $100 million, then you know that your target revenue run rate to have an optimal exit should be around $20 million.

The second thing you learn in this space is what the revenue multipliers have been. If you create a value oriented strategic plan, you may be able to sell at the higher end of the multiples you find. If you just build a company that focuses on customers but not the acquirer, then you may end up with lower multiples. I call this principle the "second customer" principle, meaning that you need to simultaneously build your company to serve the first customer who buys your digital health product, and also to provide maximum value to your "second customer" who buys your company. These value propositions are not the same and should be considered simultaneously in any important strategic decision.

You will find that it is difficult to locate much of this information. If you have incomplete information on some transactions, that is ok. Go ahead and use them to fill out the table. Some information is better than none at all. You can find some of this information in the SEC EDGAR database online, or at Pitchbook, CBInsights, Crunchbase and other data sources (Table 5.3).

Your Team is the next section. The team is NOT the same team you might have on a pitch deck slide. You should identify the gaps in your team that need to be filled to achieve an optimal exit. These people may be consultants or advisors, or they may be full time on your staff. Examples include lawyers, accountants, investment bankers, CEOs with exit experience, etc. By identifying and engaging these individuals now, you can use them to build your exit strategy as well as to execute on it.

Exit timing is one of the most important issues to consider because you never know when an acquirer might come knocking on your door. You should be thinking about your value proposition to acquirers and how that changes over time. Early on in your startup, the value may be for the technology, patents or employees (an "acquihire" is an acquisition just to get your team). You should be thinking about that value proposition as it evolves to include customers, distribution channels, cash

Table 5.3 Exit strategy canvas

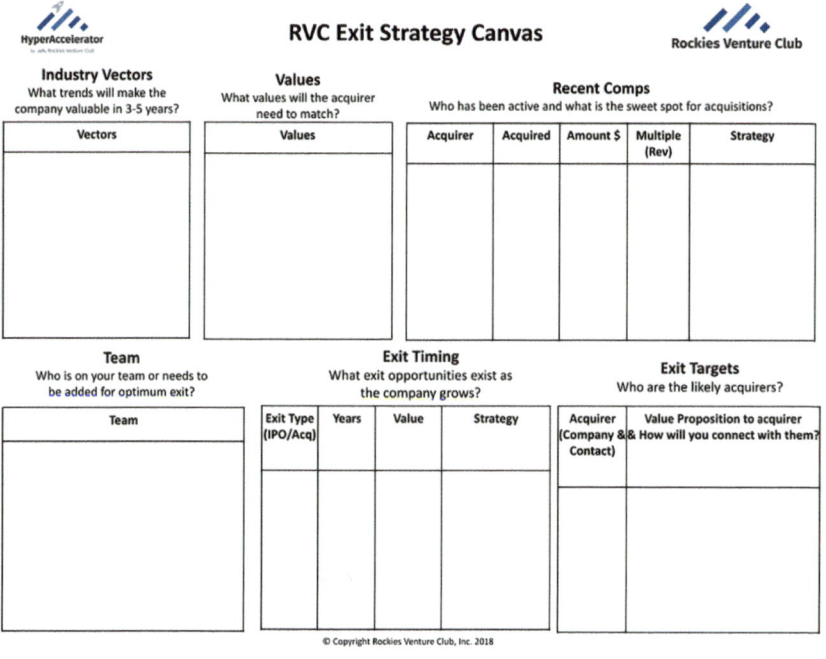

© Copyright Rockies Venture Club, Inc. 2018

flow, new technology or other competitive advantages. It's a good idea to always know what your company is worth, so when an offer does come along, you know if it's a fair one or not.

Exit Targets is the final segment to complete. You will want to identify who are the likely acquirers of your company. You should identify not only the company that will do the acquiring, but the people inside the company who will lead the decision making process. This is different for all companies, so you may need to do some research. In some cases it comes from the CEO or CFO, others have strategy departments, M&A groups, corporate development teams, or product managers.

Once you have identified the people you need to know, it's time to do some research. Get on LinkedIn and connect to them. Join the LinkedIn groups that they are members of. Find out what conferences and trade shows they attend. Read their blogs and find out how they think. Write your own blogs and send them to your contacts. Be a thought leader in your industry and get known for that. M&A is much like venture capital because it is a people oriented business. Corporate Development teams like to get to know you 6 or 12 months before they consider making an offer, so starting the relationships early on in your company life-cycle is a really good idea.

Once you have completed the Exit Strategy Canvas, you can use it to help make decisions, make a better story for your pitch deck and to drive alignment between your team members, board members and investors. One investor I know asks to have a review of the exit strategy at every board meeting. It does not need to take a lot of time, but it ensures that everyone is still on the same page for this important piece of your company's strategy.

Remember, exit strategy is the number one filter that investors have for making investments, so having a well-researched exit strategy is your best strategy for raising capital for your business.

There are many other factors for you to consider in your fundraising strategy including putting together a killer pitch deck and presentation style, building a team, developing a prototype or MVP of your product, getting your legal house in order, preparing for due diligence so it goes smoothly, refining your strategic execution plan, validating your customer value proposition, writing up a draft term sheet so you're always ready to close on an investor meeting and much, much more. We have covered some of the more complex topics here that apply especially to digital health startups and there is a wealth of resources that serve the needs of all startups that I would encourage you to become familiar with.

Funding your startup is hard—good luck!

Chapter 6
The Role of Artificial Intelligence in Digital Health

Anthony Chang

Artificial Intelligence: Basic Concepts

Intelligence can be defined as the ability to learn or understand or to deal with new situations or to apply knowledge or skills to manipulate one's environment. These definitions have interesting implications for artificial intelligence. Perhaps the best definition of artificial intelligence is the one conjured by the American cognitive scientist Marvin Minsky: the science of making machines do things that would require intelligence if done by man (woman).

Artificial intelligence can be categorized as weak vs. strong: weak (or specific, narrow) AI pertains to AI technologies that are capable of performing specific tasks (like playing chess or *Jeopardy!*) and strong (or broad, general) AI, also called artificial general intelligence (or AGI), relates to machines that are capable of performing intellectual tasks that involve human elements of senses and reason. The public perception of artificial intelligence, however, continues to be that of the menacing robots that threaten mankind (such as HAL in *2001: A Space Odyssey* or *The Terminator*). Recently, this perception is modified to that of the more sophisticated and complex artificial intelligence-inspired but humanoid robots seen in the movies *Her* (2013) and *Ex Machina* (2015).

Machine learning (and its specific domain deep learning) are not synonymous with artificial intelligence but are rather types of AI methodology. AI, however, does overlap with data science and data mining as well as big data. Other AI methodologies can include cognitive computing and natural language processing. Cognitive computing (as exemplified by IBM's Watson cognitive computing platform) can involve a myriad of AI tools that simulates human thinking processes while natural

A. Chang (✉)
The Sharon Disney Lund Medical Intelligence and Innovation Institute (MI3),
Children's Health of Orange County, Orange, CA, USA

language processing involves connecting human language with computer programmed understanding.

A Brief History of Artificial Intelligence and Its Role in Medicine

It is the British mathematician and computer scientist Alan Turing, however, who would be considered the progenitor of artificial intelligence with his pioneering works that included his theory of computation and his work on computing machines [1, 2]. His most valuable contribution was his deciphering of the German Enigma machine during the second World War at Bletchley Park using machine intelligence (portrayed in the film *The Imitation Game*). The eponymous Turing Test is a test of machine AI's ability to pass as a human.

In 1956, mathematicians and scientists gathered at the seminal Dartmouth Conference and it is the proposal for this august gathering that the term "artificial intelligence" was coined by the Stanford computer scientist John McCarthy. This summer conference and its discussions is widely thought to be the birth of AI as an interdisciplinary field.

Following this early epoch of machine intelligence, two AI "winters" in the 1970s and then subsequently in the following decade occurred due to concomitant lofty expectations and suboptimal realities, resulting in an overall disappointing outlook on AI. Main shortcomings include the lack of a theory-to-use coupling as well as the inadequate integration of the existing AI techniques into workflows to achieve user support.

Initial efforts in artificial intelligence and its application in medicine began in the 1960s and focused mainly on diagnosis and therapy. Among the best known early works on AI in medicine was the Stanford physician and biomedical informatician Edward Shortliffe's innovative heuristic programming project MYCIN. This pioneering work was a rule-based expert system (written in the Lisp programming language) that had if-then rules; these rules yielded certainty values that mimicked a human's expertise (such as recommended selection of antibiotics for various infectious diseases) [3]. The knowledge from a human expert was entered into a knowledge base, which in turn was connected to an inference engine. The non-expert user then queries a user interface that was coupled to the inference engine. The advice was then given to the user via this user interface.

The Current Era of Artificial Intelligence and Its Impact on Medicine

The data mining and machine learning focus in the 1990s slowly revived the field of AI and this era was best symbolized by IBM's supercomputer Deep Blue, which defeated the reigning world chess champion Gary Kasparov in 1997. Another IBM supercomputer, Watson (named after its first CEO Thomas Watson), with access to over 200 million pages of content and developed in IBM's DeepQA (question and answer) project, easily defeated the human champions Ken Jennings and Brad Rutter on February 14, 2011, on the game show *Jeopardy!*. In a similarly dominant fashion, the AlphaGo program of DeepMind easily defeated the human Go champion Lee Sedol in March 2016, thus heralding a new era of AI with deep learning.

The recent advent of an AI "trinity" that consists of: (1) the increasingly large volumes of available data that requires new computational methodologies (or simply "Big Data"), (2) the escalating capability of computational power (with faster, cheaper, and more powerful parallel processing that defied Moore's Law) and cloud computing (with nearly infinite storage), and (3) the emergence of machine and deep learning with its variants have together promulgated this new dawn of AI.

Algorithms The advent of complex and efficient algorithms (sets of steps to accomplish certain tasks) that are available for not only calculations and data processing but also automated reasoning has advanced the capabilities of machine intelligence. Examples of complex algorithms that are in current use include Pixar's coloring of 3D characters in virtual space (rendering algorithm) and NASA's operations of the solar panels on the international space station (optimization algorithm).

Big Data Data have escalated in a myriad of ways to the point that traditional data processing applications are no longer adequate. The four "V"s of big data often discussed are: (1) volume (over 40 zettabytes, or the equivalent of 40 trillion gigabytes, are expected to be in existence by 2020 with internet of things accelerating this growth), (2) variety (videos, wearable technology, tweets, and structured vs. unstructured types of data can create a digital chaos), (3) velocity (speed data is accessed such as with streaming data and over 20 billion network connections by the end of this year), and (4) veracity (uncertainty of data is not only costly but leads to inaccurate conclusions). Additional "V"s in big data include: value, visualization, and variability.

Cognitive Computing Cognitive computing uses machine learning, pattern recognition, and natural language processing (NLP) as well as other AI tools to mimic the human brain and its self-learning capability. The IBM supercomputer Watson with its victory in the game show *Jeopardy!* against human champions in 2011 heralded the era of cognitive computing with its potent NLP and knowledge representation and reasoning capabilities along with machine learning [4]. The supercomputer can scan 40 million documents in 15 s.

There is sometimes understandable confusion between AI and cognitive computing. While AI does not intentionally mimic human thought processes, cognitive computing with its origin in cognitive science, does attempt to simulate the human problem-solving process in a computerized model via AI tools such as machine learning, neural networks, and natural language processing as well as sentiment analysis and contextual awareness. While the present day virtual assistants are preprogrammed collection of responses, a cognitive system can yield a more thoughtful "human" response in the near future.

Machine Learning Machine learning is an increasingly popular sub-discipline of AI and focuses on big data. In machine learning, a computer uses algorithms to find patterns in data. The sophisticated algorithms are used to interpret data (from a "training set") with the use of classifiers (features or attributes that are used to classify the subjects in a process called feature extraction) in order to make predictions (from an initial "test set" first followed by new datasets).

In other words, the features are predictor variables with labeled outcomes. In short, the four steps of machine learning are: data pre-processing, feature extraction, machine learning algorithm, and predictive model as the last step.

Machine learning is usually categorized into three types of learning:

First, **supervised learning** take raw data and use an algorithm to predict the outcome based on a prior training set of data that are labeled. These supervised learning methodologies lead to classification and regression. Classification leads to categorization of output variables whereas regression leads to numerical representation of output variables. These supervised learning methodologies include: support vector machines (SVM), naive Bayesian classifiers, k-nearest neighbor (k-NN), linear and logistic regression, and decision trees methods (like random forest).

Second, **unsupervised learning** take unlabeled data and use algorithms to predict patterns or groupings in the raw data set. These unsupervised learning methodologies lead to clustering or association. Other questions unsupervised learning can answer include segmentation and dimension reduction.

In addition to the aforementioned supervised and unsupervised learning, a third type of machine learning is **reinforcement learning**. In this type of learning, the model finds the optimal method to achieve the most desirable outcome analogous to humans attempting to attain the highest score in a game. In other words, there is a positive and negative feedback to the solution of the algorithm so reinforcement learning is well suited for decision process. Reinforcement learning is the methodology that AlphaGo utilized in its defeat of the human Go champion and may be an asset for biomedicine as it is designed to make decisions in an uncertain environment.

There are several limitations with machine learning. A common issue with machine learning resides in its "black box" characteristic- for those who are not data scientists, it is difficult to understand the data science in the machine learning process [5]. Some of the higher prediction accuracy machine learning methodologies (deep learning, random forest, support vector machines, etc.) have the least explainability whereas others (Bayesian belief nets, decision trees) have more explainability (but lower prediction accuracy). There is an ongoing effort to elevate explainability in the form of "explainable AI or XAI") while maintaining (or even increasing) prediction accuracy with a new suite of techniques.

Deep Learning In 2012, the team from University of Toronto used a deep learning algorithm with 650,000 neurons and five convolutional layers to reduce the error rate in half during a computer vision challenge [6]. Andrew Ng of Stanford and Google and others synthesized huge neural networks by increasing the number of layers and neurons to enable large data sets to be trained to promulgate deep learning [7–9].

Whereas traditional machine learning flow has feature extraction followed by machine learning algorithm that leads to output, deep learning flow involves an artificial neural network that can combine feature extraction with the classification as one step. Machine learning, compared to deep learning, is relatively easy to train and test but its performance is dependent upon its features and is limited even with increasing volume of data. On the other hand, while deep learning can learn high-level features representation, it does require large amounts of data for training ("big data") and can be expensive from a computation usage perspective. In addition, deep learning are more difficult to comprehend as the algorithms are largely self-directed.

All of the aforementioned tools in the panoply of AI technologies are essential to deliver "intelligence-based medicine" as the tools will enable the narrowing of the gap in knowledge.

Current Concepts of Artificial Intelligence in Medicine

How Doctors Think In Jerome Groopman's *How Doctors Think* [10], he aptly described several deficiencies in the way physicians think. One such mechanism is confirmation bias, which is the tendency for physicians to search for information that confirms one's preexisting hypothesis. In Sherlock Holme's parlance: "It is a capital mistake to theorize before one has data. Insensibly one begins to twist facts to suit theories, instead of theories to suit facts." Another example of cognitive error is the availability heuristic or an intellectual shortcut that relies on immediate recall when evaluating a situation. The myriad of human biases and heuristics can potentially be neutralized with an AI-supported strategy in decision-making process.

Comparing Doctors and Data Scientists Daniel Kahneman, the Nobel Prize-winning psychologist noted for his work on decision making, described System 1 vs. System 2 thinking (fast and experiential vs. slow and analytical, respectively) [11]. This dichotomy conveniently delineates some of the key differences between clinicians (prone to System 1 thinking) and data scientists (with their affinity for System 2 thinking). For example, physicians often rely on a fast intuition-based "System I" thinking that is based on experience and accumulated judgment. Data scientists, on the other hand, more frequently approach problems with slower and more logical progressive thinking that is rationality-based "System 2" thinking. Medicine ideally should perhaps incorporate both types of thinking and individualize decisions based on how much of either type is appropriate. This strategy will minimize the pitfalls in diagnosis and treatment due to inherent heuristics and biases in clinicians [12].

The Conundrum of Healthcare Data The current imbroglio in health care data is highlighted by an escalating volume of unstructured, heterogeneous medical data with little embedded predictive analytics or machine learning [13, 14]. The complex portfolio of health care data includes not only electronic medical records (patient encounters, vital signs, laboratory results, prescriptions, etc.) but also advanced imaging studies (such as MRI, CT scans, and echocardiograms and angiograms) [15]. In addition, it is estimated that about 80% of health care data is unstructured [16]. Lastly, current estimate of health care data volume is above 150 exabytes in volume and escalating rapidly [17].

Despite the large volume, variety, and velocity of big data in biomedicine, there is little dividend in the form of information from this health care big data [18, 19]. Yet, there are opportunities for utilizing health care big data to reduce costs: high-cost patients, readmissions, triage, decompensation, adverse events, and treatment optimization [20]. This situation will soon be far more complex and daunting with the advent of data "tsunamis": genomic data (as a result of the high throughput next generation sequencing) [21] and physiologic data (from home monitoring and wearable physiologic devices) [22].

Artificial Intelligence in Digital Medicine

The Perfect Storm The physicians are facing the perfect storm: exponentially increasing medical knowledge, more patients with higher degree of complexity of chronic diseases with increasingly more data, and high level of stress and burnout from the mounting burdens of EHR and workload. There is a myriad of reasons that physicians in any subspecialty could benefit from incorporation of AI into their practices. First, the amount of medical knowledge is exponentially increasing and doubling at a rate of a few months, and yet physicians do not have enough time to read and maintain their knowledge capacity. AI can be a useful knowledge "partner". Second, AI can help organize and facilitate the care of chronic diseases in many of the patients especially as they have more relevant data from disparate sources such as genomic sequencing and wearable technology. Lastly, physicians have currently a high rate of stress and many are facing or having had burnout from their careers. The use of AI can mitigate the EHR burden and simplify their workload.

Digital Medicine Digital medicine and health herald the era of technological advances such as apps, wearable technology and remote monitoring, telemedicine and communication tools, and other diagnostic devices to affect a more optimal quality of care as well as a more timely response to any situation. An essential part of digital medicine and wearable devices is the data mining of the incoming data for anomaly detection, prediction, and diagnosis/decision making [23]. The data mining process for wearable data includes a feature extraction/selection process for modeling/learning to yield detection, prediction, and decision making for the clinician. Expert knowledge and metadata can influence modeling and learning.

The advent of wearable devices and sensors to continuously track physiologic parameters can provide an overall patient care strategy that will improve outcome and lower healthcare costs in cardiac patients with heart failure [24]. This new paradigm of cardiovascular disease management can also improve the physician-patient relationship. Machine learning algorithms have also been applied to large-scale wearable sensor data in neurological disorders such as Parkinson's disease to significantly improve both clinical diagnosis and management [25]. This sensor-based, quantitative, objective, and easy-to-use system for assessing Parkinson's disease has potential to replace traditional qualitative and subjective ratings by human interpretation.

AI in Digital Medicine   The overarching theme in digital health and medicine in the use of AI is orchestrating, storing, and interpreting the huge amounts of data derived from the devices to facilitate acute and chronic disease diagnosis and management via AI-enabled acquisition and interpretation of data. This strategy will both increase the ability to proactively intervene when appropriate as well as decrease the burden on both the patient and the caretakers when the decisions are relatively straightforward. Until recently, there is a paucity of reports in digital medicine and AI that clearly demonstrates not only proof of concept in applying AI to an app or device but also clinical benefit. As a matter of fact, a prior editorial in *Lancet* cautions the use of AI in digital medicine and strongly recommends a continual evaluation of digital health interventions for both clinical effectiveness and economic impact [26].

A recent state of the art review of digital health technology and artificial intelligence emphasized that the future will be about personalized risk assessment with machine learning [27]. Another review in this domain on the concept of a medical internet of things (mIoT) in digital healthcare that is imbued with AI-related tools [28]. In order to reduce overall costs for both prevention and management of chronic diseases, devices are needed to execute this strategy: to monitor health biometrics, to auto-administer therapies, and to track real-time health data during therapy. Along with these devices, mobile applications for access to medical records as well as tools for telemedicine and telehealth for this new paradigm of medical IoT. All of these devices and equipment will need an AI-centric strategy for data integration and interpretation for delivering optimal healthcare advice and direction. While chronic diseases such as diabetes care can benefit greatly from a coordinated and efficient strategy, use of technology including AI remains fragmented at present due to a myriad of issues: lack of supportive policy and regulation, unsustainable reimbursement, inefficient business models, and concerns regarding data security and privacy [29].

The Future of AI in Digital Medicine   There are other AI technologies that will be very useful for digital medicine in the near future. There is exciting work on pushing AI "peripherally" to devices even at the microprocessor level. This artificial intelligence of medical things, or AIoMT, provides a portfolio of "intelligent" devices for the future of chronic disease management as well as population health strategies.

The internet of things becoming internet of everything (IoE) with edge AI will be invaluable for chronic disease management and population health in the future. There is already discussion about how neural nets can be located on a microprocessor (termed "tinyAI" by MIT researchers) [30].

The future development of AI in healthcare will be in two directions: Towards a centralized cloud for analytics and concomitantly towards a peripheral network with AI embedded in many devices and sensors. This will be the AI equivalent of a brain and peripheral nervous system. In addition, the limitations and nuances of existing electronic medical records in current state demands a disruptive technology in the future. One such promising technology is graph databases coupled with knowledge graphs to create a paradigm shift in how electronic medical records are structured and curated. Both IoE and graph databases will be particularly useful when federated learning becomes more common as a methodology to collect and share data. Federated learning consists of edge devices with local data that can train their own copy of the model from a central server, and only the parameters/weights from these models (but not the data) are sent to the global model [31].

Multimodal AI, such as combining perception and linguistic capabilities of machines, can increase the potential for AI to deal with the complexities of healthcare (see Figs. 6.1 and 6.2) [32]. The advent of GPT-3 will be an asset to a more sophisticated AI to better understand and adapt to the world. In the area of medical education and clinical training, not only AI in and of itself but also in combination with extended reality can be extraordinarily effective in educating and training

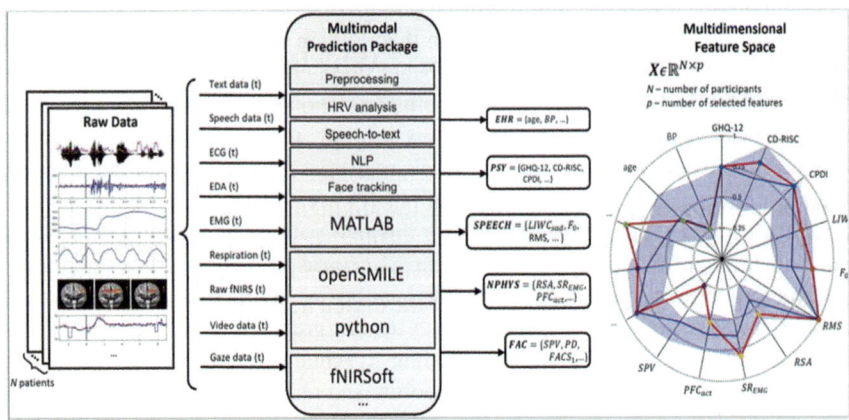

Fig. 6.1 *Multimodal Artificial Intelligence.* Multimodal data acquisition in real-time is the input with feature computation after collection of data from several different sources in patients with COVID-19. General Health Questionnaire (GHQ-12), Connor-Davidson Resilience Scale (CD-RISC), COVID-19 Peritraumatic Distress Index (CPDI); NLP feature LIWC "sad," voice fundamental frequency (F0), voice root mean square (RMS); respiratory sinus arrhythmia (RSA), EMG-based startle reactivity (SREMG), prefrontal cortex activity (PFCact); saccadic peak velocity (SPV), pupil dilation (PD), a feature related to facial action coding system (FACS). (From Cosic K et al. AI-Based Prediction and Prevention of Psychological and Behavioral Changes in Ex COVID-19 Patients. *Front Psychol* 2021; 12:782866.)

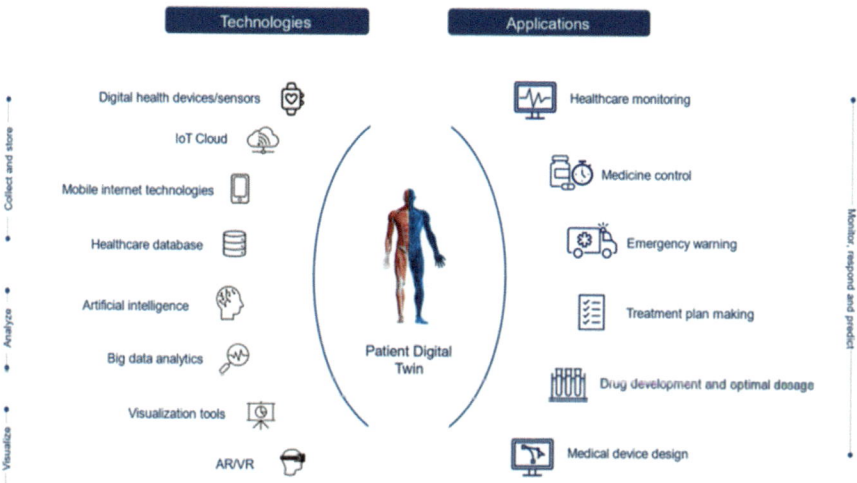

Fig. 6.2 *Digital Twin*. Digital twin will be the ultimate embodiment of digital health in the future as it provides real-time information interchange between the person and the environment . (From Armeni P, Polat I, De Rossi LM et al. Digital Twins in Healthcare: Is It the Beginning of a New Era of Evidence-Based Medicine? A Critical Review. *J Pers Med* 2022; 12(8): 1255.)

clinicians; adding an AI dimension to extended reality can be termed intelligent reality. Along with this virtualization of clinical medicine and healthcare can be AI imbued in the digital twin concept for both the patient as well as the health system so that this concept may be the essence of digital health in the future [33].

In conclusion, the pandemic has provided us with new insights into how to deliver population health with digital tools and machine learning. The future of artificial intelligence in digital medicine is extremely propitious with a myriad of advanced AI such as digital twins, health learning system, and deep reinforcement learning that will need to be in synergy with clinicians to allow data to be an enabler of new knowledge and intelligence in biomedicine and healthcare. All healthcare data will need to be liberated and shared without any obstacles so that AI can be ubiquitous and invisible in the future health care arena and discover new knowledge from all sources of data and information. In addition, there needs to be an interface between clinicians with data and computer scientists with analytics to assure a data-to-information continuum and eventually a knowledge-to-intelligence transfer. Finally, we need to promulgate a human-machine synergy via a clinician-data scientist collaboration without hubris to push future healthcare and medicine to the highest echelon.

With AI in digital medicine and healthcare, it is not human versus machine, but human *and* machine in this brave new world of digital health.

Acknowledgement I would like to express my deep gratitude to Ms. Monica Suesberry, my assistant, for her support for the work on this chapter.

References

1. Turing AM. On computable numbers, with an application to the Entscheidungsproblem. Proc Lond Math Soc. 1937;S2–42(1):230–65.
2. Copeland J. The essential turing. Oxford: Oxford University Press; 2004.
3. Shortliffe EH, David R, Axline SG, et al. Computer-based consultations in clinical therapeutics: explanation and rule acquisition capabilities of the MYCIN system. Comput Biomed Res. 1975;8(4):303–20.
4. Chen Y, Argentinis E, Weber G. IBM Watson: how cognitive computing can be applied to big data challenges in life and science research. Clin Ther. 2016;38(4):688–701.
5. Gunning D. Talk at DARPA. 2016.
6. Krizhevsky A, Sututskever I, Hinto GE. ImageNet classification withDeep convolutional neural networks, vol. 1. La Jolla, CA: Neural Information Processing Systems Foundation Inc; 2012. p. 4.
7. LeCun Y, Bengio Y, Hinton G. Deep learning. Nature. 2015;521:436–44.
8. Porter J, editor. Deep learning: fundamentals, methods, and applications. New York: Nova Science Publishers; 2016.
9. Arel I, Rose DC, Kanowski TP. Deep machine learning—a new frontier in artificial intelligence research. IEEE Comput Intell Mag. 2010;5(13–8):1556–603X.
10. Groopman J. How doctors think. Boston: Houghton Mifflin; 2007.
11. Kahneman D. Thinking, fast and slow. New York: Farrar, Straus, and Giroux; 2011.
12. Klein JG. Five pitfalls in decisions about diagnosis and prescribing. BMJ. 2005;330:781–3.
13. Chang AC, et al. Artificial intelligence in pediatric cardiology: an innovative transformation in patient care, clinical research, and medical education. Cong Card Today. 2012;10:1–12.
14. Roski J, et al. Creating value in health care through big data: opportunities and policy implications. Health Aff. 2014;33(7):1115–22.
15. Weil AR. Big data in health: a new era for research and patient care. Health Aff. 2014;33:1110.
16. Healthcare Content Management White Paper. Unstructured data in electronic health record (HER) systems: challenges and solutions. 2013. www.datamark.net.
17. Hughes G. How big is "big data" in healthcare? SAS blogs. 2011.
18. Jee K, et al. Potentiality of big data in the medical sector: focus on how to reshape the healthcare system. Healthc Infrom Res. 2013;19(2):79–85.
19. Schneeweiss S. Learning from big health care data. N Engl J Med. 2014;370:2161–3.
20. Bates DW, et al. Big data in health care: using analytics to identify and manage high-risk and high-cost patients. Health Aff. 2014;2014(7):1123–31.
21. Feero WG, et al. Review article: genomic medicine—an updated primer. N Engl J Med. 2010;362:2001–11.
22. Chan M, et al. Smart wearable systems: current status and future challenges. Artif Intell Med. 2012;56(3):137–56.
23. Banaee H, Ahmed MU, Loutfi A. Data mining for wearable sensors in health monitoring systems: a review of recent trends and challenges. Sensors (Basel). 2013;13(12):17472–500.
24. Steinhubl SR, Topol EJ. Moving from digitalization to digitization in cardiovascular care: why is it important, and why could it mean for patients and providers? J Am Coll Cardiol. 2015;66(13):1489–96.
25. Kubota KJ, Chen JA, Little MA. Machine learning for large-scale wearable sensor data in parkinson's disease: concepts, promises, pitfalls, and features. Mov Disord. 2016;31(9):1314–26.
26. Is digital medicine different? Editorial. Lancet. 2018;392:95.
27. Javaid A, Zghyer F, Kim C, et al. Medicine 2032: the future of cardiovascular disease prevention with machine learning and digital health technology. Am J Prev Cardiol. 2022;Dec 12:100379.
28. Dimitrov D. Medical internet of things and big data in healthcare. Healthc Inform Res. 2016;22(3):156–63.

29. Fatehi F, Menon A, Bird D. Diabetes care in the digital era: a synoptic overview. Curr Diab Rep. 2018;18(7):38–47.
30. Website: https://tinyml.mit.edu/ (2022).
31. Rieke N, Hancox J, Li W, et al. The future of digital health with federated learning. NPJ Digital Health. 2020;3:119.
32. Cosic K, et al. AI-based prediction and prevention of psychological and behavioral changes in ex COVID-19 patients. Front Psychol. 2021;12:782866.
33. Armeni P, Polat I, De Rossi LM, et al. Digital twins in healthcare: is it the beginning of a new era of evidence-based medicine? A critical review. J Pers Med. 2022;12(8):1255.

Chapter 7
Getting Reimbursed for Digital Health

David D. Davis

Disclaimer

This work was prepared by the author in his personal capacity. The views and opinions expressed in this chapter are the author's own and are not intended to represent or reflect those of his employer, W. L. Gore & Associates.

Overview

Reimbursement in the digital health world can come from two types of payors, the individual user or a third party, for instance, an insurance company or a government payor, i.e., TRICARE, Medicaid, and Medicare. Third-party payors have been hesitant to reimburse digital health in the past; however, we are in the midst of a sea of change elevated by the COVID pandemic. COVID provided the platform for digital health to prove the value proposition that digital health entrepreneurs have been promising. The results were resounding positive. The digital health wave is gaining momentum, and we are on the cusp of digital health becoming mainstream.

Reimbursement within digital health is a two-edged sword, as entrepreneurs who want the freedom to build and create payment by a third party always makes more regulations, rules, and medical policies that could prohibit or immediately slow the ability to reach patients. Many within the digital health community will argue this industry can survive without third-party reimbursement by pointing to the success of digital watches, digital scales, and blood pressure cuffs. Conversely, some within

D. D. Davis (✉)
W.L. Gore & Associates, Newark, DE, USA
e-mail: davdavis@wlgore.com

© The Author(s), under exclusive license to Springer Nature Switzerland AG 2023
A. Meyers (ed.), *Digital Health Entrepreneurship*, Health Informatics,
https://doi.org/10.1007/978-3-031-33902-8_7

the community will argue the only way to move the industry forward is to receive the appropriate reimbursement will only come from third-party payors.

Digital health's challenges to reimbursement come from within today's reimbursement framework. The fee-for-service model rewards healthcare providers for completing procedures and services by considering the provider's work, time, and effort. Quality is not a consideration in this model. Therefore, payments for services are identical for different levels of quality. Many digital health services may reduce the provider's work, time, and effort, which may lower the reimbursement to the provider—creating these efficiencies that penalize the provider instead of rewarding the provider for working more efficiently. Digital health is better when most third-party payors follow a value-based reimbursement model that incentivizes outcomes over volume. In the US, many private payors are moving to a value-based model. Medicare is moving much slower due to the political sensitivity of changing the US health system.

Introduction to Medicare

Medicare is the primary payor in the US for most medical technologies, devices, and services. Medicare's payment system is well documented and updated annually at its website, www.cms.gov. Medicare publishes policies, payments, and national and local coverage decisions along with the reasoning for the findings and the research used to support the decisions on the website. Due to the public nature of the decisions, many private payors will adopt Medicare policies. Private Payors are not required to publish any of this information, and many do not allow the public view of this material.

Medicare Is the US Federal Health Insurance Program for

Patients ages 65 or older, or a person receiving disability for the past 24 months, or a person diagnosed with End-Stage Renal Disease (permanent kidney failure requiring dialysis or a transplant, sometimes called ESRD).

Medicare offers Hospital and Medical Insurance as well as Prescription Coverage. Part A (Hospital Insurance) and Part B (Medical Insurance). Most beneficiaries (patients) are eligible for premium-free Part A if they have worked or are a spouse of someone who has worked and paid Medicare taxes for more than 10 years. Typically, for someone who has worked or a worker's spouse, once a beneficiary reaches 65 years of age, Part A Hospital Insurance is provided, free of charge. Next, the beneficiary can purchase Part B, Medical Insurance, for a monthly premium. There is an additional monthly fee if the beneficiary wants to receive prescription drug coverage. Each calendar year, beneficiaries are allowed to opt-in to traditional Medicare (Part A and Part B), or they can elect to use Part C (Medicare Advantage). Private insurers provide a Medicare Advantage plan or an MA plan. These plans are similar to HMO and PPO-type services. In recent years, these plans have increased in popularity and make up more than 40% of the Medicare population.

- Medicare Part A (Hospital Insurance):
  Part A covers inpatient hospital stays, care in a skilled nursing facility, hospice care, and home health care.

- Medicare Part B (Medical Insurance):
  Part B covers doctor's services, outpatient care, medical supplies, and preventive services.

- Medicare Part C (Medicare Advantage Plans):
  A health insurance plan provides Medicare benefits through a private-sector health insurer. Medicare Advantage Plans replace Part A and Part B benefits.

Medicare Advantage Plans include:

- Health Maintenance Organizations
- Preferred Provider Organizations
- Private Fee-for-Service Plans
- Special Needs Plans
- Medicare Medical Savings Account Plans

Medicare Part D (prescription drug coverage).
  Part D adds prescription drug coverage to:

- Original Medicare
- Some Medicare Cost Plans
- Some Medicare Private-Fee-for-Service Plans
- Medicare Medical Savings Account Plans[1]

Commercial Payors

Commerical payors, such as Blue Cross Blue Shield, Aetna, and United Healthcare, are private medical health insurance companies. Traditionally, a percentage of the premiums are paid by the employers of the insured.

What Is Reimbursement?

Reimbursement can be defined as third-party payments to the provider for medical services rendered. Reimbursement has three main components: coding, coverage, and payment. These components are necessary to achieve reimbursement.

---

[1] Centers for Medicare and Medicaid Services (2018) Medicare Consumer Information. https://www.medicare.gov/sign-up-change-plans/decide-how-to-get-medicare/whats-medicare/what-is-medicare.html, Accessed 1 Aug 2018.

Coding

Coding is simply the language used between the provider and third-party payor. Coding allows the provider to tell the insurer what was needed and why accurately. This system is called HCPCS (hick-picks) or the Healthcare Common Procedural Coding System. The same legislation that created HIPAA (Health Insurance Portability and Accountability Act of 1996) also formally cemented our code sets. Before HIPAA, many insurance companies created their codes; this created a nightmare scenario, as many providers were unsure what code to choose for what insurance company. The code sets today are used to classify medical diagnoses, procedures, diagnostic tests, treatments, equipment, and supplies. A unique code identifies each service or treatment; this code is then placed on a billing form and sent electronically to the insurance company.

CPT

CPT stands for Current Procedural Terminology. The CPT provides procedural codes when performed by a licensed medical professional. The American Medical Association creates and maintains the CPT codes. The following categories differentiate the codes.

Category 1 CPT codes describe proven technologies that are FDA approved and available in the marketplace today.

Category 2 CPT codes describe well-established measurements supported by medical societies, national guidelines, and evidence-based measurements.

Category 3 CPT codes are procedures or services that are currently or recently performed in humans.

ICD-10

ICD-10 stands for International Classifications of Diseases, tenth Edition. This book has two distinct parts; CM (clinical modifications) are diagnostic codes. PCS (Procedural Coding System) are inpatient procedure codes.

Physician Coding

Physicians are always paid and coded separately from the hospital coding and payment. This payment represents their professional services' skill, work, and effort. The physician will utilize a CPT code describing the service or procedure and an ICD-10-CM code describing the patient's diagnosis.

Table 7.1 Coding system by place of service

Place of service	CPT	ICD-10-CM	ICD-10-PCS
Physician service	X	X	
Hospital inpatient		X	X
Hospital outpatient	X	X	

Hospital Coding

Before choosing the correct code in a hospital setting, one must determine if the patient is an inpatient or an outpatient. The provider will decide if this patient will likely stay in the hospital for less than 24 hours; if that is the case, the patient will be considered an outpatient. If the patient ends up staying longer than two midnights, then the patient will be viewed as an inpatient based on the Medicare "2 Midnight Rule", which states that if a patient is in the hospital for two midnights or more, this patient is now an inpatient. Table 7.1 illustrates the coding changes between an inpatient and an outpatient.

Coverage

Insurance coverage is not the same as coverage in the reimbursement world. Insurance coverage tells us if the patient has insurance. Reimbursement coverage is the payor recognizing the medical services of the provider as appropriate within the medical policy of the beneficiary. One important point to remember, just because a device has FDA coverage does not automatically mean you will receive CMS or commercial insurance coverage.

Medicare Coverage

Medicare coverage is limited to items and services that are reasonable and necessary for the diagnosis or treatment of an illness or injury (and within the scope of a Medicare benefit category). National coverage determinations (NCDs) are evidence-based processes with opportunities for public participation. In the absence of a national coverage policy, an item or service still may be covered by Medicare at the discretion of the Medicare contractors based on a local coverage determination (LCD).[2]

The Social Security Act of 1965 created what is known today as Medicare; within the act, Congress authorized Medicare to pay for services that meet the criteria of "medically necessary and reasonable ." Legislation has been created that allows

---

[2] Centers for Medicare and Medicaid Services (2018) Medicare Coverage Determination Process. https://www.cms.gov/Medicare/Coverage/DeterminationProcess/index.html, Accessed 1 Aug 2018.

Medicare to determine "medically reasonable and necessary" by examining the services more closely and using outside sources to assist as necessary.

National Coverage Determination

National Coverage Determinations are made through an evidence-based process, with opportunities for public participation.[3] Any manufacturer or entity can request an NCD through a formal request to the CMS. The downside risk of using this process is if the device or service in question receives a national non-coverage decision, then the product or service will not be covered by Medicare and possibly no other insurer. All National Coverage Decisions can be found on the CMS website.

Local Coverage Decision

Without an NCD, each local Medicare administrative contractor (MAC) may cover services at their discretion. Medicare is flexible with these coverage decisions since it is known that all medical decisions may vary by geography. The downside of applying for an LCD is much less than an NCD. A denial at the local level will not allow you to serve beneficiaries within that region until you can show better evidence. A negative response at one MAC will not carry over to the next MAC. One would still be allowed to apply to another region. A favorable coverage decision would only apply in the area where it was accepted. This decision would not be a nationwide acceptance. All local coverage decisions can be found on the CMS website.

MAC

Medicare Administrative Contractors are commercial health insurers awarded a geographic jurisdiction process to process claims on behalf of Medicare. The Medical Directors at these MACs will be the gatekeepers to the local coverage decisions. Currently, there are 12 MACs that process Part A and Part B claims.

---

[3] Centers for Medicare and Medicaid Services (2018) How to Request an NCD. https://www.cms.gov/Medicare/Coverage/DeterminationProcess/howtorequestanNCD.html, Accessed 1 Aug 2018.

Commercial Payors and Digital Health Coverage

Digital health has proven to be a technology that can drive economic value for the commercial payor. Most commercial payors are public companies; these companies are obligated to the shareholders to return earnings and create shareholder value. The value proposition is different for digital health than for standard services. In our traditional healthcare system, insurance companies can create shareholder value by reducing the number of paid services.

Digital health entrepreneurs need to identify the value they can drive for these companies across populations or their entire business; thinking holistically about the value proposition will help one overcome the traditional coverage problem that focuses on individual patients. However, you should always have alternate strategies and not dismiss the individual patient. Understanding how the system works allows one to think strategically on multiple fronts.

On the individual patient level, a favorable coverage decision by Medicare may result in a positive coverage decision for many commercial payors. With commercial payors, Medicare coverage carries a significant amount of weight; attempt to find ways to utilize your service within the Medicare population. Commercial payors have more leniency and are not bound to legislation that may inhibit Medicare coverage of a digital health service. Commercial payors may be the only coverage you are looking to obtain in your favor if you are targeting patients under 65, for example, a service dedicated to pediatrics.

Coverage Challenges to Digital Health

Traditionally, digital health services' main challenge was coverage by the Medicare program. During the COVID pandemic, Medicare allowed for many digital health programs to be covered temporarily. Services include virtual visits, remote patient vitals, and others. This temporary coverage created space for digital technologies to demonstrate the economic value that the largest payor in the US has missed. Medicare has turned many of these coverage decisions from temporary to permanent.

Coverage has been the Achilles' heel of many medical devices because payers do not want to pay for unproven technology. The only way to combat this hurdle is to collect data that proves your value proposition. Once you have collected data, the next step is then to turn the data into a peer-reviewed published article. This level of evidence will be necessary to overturn coverage decisions. The bottom line with coverage, having the data to prove the value of the technology is the way to overcome any coverage challenge.

Payment

Many terms unique to the healthcare system are not common knowledge outside of the industry. These terms can have different meanings within different applications. The word payment could be the patient paying the insurance company, for instance. Here are the definitions within the context of healthcare insurance:

- Payment: The amount of money transferred from the payor and the patient to the provider to perform a unique medical service, procedure, or test.
- Co-Payment: The amount or percentage that the patient pays to the provider.
- Deductible: The amount the patient must pay before the insurance plan pays.

You may wonder how payment works for the digital health company, as the definitions above never mention a flow of funds for a digital service. In our legacy healthcare system, the digital health entrepreneur would approach a provider to utilize and pay for the service. The provider would then bill the insurance company for the service and receive payment. Therefore, the digital health entrepreneur wants to ensure the insurer will reimburse their customer for the service.

Medicare Payment

Medicare has many different payment structures developed to determine the appropriate price to pay providers. Understanding the basics of these payment systems is necessary for creating a reimbursement strategy for any digital health platform. We will cover the payment structures for the following places of service: physician facility payment, physician non-facility payment, hospital inpatient, and hospital outpatient.

Physician Payment

Physicians are paid within the Physician Fee Schedule (PFS) rules. The PFS is updated quarterly. Resource-Based Relative Value System, or RBRVS, is the name that describes this system. RBRVS pays the appropriate amount for the resources used during the procedure or service. There are three components used: Physician work is the skill, work, and effort required to complete a procedure, practice expense (office resources utilized during the procedure or service), and professional liability insurance. Each service is relative to another; for example, you would expect a coronary stent procedure to pay less than an open coronary cardiac bypass.

Physicians perform services within their offices, where they will utilize and pay for the resources used to complete the procedure. Alternatively, if a physician operates in the hospital, the hospital pays for the equipment, utilities, and the building.

Therefore, Medicare will pay the physician only for the services performed at the hospital, not the equipment or facilities. In the PFS, these two categories are called facility and non-facility payments. The facility payment is the payment the physician will receive when performing services at the hospital. Non-facility payment is the payment for performing services within their office setting.

Hospital Inpatient Payment

The system Medicare uses is called the Medicare Severity-Diagnosis Related Group or MS-DRG. One MS-DRG is assigned and paid per discharge. The hospital sends Medicare the appropriate ICD codes for the patient encounter. Medicare then uses grouper software to group them into one MS-DRG. The hospital does not choose an MS-DRG. to send to Medicare; this is a common misnomer. There is no line-item reimbursement for services at the hospital. Digital health services designed to aid the provider in the hospital most likely will not affect the MS-DRG., therefore, not allowing for any additional payment to the hospital for the service.

Hospital Outpatient Payment

APC or Ambulatory Payment Classification is the Hospital Outpatient Payment. Medicare will pay for multiple APCs; Medicare will reduce the payment by 50% for any procedure after the first.

Payment Challenges to Digital Health

Suppose your digital health service is a disruptor and eliminates the physician's work or reduces the resources used by the physician. The result will be a lower physician payment or no payment. Digital health service payments are not related to the amount of savings you are attempting to deliver to the system.

For example, to illustrate this point, a digital health entrepreneur creates a new sensor implanted subcutaneously on the shoulder. This new sensor is part of a system that will send a daily status report to the physician's electronic medical record daily, informing them of sensor placement, patient activity, and the patient's blood flow velocity, which was proven useful for this new technology. This new sensor can notify the provider if the patient is at high risk for a stroke with enough advanced notice to treat with a pharmaceutical agent instead of an operation. This implant requires cauterization, and it is necessary to implant at the hospital; the patient can safely leave after the sensor has demonstrated to be stable, typically

3 hours following the implant. The AMA granted a CPT code for the insertion of the sensor and a second CPT code for reviewing the daily status of the patient over 3 months. Medicare has given this technology coverage and pays for the insertion and monitoring. Using this example, here is the potential reimbursement/ payment pathway.

The digital health company would sell the sensor to the hospital then the physician implants the device. This activity would trigger the following reimbursable events. The physician's office and the hospital will bill the insurance company with the new CPT code for the sensor, along with the appropriate diagnosis code. The physician will receive payment from the patient's insurance company and co-pay. The hospital will receive compensation from the patient's insurance and co-pay. Next, the patient has had the sensor for 3 months, and the physician has received the daily reports in the electronic medical record; the patient and the sensor are both unremarkable for this period. The physician would notate this in the patient's chart. This activity would trigger a reimbursable event, and the office will bill the insurance for the CPT code for monitoring; along with the diagnosis code, the office will receive payment from both the insurance company and the co-pay from the patient.

Creating Your Strategy

Think About Reimbursement Early

Most entrepreneurs and medical device executives always consider FDA qualifications. They will set out to create a regulatory strategy while not appreciating that providing customers with a pathway for third-party payment is just as important, if not more so.

Remember, if your service is considered substantially equivalent to another device from the regulatory agency, there is a high degree of certainty that the reimbursement will be the same. It is imperative to start and plan the reimbursement strategy development at the same time as the regulatory strategy or earlier.

Talk to the Payors

There are many private payors today interested in working with digital health partners. Many companies have created digital health venture funds to invest in new companies. These meetings allow entrepreneurs to discuss your new technology, the benefits the payor will experience with your product or service, and the level of evidence needed to penetrate these markets. Many private payors see the savings from these digital health initiatives and are eager to partner with or purchase the technology.

Clinical Trials

First, as you build your clinical trial for FDA approval, always include as many elements of economic data as possible. This data will serve many purposes but will drive the economic value story necessary with hospitals and payors. The financial and clinical data elements that, at the least, need to be considered are costs, insurance payments, and quality of life measures. Also, consider any appropriate data element where one can observe comparable measures. This data will be helpful for future white papers and health economic studies related to economic value.

Code Selection

Research and identify if any appropriate existing codes describe the technology or service. If a code fits the description, then the next step is to contact the physician specialty society for that code and have them verify that the code would be appropriate for the technology. Written verification from a specialty society is necessary for providers, hospitals, and insurance companies to prove this is the correct code. The next step is researching the ICD-10, available on the CMS website.

A new code will be necessary for other services not described by a code.

A category 1 code requires the following:

- All devices necessary for the performance of the procedure of service have received FDA clearance or approval when such is required for the performance of the procedure or service.
- The procedure or service is performed by many physicians or other qualified health care professionals across the United States.
- The procedure or service is performed with a frequency consistent with the intended clinical use (i.e., a service for a common condition should have a high volume).
- The procedure or service is consistent with current medical practice.
- The clinical efficacy of the procedure or service is documented in the literature that meets the requirements outlined in the CPT code-change application.

The following criteria are used by the CPT Advisory Committee and the CPT Editorial Panel for evaluating Category 3 code applications:

- The procedure or service is currently or recently performed in humans AND

  At least one of the following additional criteria has been met:

- The application is supported by at least 1 CPT or HCPAC Advisor representing practitioners who would use this procedure or service (or)
- The actual or potential clinical efficacy of the specific procedure or service is supported by peer-reviewed literature which is available in English for examination by the CPT Editorial Panel (or)

- There is:
- At least 1 Institutional Review Board approved protocol of a study of the procedure or service being performed
- A description of a current and ongoing United States trial outlining the efficacy of the procedure or service or
- Other evidence of evolving clinical utilization

Which would you choose for new technology?
CPT category 1 code

- It takes approximately 3 years to obtain.
- Coverage: beginning assumption from payers is a high level of evidence.
- Payment amount assigned by Medicare.

CPT category 3 code

- Approximately 6–18 months.
- Coverage: the beginning assumption is unproven and not covered.
- Medicare will assign no payment amount
- The claim will only be paid on appeal through the MAC.

CPT codes granted a category three status cannot be granted category one status until all the criteria are satisfied for a category one code. Procedures and services are not mandated to start at a category three; there may be certain instances when collecting all the necessary data and then applying for a category one code is more advantageous than starting with a category three.

Once a code has CPT category one status, the AMA and CMS take the code through the RUC (RVS Update Committee) process and apply the appropriate resources to the CPT code to have a payment amount. Category 3 codes have no payment attached and are not involved in the RUC process.

Obtaining Coverage for Your Service

Coverage strategy first requires research. Reviewing medical policies for both Medicare and the top 10 commercial payors in the US gives visibility into the coverage situation that one is entering. Coverage research is also an excellent opportunity to see how the payors recommend coding a service. The appropriate CPT/ICD-10 codes are in the coverage policy.

Once the research is complete and data has been gathered, the coverage strategy becomes more evident. The following statements and questions can help formulate an action plan for the strategy.

- Start by contacting private payors with similar policies that are favorable.
- If the technology is ground-breaking, it may be best to contact a small insurance company first to gather thoughts and perspectives.

- For digital health, California insurers may be more receptive to new ideas than the northeast. There may be focused areas for specific disease states that would be a great place to start.
- Are Key Opinion Leaders (KOL) in this area influential with payors?
- Are there patient support groups to advocate for the position?
- Are there local TV or radio stations that may want to report the story of this new digital health service?

Coverage can take many years to be successful. The best-case timeframe will be approximately 1 year. Great technologies have never been brought to market due to a lack of coverage. The entrepreneur did not have a reimbursement plan for most of these technologies and started working on reimbursement after regulatory approvals. Before COVID, this was the stage where digital health failed. Today, a new chapter is being written, and payors have never been more accepting of digital health.

Payment

Payment can be the afterthought in this process since the data will prove the correct price for the product or service. Medicare will use the submitted data for the claims on its patients to set the payment for the digital health service based on charge data. Always attempt to receive full payment for your service within the confines of the reimbursement system. Once payment has been established, it is difficult to raise it later. Consider the adverse effects of discounting before making the business decision to discount to see if the risk outweighs the benefit. Always price your product to the value provided to the marketplace and try to increase payment, if possible.

Conclusion

Building the critical reimbursement elements for any service is not easy. Still, it is rewarding to know that your service can now be utilized by patients and paid for by the insurer. Remember to develop your reimbursement strategy early and update as necessary as you move along the reimbursement pathway. Always find a way to introduce a payor to the technology; too many entrepreneurs are hesitant to share the technology with the payor community. Sharing your story can lead to many opportunities to increase your chances of reimbursement success.

Chapter 8
Legal Environment of Digital Health: Rules, Regulations and Laws that Govern Digital Health Business Design and Ownership

Jonathan A. Mintz

Introduction

The risks to all involved in digital health entrepreneurship are plentiful, limited only by one's imagination. They include, but are not limited to: product liability, breach of contract, director and/or officer liability, personal injury, personal guarantees, trademark and copyright infringement, unfair business practices, regulatory risks, etc. In the U.S., these risks often manifest themselves in civil litigation, with a significant risk of a large jury verdict.

Unlike most common law countries such as the U.K. and other Crown Dependencies, the U.S. gives potential plaintiffs easy access to the courts in two significant ways: (1) Contingency fees, which permit lawyers to accept cases with little out of pocket cost to the plaintiff (typically only the nominal filing fees required to file a complaint); and (2) No "loser pays" consequence for unsuccessful plaintiffs. In most common law jurisdictions other than the United States, the loser in litigation must pay the winner's costs, including legal fees, which is a significant deterrent to bringing frivolous litigation. Thus, there is little or no financial deterrent to file a lawsuit, and yet it costs tens of thousands or even hundreds of thousands of dollars for the defendant get out of a lawsuit—even where that suit has no merit!

Perhaps just as significantly, as a general rule many Americans do not accept that sometimes bad things just happen (i.e., it's always someone else's fault), and juries frequently accept as their role redistributing wealth from those who have it to those who have been injured. Thus, one can do absolutely nothing wrong and still find themselves on the wrong side of a very large judgment.

As a result, the United States is one of the most litigious countries in the world, and many times juries award large judgments in cases where the facts establishing

J. A. Mintz (✉)
Evergreen Legacy Planning, LLP, Evergreen, CO, USA
e-mail: JAM@EvergreenLegacyPlanning.com; http://www.EvergreenLegacyPlanning.com

© The Author(s), under exclusive license to Springer Nature Switzerland AG 2023
A. Meyers (ed.), *Digital Health Entrepreneurship*, Health Informatics,
https://doi.org/10.1007/978-3-031-33902-8_8

liability are scarce. Moreover, the laws of many states (like California) tend to favor creditors over debtors, with the result that those with any wealth are a target, and the greater the wealth the larger the target. Therefore, protecting one's hard-earned wealth should be a critical component of their estate planning. For digital health entrepreneurs, this includes strategic business formation and ownership planning as well.

Fortunately, many of these risks can be addressed through insurance and legal structures. This chapter explores these solutions in greater detail.

Insurance

The first line of defense against many of the risks faced by digital health entrepreneurs is frequently insurance. For example, practicing physicians obtain malpractice insurance against claims of malpractice, whether real or fabricated. Similarly, directors and officers of digital health entrepreneurship companies can protect against claims against them in these capacities through Directors and Officers (D&O) Liability Insurance or Errors and Omissions (E&O) Liability Insurance.

Moreover, all digital health entrepreneurs should consider umbrella liability coverage for all of their activities. Umbrella liability coverage is an inexpensive first or second line of defense for all types of potential claims faced by digital health entrepreneurs, including claims that arise from activities both in and out of their business. For example, if the digital health entrepreneur owns rental properties in her name (a bad idea, as discussed below) and a tenant is injured on the property, an umbrella policy *may* provide coverage against any claims arising from that injury. Note the italicized "may"—the downside with umbrella coverage is there are typically exclusions that preclude coverage; for example, most policies exclude coverage for intentional acts, such as a crime.

Further, while it is relatively inexpensive and thus all digital health entrepreneurs should purchase as much umbrella coverage as possible, umbrella policies have relatively low policy limits, typically $five million or less. Thus, for larger claims, umbrella insurance will only serve as leverage for settlement. For catastrophic claims umbrella coverage will simply be inadequate and other assets will likely be available to satisfy the claim. The rest of this chapter will focus on legal structures digital health entrepreneurs can implement to minimize the risk of frivolous—and real—claims that can and frequently do have a devastating financial effect absent proactive planning.

Legal Structures

What follows is a discussion of the legal structures available to digital health entrepreneurs. The information provided below is very general in nature, and thus it should not be construed as legal advice; digital health entrepreneurs should seek the advice of a qualified professional based upon their particular facts and circumstances.

Business Entities (Corporations and LLCs): The First Step

Most digital health entrepreneurs understand the risk associated with a new venture. Thus, most new ventures are housed in a legal entity designed to limit legal exposure to the digital health entrepreneur's investment in the business. This explains why most new ventures are created as either a Limited Liability Company (LLC) or, if outside investors are contemplated, a C corporation.

These legal entities are an excellent first step in protecting against the risks associated with any new venture, digital health entrepreneur or otherwise. But housing the venture in an entity is only a first step. There are several additional steps one should take to protect against creditors of the business, often referred to as "inside creditors."

Corporations Vs. LLCs

Most digital health entrepreneurs realize that running their venture through a legal entity protects them from personal liability for claims arising within the business. In other words, the legal entity limits their liability to the business itself, absent an "alter ego" claim. Alter ego claims most frequently arise when the separate legal existence of the entity is not respected; i.e., when the entity is used as one's personal "piggy bank."

Historically, corporations and partnerships were the only entity types available to limit one's liability to their investment in the business. Corporations provide limited liability to all shareholders, but restrict the business' ability to segregate ownership and control—all voting shareholders have equal voting rights.

Alternatively, limited partnerships permit limited liability for limited partners, but the general partners of both general and limited partnerships have unlimited liability—i.e., all of their personal assets are available to satisfy a claim against the business.

In response to the perceived weaknesses of both corporations and partnerships, beginning more than 40 years ago in Wyoming, states began adopting LLC statutes that are hybrids between corporations and limited partnerships; LLCs provide limited liability for all members (owners), and through the use of a Manager or Managers, LLCs permit the separation of ownership and control. Let's explore the advantages and disadvantages of C corporations and LLCs in greater detail, since these are the two most commonly used legal entity types by digital health entrepreneurs.

C Corporations

The advantages of C corporations are significant, particularly where the business contemplates outside investors. These entities:

- Permit numerous shareholders
- Permit multiple classes of stock (e.g., preferred and common, voting and non-voting)
- Have a low 21% corporate tax rate for retained earnings

Conversely, the disadvantages of C corporations are also significant:

- Subject to double taxation—retained earnings are taxed again upon distribution to the corporation's shareholders
- No asset protection for ownership (discussed in more detail below)
- Requirement of corporate formalities

The requirement of corporate formalities is not onerous (i.e., notice of and holding an annual meeting of shareholders, minutes from that meeting, etc.), but the failure to uphold corporate formalities can be the grounds for a claim of *alter ego*, which would permit a creditor to seek personal liability from a controlling shareholder.

Note that S corporations are similar to C corporations except that with an S corporation tax election the annual profits and losses flow through to the shareholders' personal income tax returns, rather than being subject to tax at the corporation level. However, S corporations are different in that they are limited to 75 shareholders; prohibit non-resident, non-U.S. citizen owners, and are very restrictive as to the types of owners. Thus, S corporations are infrequently used in this context.

LLCs

The advantages of LLCs are also numerous. This entity type:

- Permits numerous/all types of shareholders
- Permits multiple classes of ownership interests via "Series LLCs"
- Can elect pass-through taxation or as a C Corp
- Charging order protection (discussed in more detail below)

The disadvantages of LLCs are less significant:

- Generally taxed at owner's tax rate (if a passthrough) but can elect corporate taxation if desirable
- Owners can't defer tax on income to reinvest

Thus, in this author's view LLCs (particularly Series LLCs, discussed below) provide the highest degree of flexibility, especially if established in the right jurisdiction. That said, historically C corporations have been used more often than not in this context, particularly where outside investors are considered. But because LLCs may elect to be taxed as a C corporation, it is possible to combine the flexible legal structure of the LLC with the tax benefits of a C corporation where retained earnings are contemplated.

Protecting Business Assets from inside Creditors

What if a claim arises within the business? As a general rule a creditor of the business may attach any assets of the business, including real estate, equipment, intellectual property, or any other assets owned by the business. Thus, it is imperative to also structure the business itself in such a way so as to reduce the risk of a business creditor taking the business's most valuable assets.

Therefore, it is *never* a good idea for the business to own the real estate upon which the business operates. The real estate should be owned by a separate LLC, which in turn is ideally owned by the type of trust described below. The business should then enter into a long-term lease to occupy the property, memorialized by a written lease agreement. In this way the digital health entrepreneur can retain the cash flow from the lease, if desired, upon a sale of the business. Alternatively, the real estate can also be sold, but at an additional cost to the buyer because of the long-term lease. (Note that this general rule about real estate also applies to the digital health entrepreneurs' investment real estate as well. Investment real estate, whether residential or commercial, should be owned by an LLC so that if liability arises on the investment property the risk of loss is limited to that property alone. Conversely, if the digital health entrepreneur owns the property in his or her personal name *all* personal assets will be potentially available to satisfy the claim.)

Similarly, expensive equipment (e.g., medical equipment) should be owned by a separate LLC and leased to the business, and high-risk assets like vehicles should be owned by yet another LLC so that these assets don't "taint" the business and trigger liability.

Moreover, the businesses intangibles such as goodwill, copyrights, trademarks, customer lists, etc. can all be owned by a separate LLC, with the operating business paying a royalty for the use of these intangibles. All of these separate LLCs can be bundled and sold together, or the digital health entrepreneur can retain one or more for enhanced cash flow upon the sale of the operating business.

In this way we can isolate the operating business so that all assets that would otherwise be attractive to a potential creditor of the business are unavailable. And again, the ownership interests of all of these separate LLCs should held by the trust described below.

If we structure the business in this manner the creditor's only remedy would be against the operating business, which is largely dependent upon the people running that business. This gives the business owners significant leverage to settle a creditor claim for far less than any judgment.

Protecting Business Assets from Outside Creditors

The above discussion addresses creditors from within the business. What if the creditor comes from outside the business, such as with a successful alter ego claim or as the result of a car wreck. In most U.S. jurisdictions, if you own interests in a legal entity such as a corporation or LLC, and you have a personal creditor, the courts will transfer your corporate shares or LLC interests to satisfy the creditor's claim. In other words, you will lose your ownership interest to that creditor!

For decades Delaware was the best jurisdiction for corporations because Delaware law was the best in the U.S. in this area. As a result, the vast majority of corporations were created in Delaware, regardless of where the investor(s) lived. It is important to note that one is not restricted to creating a legal entity in her own state, and it behooves one to "forum shop" to pick the best state's laws to establish a legal entity.

In addition to forum shopping, the type of legal entity is significant. As previously mentioned, historically most ventures that intend to raise capital from outside investors are established as C corporations (S corporations restrict the type and number of investors, so they are infrequently used for this purpose). Unfortunately, in nearly every jurisdiction in the U.S., shares in a corporation will be available to satisfy a personal creditor's claim. A simple example will help explain this risk.

Example: Anne is the majority shareholder in a new venture that uses blockchain technology to house digital health data. Anne was one of the first to market and thus she has a significant competitive advantage, and the venture already has significant value. Unfortunately, after working long hours, Anne was involved in a car accident on her way home, and Susan (a young professional), was killed. After a jury trial Anne was found to be at fault and a large judgment was entered in favor of Susan's estate. Due to the value of the corporation, Susan's executor asked the court to foreclose on Anne's shares, which the court granted. As a result, Anne's shares were transferred to Susan's estate to the extent necessary to satisfy the claim, and Anne lost control of *her* business.

What could Anne have done differently? Since shares in a corporation are rarely protected from creditors, did the entity have to be a corporation? Again, historically we've used C corporations when outside investors are used or contemplated, but other entities might work better in these circumstances.

If outside investors are not contemplated an LLC established in the right jurisdiction is a far better choice than a corporation. This is because in several states (including, Delaware, Nevada, South Dakota and Wyoming), the sole remedy of a creditor against an LLC interest is what's known as a "charging order." Such sole remedy jurisdictions do not allow a creditor to foreclose on the LLC interest like it can with shares in a corporation. Instead, the creditor's sole remedy is to receive whatever distributions the LLC member would have received absent the creditor.

Thus, if the LLC makes no profit distributions to the debtor the creditor gets nothing! (Note, however, that this does not preclude the LLC from paying management fees to the LLC member debtor, although these may be attached under certain circumstances.) If the debtor can avoid making distributions the debtor can use this as leverage to settle with the creditor, often on favorable terms.

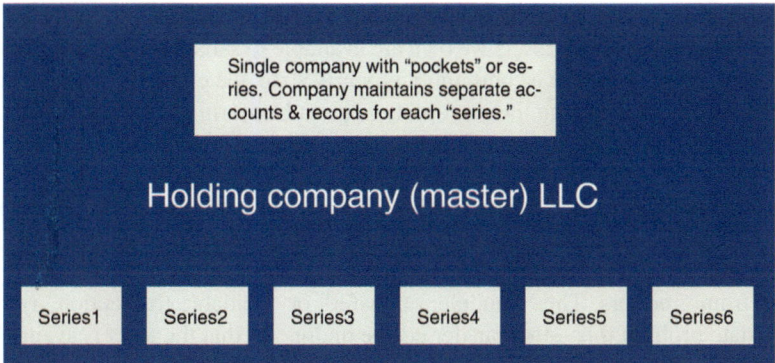

Fig. 8.1 Series LLC structure

Moreover, LLCs established in these jurisdictions provide the highest degree of privacy in that only the information for the LLC's in-state agent for service of process (typically a corporate agent) is available in the public record. Thus, in these states one cannot simply search by the digital health entrepreneur's name to learn what entities he or she owns.

What if the business contemplates outside investors with different rights (e.g., preference for distributions), such that a typical LLC will not be satisfactory? In this case the entity could be a legal entity offered in only a few jurisdictions, a Series LLC. As depicted in Fig. 8.1 below, a Series LLC acts like a holding company and subsidiary LLCs all wrapped up into one LLC, with the entity having different "series" for different investors with different rights. But again, Series LLCs are relatively new and only offered in a handful of jurisdictions.

As a result, it behooves the new business venture to be very intentional as to where it is established.

What about existing businesses and entities? Fortunately, existing entities can be "domesticated" into a state with the sole remedy of charging order protection, as either a traditional LLC or Series LLC as needed, so this analysis is also very relevant to existing businesses.

Is There an Alternative Ownership Structure?

Is there anything the founder can do to protect her ownership interest? What about the investors who have no say in the type of entity used, or the state in which it is established. Can they somehow protect their shares or LLC interests?

Fortunately, there are several steps digital health entrepreneurs can take to protect their assets, including their interests in the venture itself. Recall that only assets one owns personally are available to satisfy a creditor claim. Thus, if one doesn't own the assets yet has a beneficial interest in those assets, can we protect the assets from a potential creditor?

The answer is yes, but a more detailed explanation is warranted.

As a general rule only assets we own are available to satisfy our creditor's claim. Alternatively, if we live in a community property state, the creditor of either spouse may be able to attach community property (e.g., in California), or community property may only be available to a creditor of both spouses (e.g., Texas).

If we transfer our ownership interest away, however, that asset may be protected from creditors. I say may because in all states one cannot transfer assets for less than fair or adequate consideration to avoid, hinder or delay a creditor. Thus, one the eve of a jury verdict against them one cannot transfer their assets and have them protected from creditors. The "fraudulent transfer" or "voidable transaction" rules in every state prohibit this—the transfer can be undone so that the asset is available to the creditor.

However, what if we proactively transfer our assets when the proverbial waters are calm, when there are no claims against us and we have no reasonable knowledge of facts giving rise to any claims? Can this protect these assets from creditors?

Historically one could only transfer assets to others, or to a trust for those others, presuming the fraudulent transfer rules did not apply. However, for up to 20 years several states have permitted one to transfer assets to a trust in which the transferor is a beneficiary, and still have those assets protected from the transferor's creditors (again, presuming the fraudulent transfer rules do not apply).

Moreover, in several states the transferor can even serve as "Investment Advisor" over trust assets, such that she can have total and exclusive control over the investment decisions for the assets owned by the trust. In this way one can transfer assets proactively to protect them from future creditors yet retain total investment control over those assets.

The transferor cannot, however, retain control over distributions, as this would subject the assets to the claims of the transferor's creditors. This function is often left to an independent resident or corporate trustee in the jurisdiction where the trust is created, or the transferor can select an independent "Distribution Advisor" to initiate distributions from the trust.

Note, however, that not every state permits these types of trusts, so once again the correct choice of law for the trust is critical.

A continuation of the prior example will help explain this concept. Suppose that long before her car accident Anne transferred her interests in her blockchain company to a trust along the lines of what we've been describing established in the State of Wyoming. Presuming Anne transferred her interests long enough ago so that the transfer is not subject to the fraudulent transfer statute of limitations, Anne could be a trust beneficiary and the Investment Advisor, so that she continues to control the company as majority shareholder and yet her interests would be protected from her creditors.

Figure 8.2 depicts this structure, using a Wyoming trust to own the membership interests in the startup Wyoming LLC.

In this way we can protect the ownership *and control* of all intangible assets (those that do not have a physical presence), such as interests in LLCs, as well as many tangible assets such as shares in a corporation. Similarly, we may be able to protect real estate, particularly if that real estate is owned by an LLC.

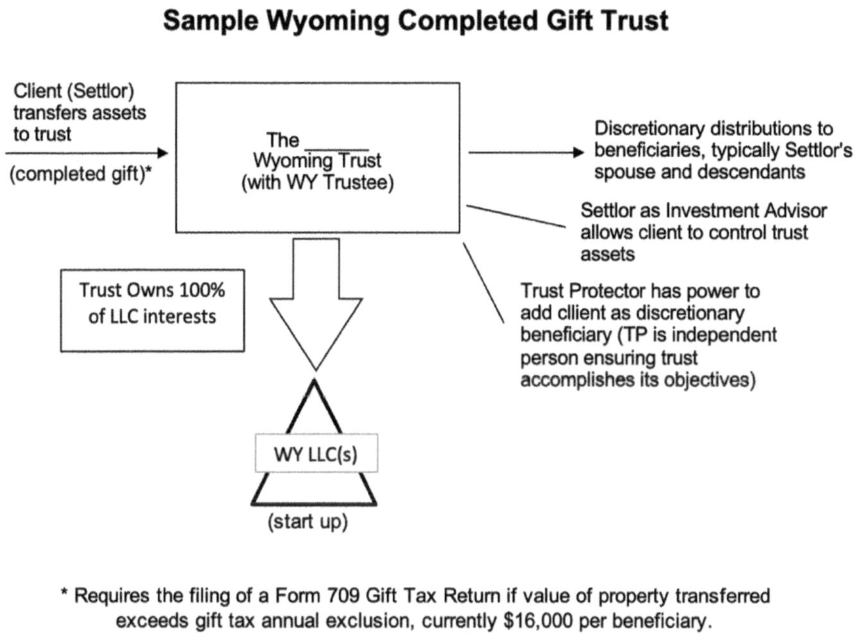

Sample Wyoming Completed Gift Trust

* Requires the filing of a Form 709 Gift Tax Return if value of property transferred exceeds gift tax annual exclusion, currently $16,000 per beneficiary.

Fig. 8.2 Sample asset protection structure

The Role of Estate Planning

Under current law, a U.S. resident or citizen can transfer up to $10 million (indexed for inflation to $12.92 M in 2023) during their lifetime or at death free of U.S. federal gift or estate tax. However, if one transfers more than $17,000 (in 2023) to any one individual in a calendar year during lifetime, the transferor must file a gift tax return (Form 709) that uses up some of the $ten million exemption. Transfers above this exemption threshold are subject to a 40% tax.

Example: Let's assume Anne's blockchain business is worth $5 million. Under current law, she can transfer the entire business to her children free of federal gift or estate tax. Note that depending upon Anne's state of residence, however, she may be subject to *state* gift or estate tax.

Alternatively, if Anne's blockchain business is worth $20 million and she desires to transfer it to her children, she cannot transfer all of the business without incurring federal transfer tax (gift or estate tax) totaling **$2,832,000** (i.e., 40% of $20 M less $12.92 M).

One must value the transfer at the current fair market value (i.e., what a willing buyer would pay a willing seller). What if, instead of waiting until the business had significant value, Anne transferred the business before it reached its current fair market value? During the start-up phase, Anne's business was worth very little, if anything; at inception a start-up has nominal value. Therefore, at inception, if Anne transferred all of her ownership interests to the type of trust described above, where

Anne could be a beneficiary and control the trust's assets as Investment Advisor, Anne could remove the value of the business completely from her estate for estate tax purposes. In other words, even if the business grew to $1 billion, all of that wealth would not be subject to federal estate tax.

Moreover, because of the protections provided by this structure, the $1 billion would also be protected from Anne's creditors (with the exception of a fraudulent transfer claim discussed above). Therefore, it is critical that digital health entrepreneurs proactively plan to protect their business interests from confiscatory taxes and creditors and predators.

And while they're at it, digital health entrepreneurs should also do their foundational estate planning: a revocable trust to avoid probate and control assets in the event of disability, plus powers of attorney for property and medical decisions, should be the foundation for every digital health entrepreneur's estate plan.

Importance of Succession Planning

The above discussion emphasis the importance of estate planning for digital health entrepreneurs. However, as with many entrepreneurs, the business may be one of the entrepreneurs most valuable assets, if not *the* most valuable asset. Where the business has significant value it is also imperative that the owners implement a carefully considered succession plan, particularly one that addresses the disability or death of owners working in the business.

Thoughtful, carefully documented planning that strategically blends business planning, asset protection, estate planning, and business succession planning must take into consideration the delicate balance of the health and protection of the venture while maximizing protection and value for each owner.

Conclusion

Digital health entrepreneurs face many risks and significant potential liability arising from those risks. However, with proactive planning using carefully considered legal structures, typically a combination of legal entities and trusts, digital health entrepreneurs can significantly reduce the business' and their personal potential exposure resulting from these risks. Moreover, with additional proactive planning, the digital health entrepreneur can protect their ownership interests (and potentially control) from being lost to one or more potential creditors, while ensuring they pay no gift or estate tax even if the value of the business skyrockets.

Chapter 9
Digital Health Intrapreneurship

Uli K. Chettipally

Definition of an Intrapreneur

From the previous chapters one has an understanding of what Digital Health is. Here we will talk about Intrapreneurship. An intrapreneur is "a person within a large corporation who takes direct responsibility for turning an idea into a profitable finished product through assertive risk-taking and innovation" as defined by the American Heritage Dictionary. The terms intrapreneur, intrapreneuring and intrapreneurship were coined by Gifford Pinchot III in 1984 [1]. It was later popularized in business magazines and in business literature where case studies were published.

Introduction

There are typically two ways companies can grow into new areas of business. One is where the company acquires or merges with another company that has the desired product, service, talent or customers in the market. The idea is that there is a potential to increase the market share by increasing the product or service line. Here the difficult work of innovation and finding a market for the offering is already done and has been tested to a degree where the risk of failure is minimized by the company that is being acquired. And hence the value of the company that is being acquired is significant. The ultimate result of this is to grow into new areas of business and increase the value of the acquiring company.

The second way is to innovate through new product and services developed by the company. Typically, the leadership of the company sets the agenda and direction of the new growth. It could be set up as a specific business unit to develop a specific

U. K. Chettipally (✉)
Innovator MD, Burlingame, CA, USA

© The Author(s), under exclusive license to Springer Nature Switzerland AG 2023   111
A. Meyers (ed.), *Digital Health Entrepreneurship*, Health Informatics,
https://doi.org/10.1007/978-3-031-33902-8_9

product or service. Sometimes it may not be clear which areas have potential for growth. Then it becomes a broader search for these areas of growth.

Typically, companies that have reached a certain level of maturity are the ones exploring these options. These companies need to be in a strong position with mature markets. Let's look at the life cycle of a company to understand why investment in innovation is imperative for companies to grow and thrive.

Life Cycle of a Company

Every company has a life cycle [2]. It starts with the formation of the company and ends with decline and death. This may not be evident when we observe companies for short periods of time, as some companies may have long lives sometimes lasting more than a century. There are five stages in a company's life cycle:

1. **Launch**. This is where the entrepreneurs come up with the idea for a product or a service and start building the company. The capital needs are high. And there is no revenue coming in. The idea needs to be turned into a product or service of this new company. The market needs to be tested. There is a need for investment in sales and marketing. The cash flow is negative. This puts immense pressure on the company to create value and generate income.
2. **Growth**. In this stage revenue starts to grow. So also the need for capital. There may not be any profits, as the money that is made will need to be put back into building growth. This is the phase when the company is bringing in good revenue, but the expenses are still high and at some point will break even and go into a positive cash flow situation.
3. **Shake-out**. During shake-out competition will increase. The market will reach its saturation point. And the revenues will peak. Cash flow is positive and profits are good, but there will be pressure from the competition. There may be some mergers and acquisitions. Companies that gain a strong foot hold will survive this stage.
4. **Maturity**. The company has succeeded in warding off competition and gotten into a solid financial situation where the revenues and profits are stable or decrease. Cash flow is good. During this phase companies need to figure out how to continue to grow. They need to look at new markets or new offerings.
5. **Decline**. During this phase the company's products and services loose relevance in the market place. The sales, revenues and profits decline, and the company's infrastructure becomes a burden. This leads to decline and ultimately the death of the company.

In order to maintain a company's market, revenues and profits, it needs to continuously reinvent and reimagine it's product or service strategies. This could be done by creating new business units for specific products or services, when the direction has been set by the leadership. This is often the strategic pursuit of organic growth within their core offerings. Sometimes the direction may not be clear or the company may want to explore opportunities outside of their core business. Then it is imperative for the company to set up a business unit that oversees innovation and intrapreneurship. Here, intrapreneurship can be seen as a process where individuals working for a company or organization create and develop new innovations that can potentially lead to new areas of business growth for the company. They sometimes can be paired with outside talent, but mostly work on their own internally.

Organizations that have a formal and a deliberate process and priorities are more successful in translating innovation from their internal projects [3]. The success of their innovations are tied to the effort and thought they put into the process of formalizing it, even though it is a challenge to do. Having the support roles like including research, information technology, finance and marketing coordinated will improve the rate of commercialization. Thus, strong leadership plays a crucial role at every stage and the ultimate success leading to commercialization of winning products or services.

Healthcare Industry's Challenges

Healthcare is a complex industry. It is also the largest employer of people in the USA. It consumes nearly 20% of the GDP. But, compared to other industrialized nations, the quality of care and health outcomes do not match the amount of money spent on healthcare.

To summarize the challenges facing healthcare today, refer to "Quadruple Aim" [4]. Quadruple Aim consists of four components: (1) improving the individual experience of care. (2) Improving the health of populations. (3) Reducing the per capita cost of care and (4) Improving the experience of providing care. Each of these four goals are critical to improving the status of healthcare as an industry. Although the business model of healthcare may be at the heart of the problems facing the industry today, digitization of the processes is seen as a solution to achieving all of the above aims. Any digital health solution that does not involve one of the aims may not be seen as an improvement.

Digital Health

According to Mesko et al. [5], Digital Health can be defined as "the cultural transformation of how disruptive technologies that provide digital and objective data accessible to both caregivers and patients leads to an equal level doctor-patient relationship with shared decision-making and the democratization of care". Technologies that provide objective data, whether it is vital signs, genomic or social, plays an important role. Access to data is not only available for the physician, but also to the patient. The decisions are made by both the doctor and the patient, together. The ability to avail descriptive data, assess predictive information and access prescriptive knowledge for both the doctor and the patient is the key to improving health while decreasing costs. A sure way for the healthcare industry to attain these goals is through digital health.

Innovation as a Strategy

Healthcare companies have enjoyed a good run of healthy growth over the past few decades. They did not have to change much in terms of how they did business. Now they are being forced to change. There are several reasons to innovate [6]:

1. **Increasing competition**. Existing competitors are innovating to capture a larger market share. Nimble startups, pharma companies, technology companies and global competition are some of the forces that are increasing the pace of innovation. Healthcare companies that have had a stable business with huge infrastructure are facing challenges from new companies that are lean and technology driven. Technology has helped speed up globalization and thus increase competition.
2. **Consumer expectations**. Consumers now have access to more knowledge and services, thanks to technology. They are now expecting personalized, efficient and inexpensive services. Companies that can provide all of the above with convenience are going to be the winners. Consumers can now share information through social media which drives more engagement for the companies that can innovate in this area and reap the benefits.
3. **Advancing technology**. It is now possible to automate a lot of the processes that used to take manual labor to accomplish. Technology is getting smarter, faster and cheaper. Legacy companies that do not have modern technology will be at a disadvantage, not only due to lack of sophistication but with increased cost and inefficiency, they become less profitable. With smarter technology the cost of doing business decreases due to increased efficiency and decreased need for human labor.
4. **Aging population**. With improving conditions, populations are living longer. As population gets older, their health deteriorates and the cost of taking care of them increases. It may take five to ten times the cost to take care of an older patient compared to a younger patient. This puts an additional burden on legacy companies that have nurtured their patients over the past few decades. With increasing cost of medical technology and newer, expensive drugs the pressure keeps mounting.
5. **Changing environment**. There are several external factors that are changing the business environment where healthcare companies operate. From regulatory hurdles to changing business models, companies are faced with difficult decisions like embracing their core competencies versus venturing into new areas of business. If they make no changes, there is the risk of becoming obsolete and irrelevant. If they make changes, there is the risk of that venture failing in the market.

How to Do Innovation

One thing is for sure—companies cannot stay where they are and expect to conduct business as usual and still remain in business. So, what are the ways companies can grow and remain relevant in the market place? There are three things that companies can do to stay relevant, grow into new markets and thrive amongst competition [7]:

1. **Increase investment capacity**. This can be done by revitalizing their core businesses. These are the services and products that have helped them succeed so far and generate revenue. The systems need to be made more efficient. Costs need to be trimmed. New technology needs to be used to automate or speed up processes. Make a firm commitment to their customers to buy their loyalty.
2. **Foster innovation internally**. Encouraging the current employees to participate in the innovation process. People working in the front lines understand the problems intimately. They may also come up with solutions that can solve the problem. Encouraging them by giving them protected time to innovate and changing the overall culture to nurture innovation at various stages is helpful.
3. **Create synergies between old and new**. Once new lines of product or service are created, building synergies to support the new and move the old towards the new moves the whole organization forward. Using existing support services to support the new business and repurposing some of the resources can have a beneficial effect on the newly created service or product lines. Sometimes they may have to let some of the old processes die to make room for new processes.

A Good Innovation Process

Here we are describing the innovation process as not just coming up with ideas or solutions, but to actually create a product or service that can be commercialized [8]. Innovation involves taking risks. A good innovation process should be designed to decrease the risk of intrapreneurship. We can look at innovation process as a funnel. Not all ideas can solve problems. Not all solutions can become products and not all products can be commercialized or scaled. As we go from product to a scaled product, there will be many ideas that cannot reach the market, which is the ultimate destination. In other words, there is a risk of failure or risk of not reaching the ultimate goal. A lot of work needs to be done before an idea becomes a product. This process is called de-risking. Methodologies like the Lean Start-up that have become popular in de-risking the startup process can be used in an Intrapreneurship program.

There are three main components of the Lean Start-up Process [9].

1. **Business model canvas**. Here the intrapreneurs sketch out what their hypotheses are while they are just starting out on their projects. The creation of the traditional business plan is discouraged. And the reason for that is the numbers and projections in a business plan are based on assumptions. So it is better not to get

too far in planning before those assumptions are tested to be true. The idea is to clearly express the value one is creating for the company and its customers.

2. **Customer development**. In this phase the intrapreneur has to go out and talk with several potential customers, distributers and partners. One is trying to understand how and whether the solution that is being proposed satisfies or solves a customer problem. By talking with customers early on, one might get a better understanding of the market fit of the solution. Customer development can also tell early on whether there is a problem and whether the solution being proposed will be successful or even needed. A lot of emphasis is put on customer research to come up with features and pricing for the product before it is built.

3. **Agile development**. Developing the product and features iteratively is the core work that occurs during this phase. It goes hand in hand with the previous phase where customer feedback helps design and develop the product. This reduces unnecessary expenditure of effort and resources on features that are not needed. It also helps in reaching the stage of minimum viable product or MVP. The idea is to go to market with a product with just the basic features and give it to customers. As one gets feedback from the customers, then develop more features that the customer actually needs. It is designed to decrease time to market and wasted money on product development.

The Purpose of an Intrapreneurship Program

Research has shown that a formal and structured process that has been set up deliberately to promote innovation and entrepreneurship is more successful [3]. The lack of a formal process fails to bring ideas to reach commercial success. The principles behind these processes are to:

1. **Decrease the risk**. Innovation is a risky business. Seventy-five to ninety percent of the start-ups fail. The purpose of an intrapreneurship program is to decrease this risk. Starting from problem discovery to commercial success, there are several steps that need to be completed to de-risk the process. The idea is to invest in the journey incrementally as the idea progresses through various steps to ultimately become a successful product.

2. **Make evidence-based decisions**. Research should be a closely intertwined with the intrapreneurship process. Research may involve qualitative research like speaking with customers, getting input from focus groups to quantitative research like doing retrospective data study or doing an outright clinical trial to evaluate tools developed. All decisions should be based on evidence.

3. **Figure out the business model**. Business model has to be thought through and decided upon, before launching the product. Even the greatest product may not survive if the business model picked is not right. This may require detailed analysis of the value proposition for the customer and the company. If a product cannot be sold while making a profit, it cannot survive in the market.

4. **Be O.K. to fail**. Processes should be designed in such a way that if an idea is going to fail, it will fail early. There should not be any negative consequences attached to failure. In fact early failure should be encouraged. This saves a lot of effort, money and time. The team can pursue other ideas and not waste their time on something that may not work out in the end.

Structure of an Intrapreneurship Program

There are several types of formal structures that organizations can set up to encourage innovation and support intrapreneurship. The type of structure depends on what stage of innovation journey the organization is going through and how seriously it is pursuing this. Here are the most common ones in the order of involvement and investment:

1. **Innovation lab**. An innovation lab is a dedicated space allocated for the purpose of encouraging innovation. The theme for innovation is loosely structured. There are no rigid rules about what projects can or cannot be a part of the lab. There are no timelines or financial support other than having basic supplies. Outcomes may not be tracked. The downside of this structure is that there is no serious thought to what happens to the innovations if they are successful. Some critics call this "Innovation Theater" for this reason.
2. **Incubator**. An incubator is a more formal structure where innovators are given more support. The duration may be well defined and there is a definite end point. The support typically includes mentoring, meeting and office space, access to experts and investment networks. They may not provide financial support directly to the projects. They may offer to fund some of the projects that have proven to be successful.
3. **Accelerator**. An accelerator may have all the support structures with the addition of early stage financing and a competitive application process. The timeline is comparatively shorter and has a regular calendar with a definite graduation day. If successful, the team is expected to launch the company and raise funding from angel and venture capital groups. An equity stake is taken by the host company. And there are various combinations and variations of the above models.

Creating Space for Innovation

Ultimately, the level of support that the organization provides to its intrapreneurs depends on the strategic priority of innovation for that organization. Innovators and intrapreneurs in established companies face tremendous cultural challenges. What is needed to run a company's core business is very different from running an innovation space. Ultimately, it boils down to leadership. There are several "spaces" that company leaders need to create for an intrapreneur, other than the physical space, to succeed in a corporate setting according to Tendayi Viki [10]:

1. **Strategic space.** Innovation and intrapreneurship should be part of the main strategy that the company is planning to grow in the future. If that is not the case, then innovations are bound to stagnate once created. Leaders need to have a clear vision on the strategic growth areas that intrapreneurs can then focus on exploring.

2. **Portfolio space.** Portfolio space refers to making space for products whether they may be core vs. adjacent vs. transformational. Having a vision of the future on how the current company portfolio will change based on market opportunities is a leadership function.

3. **Financial space.** Providing protected financial support to these ventures is critical to their success. Some entities have made that decision by separating the innovation arm from the main company with separate leadership. Sometimes these projects need longer term support than the annual cycles that organizations have.

4. **Management space.** Intrapreneurs use very different methods compared to running a typical business. There is a lot of experimentation and iteration that needs to happen. So, there are different set of tools that help intrapreneurs guide their journey through product development.

5. **Time space.** Innovation needs protected time for intrapreneurs to use. A lot of frustration ensues when that is not available. Companies that can provide this dedicated time for innovation have seen more successes. Again, it falls on the leaders to provide this time to encourage innovation.

6. **Learning space.** Intrapreneurs need to learn and develop new skills. The traditional ways of working that helped them in their previous jobs may not be useful in their innovation journey. Investing in building these new skills needs to be a priority to be able to use time productively. Creating mentorship is one way to do this.

7. **Space to fail.** Innovation is about taking risks and trying out various ideas. Not all ideas succeed. Having this knowledge and putting it into practice creates a space for intrapreneurs to not get scared and to try a variety of ideas. The more ideas one goes through and learns from, the higher the chance of success of the next idea.

8. **Space to scale.** Innovation process may help develop products successfully, but the product needs to find a place to be implemented and to grow. Finding a fertile environment becomes critical for the new product to flourish. Sometimes, the organization cannot find a way to scale it or is unwilling to scale it. There may be several reasons for it. The product may not fit with their current strategy, or it may make current, successful product obsolete. This is a very frustrating place to be. This is why having an innovation strategy is so important even before anything is built, so that valuable resources are not wasted on something that will not be needed or used.

As we can see, all these "Spaces" need to be created by the leadership. It has to be planned deliberately, if the company is taking innovation seriously. Many times, organization's leaders do not think that far or that wide. This leads to frustration on the part of the intrapreneur because it takes up valuable time and effort to educate and convince leadership on this. Ultimately, they end up spending a lot of energy in managing the leadership.

Skills Needed for a Digital Health Intrapreneur

As discussed in the previous section, leadership plays a very important role in innovation and intrapreneurship. There are several tasks that intrapreneurs need to learn to be successful in their endeavors:

1. **Manage stakeholders**. The first task that intrapreneurs have is to manage the stakeholders. Leaders of the company being the most important stakeholders. Managing involves educating, demonstrating value, casting a vision and disseminating the success stories about the innovation. It is probably the most important responsibility, as the ultimate success of the project depends on leadership. It is also important to note that the culture of the company plays an important role. The users of your product or your customers are the second most important stakeholders. Trying to understand their pain points and problems, educating them on the benefits of your product and showing them how important they are to the innovation process goes a long way towards the success of the project. The third most important stakeholders are the funders. Keeping them updated on your progress or challenges is an important element to maintain relationship and build goodwill. Managing interpersonal relationships with managers is important to keep ego, jealousy and dogma out of the way.
2. **Learn continuously**. Intrapreneurship is a new skill. It is not taught in a clinical school curriculum. It is up to the person to learn about the technology, the business and the clinical aspects of the solution. One's prior expertise in clinical medicine is not enough to tackle intrapreneurship. It is a very different environment to work in. Things are not as clear. One needs to become comfortable dealing with uncertainty and taking small risks. Build the solution in small steps and taking time to decrease risks at each level. Learning from potential customers is key to finding the pain point and developing a solution that they will use. Once they have the product in hand, one needs to learn how they are using it and what would make it better. Also, one needs to learn from the leadership. What are the problems they are tackling? What are the priorities? Where are the budgets moving to? This knowledge will help align one's project with the organizational goals.
3. **Start small**. Starting with small projects is a great way to test the waters and also to see if it is a good fit for one's strengths and ambitions. The project could be building a new feature for a current core product or creating a small new application which is not mission critical. This experience will help develop new

relationships, provides an opportunity to learn new skills and getting comfortable doing projects that have uncertainty built into it. Not everyone will be able to thrive under these circumstances. Starting small is also a good way to show the leadership your capabilities. One can build trust and reliability through their work. This helps in getting and doing larger projects.

4. **Work smart**. It takes a tremendous effort to create something that did not exist before. It takes a special person to do the work without the guarantee that the product will work. Many hours of sweat goes into it. The satisfaction one gets from seeing a new product that one created in action is unmeasurable. But, one must be prepared to kill the project when it is not successful. It can sometimes be hard to kill one's "baby", due to the emotional investment that goes into it. Being aware and prepared of this possibility is important. Sometimes, intrapreneurs will be tempted to get into conflict with others when their project is not given the green light. It is important to remember that one is still an employee of the company and one should not attempt anything that will jeopardize their relationships, career or financial wellbeing. Frustration is a common feeling when things don't proceed the way they should or people don't understand the importance of one's project for the company. Maintaining one's physical and mental health is important. Using help when needed is critical. One does not need to do everything to get the product out. Programmers, statisticians, analysts and project managers can be hired. Some of the development work can be outsourced. It is better to avoid being the only person on the project for the above reasons. A team-based approach may be helpful to the overall success of the project.

Working with Legacy Systems

Adoption of the Electronic Health Records (EHR) have been boosted in the late 2000s with incentives from the federal government. A wealth of data resides in the EHR systems. Although these systems have not kept up with the latest advances, the data in the systems can be used for innovation in digital health. FHIR (Fast Healthcare Interoperability Resources) Specification, a new standard for exchanging healthcare information electronically from HL7 can be used to access data [11]. One needs to be aware of intellectual property issues when working with EHR companies. Variables such as access, effort and time need to be considered when working with EHRs, which may complicate some innovation projects.

Future of Digital Health

The future of digital health has amazing potential. Healthcare being one of the last industries to be digitized, there will be tremendous opportunities to grow in this field. One may or may not pursue a formal training or fellowship in informatics.

Understanding the basic principles is important. Some in the field have felt more comfortable getting a formal training. Some, who have been doing projects and are more confident in learning on the job have thrived also. The rate of change and introduction of new technologies makes any new learning obsolete very quickly. One has to be on a continuous cycle of learning. There are exciting new technologies on the horizon like machine learning/artificial intelligence, blockchain, genomics, robotics etc. that make this a very exciting time to be in business as an intrapreneur. These new technologies promise to change healthcare as we know it and bring in an era of health for our patients and wellness for our physicians and staff.

Conclusion

Intrapreneurship is a great way to make a contribution to the company's growth while fulfilling one's curiosity and building a skill set which ultimately leads to tremendous job satisfaction. It is a challenging journey, but ultimately rewarding. Preparing for it, learning about the process, managing stakeholders and keeping one's perspective on the mission will result in a successful career in intrapreneurship.

References

1. Pinchot G. Who is the intrapreneur? In: Intrapreneuring: why you don't have to leave the corporation to become an entrepreneur. New York: Harper & Row; 1984. p. 28–48.
2. Business life cycle—five stages of a business' life. In: Resources/Knowledge/Finance. Corporate Finance Institute. 2018. https://corporatefinanceinstitute.com/resources/knowledge/finance/business-life-cycle/. Accessed 31 July 2018.
3. Capozzi MM, Gregg B, Howe A. Innovation and commercialization, 2010: McKinsey Global Survey results. In: Strategy and corporate finance. McKinsey & Company. 2010. https://www.mckinsey.com/business-functions/strategy-and-corporate-finance/our-insights/innovation-and-commercialization-2010-mckinsey-global-survey-results. Accessed 31 July 2018.
4. Sikka R, Morath JM, Leape L. The quadruple aim: care, health, cost and meaning in work. BMJ Qual Saf. 2015;24:608–10.
5. Meskó B, Drobni Z, Bényei É, Gergely B, Győrffy Z. Digital health is a cultural transformation of traditional healthcare. mHealth. 2017;3:38. https://doi.org/10.21037/mhealth.2017.08.07.
6. Nolan D. 6 reasons why innovation is a survival skill. In: Blog. Innovation Excellence. 2016. http://innovationexcellence.com/blog/2016/01/05/6-reasons-innovation-is-a-survival-skill/. Accessed 31 July 2018.
7. Abbosh O, Nunes P, Savic V. Make your wise pivot to the new. Accenture. 2018. https://www.accenture.com/t20180614T101357Z__w__/us-en/_acnmedia/PDF-79/Accenture-Make-Your-Wise-Pivot.pdf. Accessed 31 July 2018.
8. Hinssen P. Innovation without execution is only ideation. https://www.forbes.com/sites/peterhinssen/2015/06/04/innovation-without-execution-is-only-ideation/#5ec328f94bc8. Accessed 25 Nov 2018.

9. Blank S. Why the lean start-up changes everything. In: Entrepreneurship. Harvard Business Review. 2013. https://hbr.org/2013/05/why-the-lean-start-up-changes-everything. Accessed 31 July 2018.
10. Viki T. Eight ways to create space for innovation. In: Leadership. Forbes. 2018. https://www.forbes.com/sites/tendayiviki/2018/05/16/eight-ways-to-create-space-for-innovation/#4d1b9a3d283c. Accessed 31 July 2018.
11. FHIR Release 3 (STU). https://www.hl7.org/fhir/overview.html. Accessed 31 July 2018.

Chapter 10
Digital Health Trends

Rubin Pillay

Meet Alex. He's 42 years old and seemingly healthy. When walking his dog, Alex is alerted about a deviation in his health condition by his wearable device and advised to see a doctor. He schedules an appointment with his family physician in one click using his smart phone. The physician reviews Alex's patient history, including the most recent information from his wearable device, performs an examination and advises Alex to see a cardiologist. Using a registry of ranking specialists, Alex receives recommendations based on his personal preference and schedules an appointment. By giving the cardiologist access to Alex's patient history, Alex enables her to review all relevant information prior to the appointment. After her examination, the specialist adds her diagnosis to Alex's patient history. Comparing Alex's patient profile against a large set of patients with the same disease and similar health profiles, she can predict that the standard surgery for this disease would be risky for Alex. The analysis shows that for Alex's specific case, a certain drug can be expected to provide the best outcomes. Because Alex has given his consent to mapping his profile against ongoing clinical studies, he is matched to a clinical trial that has shown positive results and fewer side effects than with current drugs on the market. Alex decides to enroll in the clinical trial to benefit from the new drug and to contribute his data to the research study. As part of the trial, Alex downloads an app to track specific health parameters. He uses his monitoring device to manage his physical activity, and resumes life as before, knowing that he will be notified if anything urgent arises. Meanwhile, the smart care team consisting of doctors and supporting professionals remotely monitor Alex's progress in real time through the information provided by his wearable device. They use this information to advise him on his daily plan, if necessary, and motivate Alex to continue on his prescriptions and follow his

R. Pillay (✉)
University of Alabama at Birmingham, Birmingham, AL, USA
e-mail: rpillay@uab.edu

© The Author(s), under exclusive license to Springer Nature Switzerland AG 2023   123
A. Meyers (ed.), *Digital Health Entrepreneurship*, Health Informatics,
https://doi.org/10.1007/978-3-031-33902-8_10

health plan. Alex has also given his consent for his data to be used by researchers in different organizations for the creation of new drugs and the adaption of drugs in order to help improve the lives of patients just like him.

This is the patient journey in the digital age!

With 10 billion people—that's the global population projected by 2050, and with many enjoying longer lives—the services required by healthcare systems will have to adapt and grow. No one can be certain how the industry will evolve, but with new challenges come exciting solutions. What we can be certain of is that future trends will be driven by unprecedented access to big data and a greater involvement by the patient or healthcare consumer in shaping those services to their greater benefit.

Digitalization has reached every aspect of life today and is about to change how we as a society provide and consume healthcare services. Breakthrough technologies, such as the Internet of Things, artificial intelligence, blockchain, and cloud computing, have matured and are finding broader adoption in the healthcare world. Advancements in medical technology, such as genomics, health wearables, and sensors, show increasing success in medicine. And research around nanomedicine, robotics, and medical 3D printing is promising to deliver targeted, precise, and timely healthcare services.

This new era of true digital connection is giving people greater access to health information and resources. The convergence of three main drivers is the catalyst for many healthcare organizations to start their digital transformation, with the goal to create more value for patients along the continuum of care:

- Cost pressures, demographics, and the rise of chronic diseases
- A digital, empowered, "connected" patient, who shares valuable data with the wider community
- The emergence of digital technology and advanced medical devices, sensors, and wearables for extended monitoring and prevention and more fact-based care decisions

To respond to those driving forces and capitalize on the opportunities that digitalization brings along, the traditional healthcare value chain is evolving towards a digital healthcare network. This network connects patients, professionals, and providers in real time for more responsive, patient-centric care. The digital healthcare network will be the foundation for a new, consumer-centric healthcare system in which stakeholders respond more and more to mutual, shared challenges. Its open platform for communication and integration will enable shared, connected, and fluid data among all network participants.

The transition to digital healthcare offers many opportunities for both established organizations as well as new players. All future healthcare services will need to be designed in a way that promotes the following concepts:

- Value-based care: adapting structures focusing on optimal patient outcomes at the lowest possible cost
- Patient engagement: encouraging patients to take a more responsible role in disease management and prevention

- Personalized medicine: gaining groundbreaking insights into the human body at unprecedented, highly granular levels
- Participatory research and clinical trials: including more stakeholders and a higher number of participants
- Balanced demand and supply: optimizing service offerings and eliminating waste with real-time insight and predictive

Strategic Objectives Analysis

Current healthcare models are not sustainable. For digital transformation to have a maximal impact on creating more value in healthcare, it will require quick and ongoing adaptations by healthcare providers, insurers, and life sciences organizations. What is emerging is a healthcare ecosystem, moving beyond traditional hierarchics, in which all healthcare shareholders participate and benefit. Leaders will be inspired to re-evaluate business models, business processes, and workforce structures to meet key strategic objectives, including:

- *Enhancing the patient experience*: Every patient is a consumer, and consumer expectations are bleeding into healthcare. Digital technology is changing the traditional role of patients, enabling better-informed choices regarding health and well-being. Patients can more readily access health information and diagnose their own conditions or easily obtain test results and even receive better treatment. *How can we meet the expectations of the new healthcare consumers?*
- *Optimizing outcomes for each individual patient*: Today's patients need to see value from the insight into options they have for their specific health issues, based on key performance indicators and assessments of other patients facing similar circumstances. Pure statistics are not meaningful. The demonstrated outcomes must be specifically relevant to the individual patient and his or her particular context. *How do we provide healthcare services with optimized outcomes for each individual patient?*
- *Empowering healthcare workers*: Complexity is the enemy of workforce empowerment. It can drive up costs and slow down progress. New digital tools enable the workforce to reevaluate how they work and get the most out of their professional training, freeing them from paperwork to focus on patient care. *How can we restructure and empower our workforces to allow them to perform at their best?*
- *Increasing their organization's operational efficiency*: Providers are under constant cost pressures and resource constraints. A next-generation digital core will be the foundation for a smarter business—leveraging Internet of Things (IoT) and machine learning for higher automation and offering cockpits with embedded analytics, prediction, and simulation to ensure a more agile nervous system for the entire organization. *How do we remove unnecessary cost and waste and free resources for innovation and better patient care?*

- *Applying data-driven clinical innovations*: The most dramatic change in the digital economy will be driven by hyperconnectivity and Big Data science. These will transform nearly every business model in healthcare. The ability to monitor patients, collect health data, and react early to, or even predict, medical conditions, independent from physical constraints, will massively change the healthcare value chain and the way healthcare professionals deliver care to their patients. *How can we move from a mainly experience-based healthcare model to delivering personalized medicine based on real-world evidence?*

The starting point of the digital journey is the ability to reimagine everything. To help you reimagine your organization, you can think along three core dimensions: business models, business processes, and work environment. These dimensions can be evaluated by using the concept of value-based care and asking two basic questions:

- Are we improving patient outcomes?
- Are we reducing costs?

Business Model Trends

Healthcare is evolving from the optimization of single providers to building a community of specialists that collaborates in a wider ecosystem. By harnessing the flexibility of digital and, in particular, cloud-based solutions, the healthcare industry can find new ways to help professionals and consumers jointly create more comprehensive, patient-centric, and cost-effective healthcare.

Digital technology provides an opportunity to *integrate the care continuum* to elevate quality of care and health consumer interaction by orchestrating one-dimensional, single-step care providers into communities of care. The goal is to ensure targeted and personalized responses across the spectrum of service providers. Digital services can help patients navigate the healthcare system, foster prevention and manage chronic diseases, and empower them to take an active role in monitoring and managing their health. Real-time analytics can provide insights into the population and trends and help clinicians and researchers make good decisions at the moment of necessity.

Healthcare providers can lead in patient outcomes through *specialization* rather than offering a wide selection of services. To adopt this business model, organizations need to know their key strengths (such as units leading in patient outcomes), and identify noncore services to shed. This could include investing in clinical research, attracting new patients seeking specialized, high quality care, leveraging economies of scale through a higher volume and exchanging specialized knowledge within the ecosystem.

By harnessing digital technologies and electronic medical records from various sources, clinics can unveil new clinical insights from large populations beyond traditional clinical trials. This will help inform patient care with lessons learned from previous cases, optimize and personalize clinical treatment and increase transparency of clinical outcomes.

Connectivity also enables providers to offer innovative healthcare services to address the needs of the new healthcare consumers by leveraging new channels and accessing new market segments like corporate health to help companies keep the workforce healthy and productive, medical tourism aimed at offering high-quality, specialized services at attractive prices to patients willing to get healthcare abroad and retail healthcare which will offer standard services at convenient locations and office hours.

Leveraging real-time digital platforms will also create opportunities aimed at eliminating inefficiencies in healthcare delivery by brokering resources within healthcare networks. Stakeholders can connect beyond traditional channels to match supply and demand better using the digital age to close the gap. These would include amongst others, optimizing appointments.

Business Process Trends

With new business models opening the doors to increased collaboration across the digital healthcare network, processes are arising that provide solutions at every stage of healthcare—preventative, curative, and educational.

Digital technologies, such as sensors and mobile devices, help the patient and the care team to monitor conditions and behavior in real time and react faster and more effectively. We will thus be able to create effective preventive healthcare by empowering and motivating patients to take responsibility for their health. Engaging patients in disease prevention will result in better health outcomes.

With digitalized solutions, healthcare professionals can underpin clinical decisions and diagnostics with real-world evidence. They can gain new insights into our physiology, biology, and anatomy. By sharing health information over the digital health network and combining it with relevant clinical research, we can rely less on experienced-based medicine and find the root causes of diseases [1]. This includes:

- Outsourcing of highly specialized diagnostics
- Identifying and accessing relevant clinical research
- Eliminating duplicate testing
- Making patients a trusted source of valuable health information

Remote patient monitoring is among the top ten use cases that will drive IoT growth through 2020 across all industries [2]. Through delivery of telemedicine services with digital and interactive technologies, organizations can virtualize care venues, continuously track relevant biological signals, and facilitate early detection and prediction of health issues—extending their impact beyond traditional borders.

Digital technology will also help us meet health consumer expectations for individualized care. Medication and treatment can be tailored to each patient, promising better health outcomes, for example, by matching doses and active ingredients to individual genetic profiles rather than the general population. Leveraging the digital healthcare network, patients and providers will jointly define actionable health plans, agree on individual health goals, and use technology to monitor progress and react to deviations in real time.

When live data from all critical resource categories becomes available in the digital healthcare network, physical assets, care teams, and the patient can be planned simultaneously, even across organizational borders. Data capture can be automated through machine-to-machine communication and connected medical devices in real time. Advanced resource planning combines actual status with simulations and what-if scenarios thereby enabling us to manage resources smartly, efficiently, and in real time.

Connectivity also empowers the workforce with real-time insights and communication. Organizations can enjoy full transparency and real-time insights into all care activities and across all care team roles and care venues. New technology makes it possible to eliminate repetitive hand-over of tasks and error prone manual transmission of information. Lightweight, enterprise-grade communication tools provide professionals the same level of convenience they experience in their private lives.

The Future of the Work Environment

People working in healthcare do so because they feel it is their calling, even a dream job. Yet the burgeoning healthcare infrastructure prohibits them from giving hands-on, effective care. With digital technology, they will find new opportunities to do their job better and grow in their profession. They will also be able to actively contribute to the solutions of the future, creating the next cycle of proactive care.

In the new digital healthcare network, a physician's responsibilities will go beyond one-off diagnostics to include advising and coordinating along the continuum of care. Access to relevant clinical and research information combined with advanced clinical decision-support systems will help empower physicians to evolve into a new role of trusted facilitator. Whether rule-based or through insights from smart data, the digital health network will provide a new level of clinical decision support to healthcare stakeholders to make the best decision for each patient based on real-world evidence thereby driving better outcomes.

Human interaction will continue to be key in healthcare. Digitalization will enrich this interaction for better patient outcomes and more efficient deployment of scarce medical resources. Supporting technology, such as sensors, speech recognition, and automated documentation, releases nurses from traditional, routine tasks, freeing them up for more time with patients. They can focus on value adding activities, such as interaction, providing advice, and planning recovery, making for an improved patient experience.

Employers aim to create work environments that foster open communication across specialties. Mutual knowledge sharing based on proven patient outcomes will create a new generation that questions hierarchies and assumes shared responsibility. Digitisation encourages and facilitates the easy formation of collaborative and cross-functional care teams that then create clear and patient-centric key performance indicators.

Applying data-driven innovations will also extend and accelerate clinical research. Researchers use real-time analysis of clinical and genomic data, ranging from large patient cohorts down to the individual, anonymized patient. This capability allows researchers to validate hypotheses instantly and ask the best follow-up research question based on the results. Breakthrough research results can be generated in hours rather than years.

Redesigned applications enriched with machine learning and embedded analytics will not only automate back office processes, like patient billing. They will also relieve your workforce from related tedious routine tasks and help to overcome knowledge silos across departments. The automation of processes will result in smart and efficient operations.

Conclusion

Digital health has become synonymous with disruptive innovation in health care. Proponents say it has the power to transform every aspect of health and health care delivery, from improving patients' health status to the process of paying for a medical procedure. Despite that promise, digital health has yet to become ubiquitous in the U.S. health care system.

References

1. SAP. A future in digital health transforming healthcare for patients and providers. 2017. https://www.sap.com/industries/healthcare.html?source=social-atw-mailto#pdf-asset=a864cb4c-d67c-0010-82c7-eda71af511fa&page=1.
2. Accenture. Digital health technology vision 2017. 2017. https://www.accenture.com/us-en/insight-digital-health-tech-vision-2017?c=psv_digihlthrchfy17_10000004&n=smc_0517.

Chapter 11
Cybersecurity

Richard Staynings

Protecting What Matters Most

Healthcare Is Critical

Since the days of the Mesopotamia, healthcare has been considered critical to the wellbeing of soldiers and citizens, to the productivity of indentured laborers, and the health of the economy [1]. Ancient Romans are attributed with construction of the very first hospitals [2], designed initially to treat soldiers and veterans, but later extended to all citizens. In fact, the availability of good healthcare has been considered critical to every empire for nearly four millennia. In the United States it was recognized as one of 16 critical infrastructure industries by President Obama in February 2013 under Presidential Policy Directive 21 [3], which explicitly called for an update to the National Infrastructure Protection Plan (NIPP) for better healthcare protections. Other countries have similar national infrastructure plans and in all of them, healthcare is one of the identified critical industries.

Privacy and Security Regulation

The healthcare industry in nearly every country is heavily regulated. National and supra-national privacy legislation such as GDPR [4], APA [5], PDPA [6–8], governs the confidentiality of PII [9] and PHI [10]. Lacking modern federal privacy

R. Staynings (✉)
Cylera, New York, NY, USA

University College, University of Denver, Denver, CO, USA
e-mail: richard.staynings@du.edu

© The Author(s), under exclusive license to Springer Nature Switzerland AG 2023
A. Meyers (ed.), *Digital Health Entrepreneurship*, Health Informatics,
https://doi.org/10.1007/978-3-031-33902-8_11

regulation, the United States instead protects privacy via state privacy and breach notification rules for each of its 50 states and most of its 16 territories, while healthcare is specifically protected by the 1996 HIPAA Act [11] as updated by HITECH [12] in 2009 [13] and Omnibus in 2013 [14].

HIPAA was implemented to protect the confidentiality, integrity, and availability of PHI chiefly from exposure to unauthorized persons or entities. HITECH and its Omnibus rule expanded HIPAA data protection requirements, to include disclosure of data breaches of unencrypted personal health records by healthcare providers, health plans, healthcare clearinghouses, as well as related entities such as business associates and vendors. All of these entities are deemed to have either direct or indirect access to, store, transmit, or use PHI on a regular basis.

HIPAA refers to these organizations and individuals collectively as "covered entities" (CEs) and all are subject to compliance with the HIPAA Act. Standards and guidelines are defined in HIPAA's respective Privacy Rule and Security Rule, while non-compliance can result in fines of up to 1.5 million USD per year. Furthermore, breaches usually bring about a lengthy and expensive audit of security controls by HHS OCR [15] and if found lacking, result in Resolution Agreements [16] that usually feature a Corrective Action Plan (CAP) [17]. A data breach may be caused by malicious action, human error, or a failure in information handling or security systems and can cause significant harm in multiple ways, including serious physical or psychological harm, financial loss, or reputational damage.

In practice, HIPPA/HITECH has focused its attention on data privacy and the protection of confidentiality. This should be an important consideration for digital health entrepreneurs given the growing interoperability of health data between different CEs. So too should the formation of vast data lakes of medical data now mined for use across an array of AI [18] and ML [19] healthcare applications. But AI requires access to vast amounts of data for training purposes, some of it de-identified, but much of it raw medical data and therefore subject to HIPAA.

Healthcare Is Under Attack

Considered an easy and lucrative target by criminals [20], the healthcare payer and provider industry has been ravaged by hackers, cybercriminals, and pariah nation-states for decades [21]. The high value of healthcare data termed 'protected information' under HIPAA [22], is such that hackers have been able to monetize stolen information easily by the sale of personal and medical identities, health insurance, prescriptions, and much more. Easily sold or traded on a darknet full of criminal groups that specialize in identity theft, medical fraud, and the sale of prescription narcotics [23], this can be a very profitable undertaking for some. The price of information varies according to the market but a full identify can be sold for as much as $600. Compare that with a stolen credit card which was recently selling for around $0.15 each in batches of 10,000 and you can see the attraction of plundered medical information over retail, financial or other data.

Between 2009 and 2021, 4,419 healthcare data breaches of 500 or more records have been reported to the HHS' Office for Civil Rights [24]. Those breaches have resulted in the loss, theft, exposure, or impermissible disclosure of 314,063,186 healthcare records. That equates to more than 94.63% of the 2021 population of the United States. In 2018, healthcare data breaches of 500 or more records were being reported at a rate of around 1 per day. Fast forward 4 years and the rate has doubled. In 2021, an average of 1.95 healthcare data breaches of 500 or more records were reported each day [25].

According to IBM's Security's Annual Cost of a Data Breach Report [26] healthcare has had the highest breach-related financial damages of all industries for 12 consecutive years. In 2021 and 2022 cyberattacks cost providers an average of $10.1 million, up 9.4% from one year earlier. To use a 2021 example, a cyberattack cost Scripps Health based in San Diego, CA [27] $112.7 million in lost revenue and direct incident costs, with further response, incident handling, and system restoration costs continuing to come in well over a year later. Even more concerning are the massive class action law suits by a provider's patients following breach of their data or the inaccessibility of their medical records.

Of course, medical information also has an extortion value, which today is far more profitable than the sale of stolen information on the darknet. As a result, healthcare providers, have become the favored target of ransomware gangs [28]. Cyber-attacks against the availability of health systems, and health data and technology, are more than just annoying and expensive attacks however, they are 'threat-to-life' crimes because they directly threaten a hospital's ability to provide critical services to patients. As a result, this places patients at risk [29].

While the financial, operational, and reputational impacts of cyberattacks can be enormous for institutions, the medical impact for patients can be catastrophic. When patients can't get treatment, patient safety, morbidity and mortality concerns increase [30]. The availability of Healthcare IT and IoT systems is therefore of paramount concern in today's highly digital and interconnected health systems, not just for patient safety concerns, but also because of national defense, the productivity of national economies, and ultimately the sovereignty of states. Russia's November 2022 targeting of Ukrainian critical infrastructure in missile attacks, and its earlier deliberate targeting of hospitals is one such example of how loss of critical industries can impact the willingness of enemies to fight, as well as eroding the sovereignty of the Ukrainian state.

Principles of Healthcare Cybersecurity

Cybersecurity can mean different things to different people but in this case, the HIPAA Security Rule requires that HIPAA Covered Entities (CEs) protect the Confidentiality, Integrity, and Availability (CIA) of personal health information (PHI) using administrative, technical, and physical security controls. This principle is referred to as the 'CIA Triad' and forms the basis of cybersecurity across all industries. When HIPAA was written in 1996, protecting the confidentiality of PHI and the privacy of patients was given primary focus in HIPAA rules and standards, however today, with confidentiality largely already lost by overlapping cyber heists of PII and PHI, or willingly surrendered to social medial platforms, most healthcare cybersecurity professionals attach more importance to protecting the remaining 'availability' and 'integrity' of healthcare data and systems given rising patient safety concerns as discussed earlier.

Confidentiality

What is at stake when a healthcare provider is attacked by hackers? Complex US state and federal breach notification rules require that impacted individuals be notified that their personal information has been illegally accessed or otherwise disclosed. For HIPAA CEs, HHS OCR will conduct an investigation of the security in place at the time of the breach and will usually issue a corrective action plan (CAP) along with fines for any deficiencies. States' will issue their own fines, and punitive damages and class action lawsuits will make a breach an even more expensive incident. However, no one usually dies when confidentiality is lost and damage to a provider's reputation will eventually be forgotten by the community it serves, along with most of its patients, other customers, and partners. Healthcare CEOs may even retain their job following a breach and life goes on as before.

Integrity

Compare a simple breach with that of attacks against the integrity of health data. What happens when a patient's electronic medical record is changed prior to treatment, perhaps altering blood type or allergies? Unless re-interviewed and re-cross-matched, there is a risk that a post-operative patient could be transfused with the wrong blood and a transfusion reaction is mis-diagnosed resulting in the administration of an antibiotic, unbeknownst to physicians that the patient may be morbidly allergic to antibiotics. This is obviously a huge patient safety concern as could be other changes to a patient's medical history.

Other (theoretical) examples of integrity attacks include a study conducted in Israel by Ben-Gurion University of the Negev in 2019 which demonstrated how data could be intercepted between a CT scanner and its PACS stations whereby nodules were inserted or removed from DICOM images fooling 99% and 94% respectively of radiologists [31]. The impact of such a potentially malicious imntegrity attack, is obviously very concerning, resulting in needless intervention one way, and patient morbidity concerns the other way if cancerous nodules are not discovered in a timely fashion. Additionally, the introduction of fake nodules in a radiological scan of VIPs and political candidates, may be enough concern to cause victims to withdraw from planned activities or elections as the study pointed out.

Another example of PACS file integrity security was demonstrated in 2018 by CyleraLabs [32] which proved that malware could be easily inserted into the file header of DICOM files used for PACS images, and thus these widely shared images could be used as an attack vector to assault health systems [33]. The lesson to digital health entrepreneurs here is the importance of end-to-end encryption and file integrity checking. This is increasingly becoming vital for cybersecurity, even for the protection of internal communications on trusted networks.

Fortunately, we have not yet seen real life attacks of this nature, but it's quite feasible that we may in the future. The danger is that our clinical personnel are not currently trained to question or test the legitimacy of the electronic data or medical devices they work with. Nor are they trained to critically look for indicators of compromise, perhaps as the result of a cyberattack. Blind case studies, some on stage in public arenas, have proven just how ill-prepared clinical staff are to cope with medical device failure or cyberattacks, as Josh Corman and emergency physician Christian Dameff, MD and Pediatrician Jeff Tully, MD demonstrated at the RSA Conference in 2018 [34]. Indeed, it is only very recently, that medical schools have started to include very basic aspects of cybersecurity in their curriculums.

Availability

The real pain point today, however, is that of a cyber extortion attack such as ransomware against a healthcare provider. No longer is the provider simply distracted by responding to a breach or a data validity and integrity problem, but often the whole hospital or clinic is 'down for the count'. This can be devastating – financially, reputationally, and possibly result in a life-or-death issue for some patients.

San Diego based Scripps Health [35] took more than a month to recover from a ransomware attack in 2021 and lost almost $113 million in revenue [36]. However, the class action lawsuits are mounting from patients who charge that system leaders failed to keep their medical data safe from hackers, and patients were significantly inconvenienced when the provider's EPIC electronic medical record (EMR) systems were down [37]. This significantly disrupted care and forced medical personnel to use paper records. It also caused problems for other healthcare providers when Scripps' patients were forced to drive in some cases from San Diego to Los Angeles for critical and time sensitive treatments. It also resulted in expensive and wasteful duplication of tests since physicians were unable to access the patient's medical records or images. It is unknown at this stage whether other class actions may present themselves alleging physical harm by patients being denied time-critical treatments including radiotherapy and chemotherapy or if anyone died during the incident because HIT and HIoT systems were unavailable.

A similar denial of service (DOS) impacted the British NHS [38] when in 2017 many of its HIT/HIoT systems were encrypted by the WannaCry ransomware attack, attributed to the DPRK [39]. Hospitals went on divert, ambulances had to drive emergency patients much longer distances to receive care, and many surgeries, treatments, and other appointments were cancelled or had to be rescheduled – often months out. WannaCry affected at least 81 of the 236 Trusts across England - a third of NHS systems, and years later the NHS is still working to catch up on a massive backlog of elective surgeries from this period. A problem greatly exacerbated by COVID-19. WannaCry cost the NHS £92 million after 19,000 appointments were cancelled through lost productivity and data restoration costs [40]. It also was forced to spend an unknown amount on replacement of legacy IT / HIoT equipment at the center of the attack, and a further £150 million to bolster cybersecurity following the attack [41]. It is as-yet, unknown what impact WannaCry had on NHS patient morbidity and mortality [42].

In August 2022, a ransomware gang demanded € 10 million to restore Hospitalier Sud Francilien (CHSF), a 1,000-bed hospital located in Corbeil-Essonnes 28 km SE from the center of Paris, France [43]. The attack paralyzed the entire hospital depriving the population of Corbeil-Essonnes of healthcare services. The hospital, just like the British NHS before it, refused to make ransom payment to its attackers. Instead, it rebuilt all its systems from scratch taking many months to do so. Medical imaging was particularly devastated, demonstrating that medical devices were highly susceptible to the cyberattack and may have been at the core of the ransomware infection. Like most hospitals, patching of medical devices against known security vulnerabilities appears to have been lax, making these systems an easy target for hackers to establish a foothold on the medical network.

More recently, Common Spirit Health, the second largest healthcare provider in the US suffered a ransomware attack that impacted many of its legacy CHI [44] hospitals and caused massive disruption across much of the USA [45]. The organization runs 140 hospitals and more than 1,000 care sites across 21 different U.S. states. It is believed that more than 20 million Americans [46] could have been impacted by the attack, and that it may take years to fully restore and update all systems impacted.

Ransomware attacks have gone from anecdotal to the endemic with 66% of organizations having experienced an extortion attack, according to the Sophos State of Ransomware 2022 report [47]. More organizations were hit with ransomware in 2021 (66%) compared with 2020 (37%), with more victims (46%) paying ransoms and those ransoms being significantly larger than in prior years. In 2021, 11% of organizations said they paid ransoms of $1 million or more, up from 4% in 2020. As of late 2022, between 2 and 3 US healthcare providers are being hit with a ransomware attack every day so it's no wonder that both patients and the government are beginning to sit up and take note of this growing cybercrime epidemic [48].

However, the impact of a ransomware attack is much more than direct ransom costs. The costs of incident handling and response has increased dramatically. In 2019, the average cost of cleaning up after a ransomware attack was $761,000. That amount rose to $1.4 million in 2020 and $1.85 million in 2021 [49]. The fees for legal services and cyber breach insurance have also risen sharply and many insurers are now refusing to pay claims where an act of 'war' or 'cyberwar' [50] can be demonstrated. They are also paying out reduced amounts where 'contributary negligence' [51] is discovered when an organization is deemed to have inadequate security controls and protective measures in place.

Add in regulatory fines, punitive damages, credit or identity monitoring services, restitution, damages, and a growing number of class action lawsuits by individuals impacted and you have a large percentage of provider cash going out the door to cover ransomware costs irrespective of whether an extortion payment is made or not. That's money that could have been spent on improvements to patient care or improvements to cybersecurity. The costs of dealing with a cybersecurity attack are an order of magnitude more than the costs of putting in place cybersecurity measures to prevent such an attack in the first place. Yet many CEs still refuse to adequately fund their cybersecurity teams relying instead on insurance to transfer some of those risks and costs.

Of those who choose to pay the ransom, nearly half get only part of their data back, and it can take months to decrypt and validate all data exacerbating downtimes [52]. Furthermore, of those who paid ransoms, (36%) of companies went on to be targeted for a second time [53].

With rising insurance premiums and a growing list of exclusions, risk transference to insurance may no longer be an affordable or feasible option for most providers. Evidence suggests that payment of ransoms may be fueling the growth of this illicit extortion industry as attacks increased 42% year on year across the USA and 34% across the rest of the world. Interestingly, many cyber breach and liability insurers have themselves been attacked and their lists of policies downloaded by criminals. It is perhaps then little wonder when ransom demands exactly match insurance coverage limits. Use of personal machines for work (BYOD) and work from home (WFH) have also contributed to the rise in attacks according to the latest Cyber Readiness Report from Hiscox [54].

The true cost of downtime really needs to be fully evaluated including its impact on patients. Healthcare needs to do a better job of preparing for disasters, cyber incidents, or other interruptions to business continuity, and practice things like data restitution or real time failovers to hot datacenter sites, or between hybrid multi-cloud environments [55]. The reputational impact of an attack on provider and key executives is rarely calculated into the potential cost-of-loss estimates. This occurs when a hospital or other provider is unable to treat and prevent the death of a patient or introduces patient safety risks by many of its systems being down and unavailable.

So far two patient deaths have been directly attributed to healthcare ransomware attacks, though there may be more that have gone unreported as part of settlements, or have been purposely mis-classified to avoid publicity or legal suits. The first of these patient deaths occurred in 2019 when a baby was born in Springhill Medical Center in Alabama with the umbilical cord wrapped around its neck. The hospital had suffered a ransomware attack [56] the week before and its ultrasound and fetal monitoring systems were still down and therefore unable to identify potential delivery complications [57]. The baby was born with severe brain damage caused by hypoxia (oxygen starvation) and died some months later.

The second was in 2020 when a woman seeking emergency treatment for an aortic aneurysm died after a ransomware attack crippled a nearby hospital in Düsseldorf, Germany. The attack placed the hospital on divert, thus forcing the woman's ambulance to a more distant facility in Wuppertal, delaying treatment by an hour where she died shortly after arrival [58]. Physicians later determined that her chances of survival were slim at best given her condition, however that didn't stop German authorities from pursuing the Russian perpetrators on charges of negligent manslaughter.

The concern here is that in modern medicine, we are now heavily reliant upon the use of 'connected' medical technologies to diagnose, monitor, manage, and treat patients. When those systems are rendered unavailable, treatment and care declines rapidly. This is a major patient safety risk. Business continuity testing has shown that few nurses under the age of 50 can accurately chart a patient using paper and be assured that those records are complete, accurate and are entered into the EMR when systems come back up [59]. Also, (and putting fear of malpractice litigation and patient expectations aside), few physicians feel comfortable diagnosing patients without the tools and technologies that they were trained on and have become reliant upon. Evolution to digital health therefore appears to be largely one-way! [60].

Expanded Threat Surface

Digital Health Interoperability

The move to electronic patient records brought about by the HITECH Act in 2009 and CMS Meaningful Use [61] objective measures has made it much easier for hackers to access, steal or hold to ransom medical data. The opening of provider networks for the meaningful exchange of medical data with business associates and other CEs has removed the 'fortress citadel' defense of hospitals and other providers that previously existed. The advent of new AI based technologies and the massive growth in the adoption and use of connected medical and other healthcare IoT devices has further expanded the threat surface for hackers. New medical wearables and mobile health apps look set to expand this further. So too are changes in the delivery of healthcare services employing telehealth, telemedicine, and other remote medical services.

During Covid, post operative patients were sent home as soon as possible to remove them from the dangers of the pandemic raging inside of hospitals and to free up much needed bed space. The right of patients to die in their own homes, especially in jurisdictions such as Australia and New Zealand where uptake is high, means that medical beds and other equipment including remotely controlled infusion pumps, nurse call, video monitoring, and much more, is being run and operated outside of treatment facilities and in patient homes. This further expands the medical network even though only 20% of the terminally ill get to die at home in the USA, UK and Australia. Only New Zealand comes in higher at 30% [62] currently, but things may change as more people become aware of these 'rights'.

Medical and Other Healthcare IoT

Some 75% of IP connected endpoints in hospitals today are unmanaged by IT. The vast majority of these are a growing number of medical and healthcare IoT devices. These systems are usually managed by Clinical Engineering or Biomed teams. While connected hospital building management systems like elevators and HVAC – vital to patient workflows and pandemic control, are managed by Facilities engineers. Few of these teams have even dotted-line reporting into IT, so visibility by security teams is poor and distant at best, though this is thankfully changing at last. However, the BMETS and engineers who operate and maintain these devices are not currently trained on the cybersecurity risks posed by HIoT and therefore are not equipped to identify a potential indicator of compromise (IoC).

Medical and HIoT devices are growing at compound annual growth rate of over 18% [63]. This growth is being driven by the need for improved efficiency, cost containment, and a shortage of clinical staff [64]. Providers are automating nearly every function from nursing, to laboratories, to pharmacy, and to surgery. An ageing and retiring nurse population exacerbated by the pressures and risks of Covid-19, means that patients are checked now by telemetry devices, their drugs selected by pharmacy robots, dispatched to different parts of the hospital by mobile delivery robots, and dispensed by local automated and connected Pyxis cabinets. Even patient labs and other samples are sent around hospitals by mobile transportation robots that call elevators and navigate floors with apparent ease.

It is medical devices that scan patients and diagnose ailments, and devices that treat their cancers. Neurosurgery is now the domain of the da Vinci robotic surgical system, given higher levels of accuracy than possible with even the most skilled of surgical hands. Other areas of healthcare look set for automation too, as a multitude of new devices and powerful applications are developed and approved for use, many of them employing AI or ML. Some of the fastest-growing fields in the medical device industry include robotics, big data, telemedicine, and virtual reality [65].

Concerns about the Security of Medical Devices

The vast majority of medical devices were designed for their ability to reliably perform clinical tasks, not necessarily to perform those tasks or to operate on the medical network securely. The result is that most are quite insecure and have little to no native security capabilities. Most were designed only to perform that task they were designed for, and few are extensible to support updated embedded operating systems or newer more secure versions of their applications. They were launched with the necessary amount of CPU, RAM, and ROM to perform their tasks as specified, and cannot support common security supplicants like an anti-virus, or a host firewall. Some lack even the additional capacity to support a simple security patch if that changes system resource requirements.

Historic FDA rules and in particular pre-market guidance [66] was designed to encourage medical device manufacturers to improve the security of their products, but this only focussed on new devices. New FDA rules brought about by the passage of the PATCH Act of 2022 will bring about major changes to the security of new medical devices approved after Oct 1st, 2023, but these rules currently do not apply retroactively to previously approved devices. With literally millions of legacy HIoT systems in use across hospitals and clinics, and many of them amortized over a 15-to-20-year period, these riskier devices will not be retired for many years to come. This leaves providers vulnerable to the patient safety and cybersecurity risks that each of these devices introduces to the medical network [67].

What's more, while some manufacturers are good about the timely release of patches to published CVEs and other vulnerabilities, others are not. Some have been accused of being wantonly negligent by refusing to create patches for devices which have been superseded regardless of their age. Some manufacturers have suffered

FDA recalls of their devices because of serious concerns about their security [68]. And as a result, a growing specialization has emerged of highly litigious law firms who focus upon damage claims following medical device failures [69].

Lack of an agreed lifespan or support period, complicates purchases of devices since providers cannot compare one vendor product with a lifespan of 'x' years against another vendor product with a lifespan of 'y' years. So too is the question of support and the timeliness of critical patch availability, even when patches can be applied to devices or medical applications in use 24 by 7. Much of this may change as a result of new FDA rules, but for now remains a significant problem. Like most IoT systems, manufacturers price their systems based on what they can sell them for. Until recently, support overhead was not a cost consideration for most, so many devices never receive patches for their entire lifespan as that was never part of the product business plan. Since they are usually connected to the medical network this presents risks to the entirety of the health system. Unless isolated, medical devices can be used by attackers as an infiltration point, and to establish a foothold on the network from which to run malicious campaigns of data exfiltration, or for the spread of ransomware payloads to maximize the impact of an extortion attack.

Historic FDA pre-market guidance was a step in the right direction, but the FDA was not until recently empowered to fully regulate or enforce all aspects of security for medical devices. For this and other reasons the Patch Act of 2022 [70], will undoubtedly bring about changes in regulations for the security of medical and other HIoT devices. The act adjusts the balance of responsibility for security back towards manufacturers, placing the onus on them to design, test and patch devices they manufacture. This includes a requirement for manufacturers to publish an SBoM – a software bill of materials [71] for devices, so that providers can better understand risks when vulnerabilities are published in underlying software components such as embedded operating systems or their components. It also introduces the need for manufacturers to publish vulnerability disclosures and to release security patches in a timely manner among other changes.

Digital health innovators would be well advised to familiarize themselves with new and proposed legislation in the industry [72] and to the work being conducted by groups such as the Health Industry Cybersecurity Practices (HICP), and the Health Sector Coordinating Council (HSCC) / HHS 405d Task Group [73] which is a part of the Joint Cyber Working Group [74] of the Health and Public Health critical infrastructure working relationship. Innovators would also be advised to design extensibility into their innovations so as to future-proof systems against new cybersecurity risks and plan on the need for timely release of security patches and updates. They should also consider the design and service / support lifespan of innovations.

Reducing Medical Device Risks

The growing dominance of medical devices on healthcare networks has turned models of healthcare security on their head. In no other industry is there such a growth in largely unmanaged IoT. Devices that on one side are often connected to the medical network and on the other side to a live patient. They pose a unique risk to patient safety, to the integrity of the medical network, and a huge challenge for cybersecurity teams to secure as previously discussed. With many devices unable to receive updates due to hardware constraints of supporting an updated and larger embedded operating system, or even to be patched against known CVEs [75] security alternatives must be sought.

Known as 'Compensating Security Controls [76] these act as an alternative when risks cannot be directly remediated and are generally accepted by auditors including HHS OCR. This allows providers to continue to use equipment that may not yet be fully written-off on depreciation schedules and asset books often with many years of useful life left in them. It also allows providers to utilize high-risk devices, for continued rendering of care to patients, often again for many years.

One such compensating security control for medical and other HIoT devices is network segmentation through a process of isolating or enclaving 'at-risk' devices [77]. This can be accomplished in many ways, at its most basic through the firewalling of isolated medical device networks, and more effectively through network access control (NAC) [78] a feature built into modern enterprise software defined networks (SDN) [79]. This allows switch ports and virtual (AP) ports to act as mini firewalls. These are then used to lock-down access to individual devices known as 'micro-segmentation', or groups of similar devices known as 'macro-segmentation'.

However medical and other HIoT devices usually need to communicate outside of their segment or enclave to other systems. An example of this might be a CT scanner that must communicate with a PACS system for storage of images, for PACS workstations for review of images by radiologists, and links to the EMR for integration with the master patient record. However, only very specific IP ports and protocols need be opened to and from the enclave to certain pre-defined destination IP addresses. This acts as a form of object level 'ZeroTrust' [80] and reduces the threat surface for at-risk devices. It also prevents someone from using a PACS workstation to surf the web or to stream music which is usually considered a high-risk activity on FDA regulated medical equipment, and therefore is highly undesirable. NAC through a process of security group tagging (SGTs), simply drops all unauthorized data packets at the switch port for any untagged packets.[1]

The challenge for security and IT teams is to identify the needed communication profile of each device. Operating profiles are needed to create rulesets in firewalls or to populate NAC based segmentation realms [81]. Since providers usually have tens of thousands of different devices from hundreds of different vendors each with their own unique operating characteristics, this becomes a mammoth task. It is complicated further by a steady stream of new, patched, or replacement devices running different software and firmware versions that must be individually analyzed and profiles created for each of them.

---

[1] Cisco's interpretation of NAC uses security group tags (SGTs) to identify authorized network packets and enforces access at switch ports using TrustSec built into its switches. Cisco Identity Services Engine (ISE) is an application used to manage the grouping of assets and tagging of packets using SGTs. Other vendors' NAC solutions operate slightly differently but Cisco was the first to market with NAC and SDN.

A manual approach to medical device profiling is plainly unfeasible, given the time, costs and need for constant updates. Fortunately advances in digital health technology have automated this process. Through the successful application of ML-based Datatype Analysis and DigitalTwin technology [82], fragile medical devices can now be passively probed and profiled, while their virtual twins be be aggressively tested for vulnerabilities, all on a real-time ongoing basis. This facilitates the identification of changes or updates to devices when patched, and recognizes the addition of new devices as they are connected to the network. With accurate device profiles, and seamless automation and orchestration between the asset profiling tool and the network, NAC can then automatically enclave devices based upon segmentation policy, thus enabling a truly smart healthcare network. The same asset profile can be used for risk analysis and reporting of discrete devices and for improved utilization and management of HIoT. More importantly, the asset profile becomes a baseline of legitimate authorized activity so that any attempted system traffic outside of this baseline can be flagged as anomolous and appropriate alerts generated via SOC and SIEM tools.

Medical Wearables

Any medical doctor will tell you that most patients are lousy about actively managing their health and well-being on a day-to-day basis. Unless sick and in need of prescription medications, patients by and large make an appointment once a year to see their primary care physician (PCP) or General Practitioner (GP) for an annual physical. It's the only free appointment of the year for US insurance-based customers, thanks to changes brought about by the Affordable Care Act of 2010 otherwise known as 'Obamacare'. Furthermore, with the onset of high deductible health plans, many patients put off visiting the doctor or going for treatment till the end of the year when their annual deductible has finally been met. The patient-doctor interaction is therefore periodic and inconsistent, and this is the pattern that most people adopt with regard to the monitoring of their health. Wearables look set to change this by engaging patients in their own health and well-being on a daily basis.

Since its launch, the Apple Watch has been steadily adding features while gaining greater and greater market saturation. Paired with an iPhone or iPad healthcare apps, many patients now regularly check how many steps they walked and climbed each day, or their heart rate and calorific intake. Regardless of vendor, and whether consumer purchased, or hospital provided, medical wearables make excellent medical sensors and are widely being used today to monitor heart rate, body temperature, blood pressure and glucose levels.

As adoption expands, wearables will encourage still further patient engagement, making patients feel more involved in their health and well-being. It will also provide them with improved control over their healthcare treatment plans and encourage them to make better decisions without even having to consult with their care team.

With release of additional features seemingly with each new software and device version, more and more data is being acquired and uploaded to cloud based services for processing and reporting back to patients. At the same time this data is ideal for mining by AI and in particular ML and DL[2] where inferences can be drawn from the data to automatically recommend changes in patient behavior. This can be provided instantly to the owner via a simple m-Health application. As more and more consumer wearables and their healthcare apps are integrated with patient EMRs, (as Australia has done already), so the ability to share sensor data with the patient care team becomes easier. Not only that, but the data pool for each patient increases leading to improved AI outputs including early diagnosis of problems. The more data AI has access to the more complex and accurate AI based digital health solutions will become. This will likely bring about a fundamental change to healthcare and public health.

Initially considered innocuous when launched, consumer wearables as they incorporate more sensors and collect more data, become more of a concern for security and privacy professionals. Once integrated with EPRs / EHRs concerns arise as to the security and integrity of the patient record. Can consumer sensor information be trusted to be accurate. Did the owner really run ten miles or did his or her dog do so with the wearable attached to it?

Wearables lack the processing or storage capacity to run AI algorithms on the device itself so must be paired with a cloud-based service for AI data mining. Wearable devices are used primarily as data feeds or sources for smart health applications and not recipients or processors of protected HIPAA data, so risks are low compared to an unauthorized person gaining access to medical applications or the EMR. That being said, if recommendations are going to be sent down to the device for patients to read then strong authentication should be required as should encryption of data in transit to and from the wearable.

Mobile Health (m-Health)

Mobile health (m-health) is the term of monitoring patient health using mobile phones and patient monitoring devices or sensors such as an Apple Watch. SmartPhones such as the Apple iPhone also contain their own sensors such as camera, microphone, accelerometer, and gyroscope and these can all be used in healthcare-based applications [83]. Like medical wearables, mobile devices have very limited hardware capabilities so are not ideal for the running of AI. Indeed, deep learning architectures are often too computationally expensive to run on such small devices. Like wearables, m-health must be paired with a cloud-based application for the mining of data using AI.

However, given the larger form factor of smartphones, m-health is idea for reporting results and recommendations. Many providers have recently launched mobile applications for access to patient portals where appointments can be booked, and results of tests reviewed. While this is great for improved patient engagement it

---

[2] Deep Learning (DL) is part of a broader family of machine learning methods based on artificial neural networks with representation learning.

does raise questions around the security of mobile devices and the protection of HIPAA regulated data. This is especially the case if that data is persistent and stored locally, rather than just displayed via a bitmap on the screen of the device for the duration of the session only.

Precision Medicine

The convergence of AI and precision medicine promises to revolutionize health care. Precision medicine methods identify phenotypes of patients with less-common responses to treatment or unique healthcare needs. And when combined with AI's ability to draw inference to generate insights, enables an AI system to reason and learn, thus empowering clinician decision making through augmented intelligence [84]. Research reveals that humans vary widely at the genetic, biochemical, physiological, exposure and behavioral levels, especially with respect to disease processes and treatment responsiveness. This suggests that there is often a need to tailor, or 'personalize,' medicines to the nuanced and often unique features possessed by individual patients [85]. Personalizing a medicine or tailoring an intervention to a patient requires a very deep understanding of that patient's condition and circumstances, and this requires the extensive use of sophisticated assays that generate massive amounts of data, such as DNA sequencing, and here lies the security concern with precision medicine.

Unlike HIPAA protected PHI, DNA is much, more than mere non-public information, it is the essence of an individual, a unique and very detailed profile of each individual. Name, address, medical record number and many other HIPAA identifiers can all be changed and replaced in the event of a breach. A person's DNA cannot - ever! Genome sequencing and research therefore demands even higher levels of security and protection than simple PII or PHI. Given the vast amounts of data required for sequencing and identification of the unique features of each patient needed to develop and prescribe optimal personalized intervention, this becomes a highly visible security concern and one of the greatest areas of pushback around the adoption of precision medicine.

There are also questions as to who should be able to access data, for which purposes, and how this access and use should be regulated. Most of these questions to date have failed to address concerns about, for example, commercial interests [86]. The development of precision medicines is very expensive and the pressures to make this form of medicine more widely available and affordable are great. In 2016 under the Precision Medicine Initiative (PMI) special responsibility was given to the ONC [87] to "support the development of interoperability standards and requirements that address privacy and enable [the] secure exchange of data across systems." [88] The Precision Medicine Initiative: Data Security Policy Principles and Framework (PMI DSP) resulted in eight principles covering cybersecurity and data integrity which together "provide a minimum level of due care and due diligence while ensuring organizations retain the flexibility of approach allowed under the HIPAA Security Rule and the NIST CSF" [89, 90].

Precision medicine is still in its infancy, and the domain of the super wealthy who can afford the overhead of custom medications. That will change as DNA sequencing speeds up and the pool of data from past precision medications and treatments, expands to form a body of knowledge for the industry to draw upon and from which future developments can be built. The more data that is available the more can be reused including trained models. However, at the end of the day, AI's ability to advance personalized medicine will depend critically on not only the refinement of relevant assays, but also on ways of securely storing, aggregating, accessing, and ultimately integrating, the data they produce.

AI's Insatiable Need for Data

AI has an insatiable need for data, data for training, data for ensuring massive sample sizes to remove bias, and data for driving improvements to natural language processing, medical imaging, clinical decision support, and the many other applications of AI across healthcare as explored in other chapters of this book. However patient confidentiality must be maintained for regulatory compliance and patient privacy, and this is an underlying concern for digital health innovators.

Small data samples have proven ineffective for ML training. Small sample sizes also raise concerns that algorithms could be reverse engineered or that the identity of individual patients discovered. For these reasons, AI requires huge amounts of data for training and for accuracy. These requirements make it difficult to share raw medical data with researchers, which must be de-identified before data can be used. However, it's not possible to simply delete all identifying information in all cases. For example, to apply AI to tumor growth, it's necessary to associate all the studies from each individual patient. But medical data is highly valuable to criminals, even when de-identified. As more and more data feeds into these meta repositories, and more researchers mine that data, so it becomes harder to secure it.

China has been particularly interested in acquiring (usually through illicit means) these massive healthcare data lakes for its own AI development at state-owned industries. Indeed, China has made huge investments [91] and large inroads to the development of AI tools and applications in the healthcare space [92] and has focused much of its state-run and funded APT [93] hacker teams on the theft of western AI technology and training data. China is by far the world's bigger perpetrator of cybertheft [94] and much of its hacking efforts are currently focused upon the different target areas of AI [95] and healthcare data.

The importance of protecting IP of AI models, algorithms and technologies is such that it warrants a whole chapter of this book. Plainly there is a lot of national pride tied up in being first to market, and AI has become the equivalent of the 1950s and 1960s race to space between the USSR and the United States. For more information, see the chapter of this book written by Vani Verkhovsky, et al. on AI and IP.

Securing AI

AI development is widely considered to be governed by the 23 Asilomar AI Principles [96]. The sixth principle states that "AI systems should be safe and secure throughout their operational lifetime, and verifiably so where applicable and feasible." But as AI becomes ever more capable and new uses are found for it in healthcare and other industries, so the question becomes what does it mean to make AI systems safe and secure?

Plainly there are many, many uses for AI including the defense of healthcare data and systems as Anthony Chang and Dragos Ilinca have discussed in their respective chapters. A 2020 report on "Artificial Intelligence and UK National Security" commissioned by GCHQ, the U.K.'s Government Communications Headquarters, stressed the need for the UK to incorporate AI into its cyber defenses to "proactively detect and mitigate threats" that "require a speed of response far greater than human decision-making allows [97]." But if decision making is automated by AI then there is a danger that if decision making AI criteria is corrupted in some way then systems that rely upon AI for defense will fail, thus exposing both healthcare entities and national governments to the risk of attack. By the simple act of corrupting decision making by changing expected variables, adversaries can cause AI systems to make mistakes by manipulating these inputs. This is referred to as 'adversarial machine learning' [98].

Conversely, 'data poisoning' can also be used to manipulate inputs by training an AI model on inaccurate, or mislabeled data. Even the act of selectively training an AI model on a subset of correctly labeled data may be sufficient to compromise a model so that it makes inaccurate or unexpected decisions [99].

Data provenance and trust is critical for the sources of data and security around the integrity of both the supply source for that data, and the integrity of the data itself, so as to avoid internal threats around data poisoning. With these dangers in mind the US National Security Commission on Artificial Intelligence (NSCAI) has highlighted the importance of building trustworthy AI systems that can be properly audited and certified. It also emphasizes the importance of transparency, testing, and accountability for algorithms and their developers [100].

Some AI systems are in continuous training mode, intended to adapt and improve over time in response to the data these systems receive while running. This tuning of AI applications means that bad actors can continue to try to corrupt AI data streams long after development. Perhaps by launching an attack against a full production system. For these and many other reasons, AI applications should be afforded all the layered and overlapping security protections of any other live production application or IT based system.

Offensive AI and Defensive AI

AI is a powerful tool and has many offensive uses. In 2016, the run up to the US presidential election was marred by AI-based social media bots being used to manipulate various social platforms in order to undermine confidence in electoral systems and to shake the pillars of the US democracy [101]. The Brexit referendum [102] as well as French and German national elections which followed were also reportedly subject to similar attacks all attributed to Russia [103]. This pushing of false-truth narratives to manipulate popular opinion has dramatically undermined democracy, democratic institutions, and has thrown the trust-based democratic system into chaos. Furthermore, these attacks have divided and distracted western countries at a time when autocrats like Vladimir Putin and Xi Jin Ping are pushing increasingly confrontational agendas against the rest of the world. The UK decision to leave the European Union has weakened financially and militarily the EU, while resulting in a controlled crash of the UK economy.

AI is behind Deepfakes [104]—video and audio clips purporting to be of celebrities, but in reality, are almost entirely computer generated [105]. Deepfakes have been used in Business Email Compromise (BEC) attacks [106] where an AI backed interactive phone call or IM exchange with the CEO of a company instructs staff to wire money to an overseas bank account used by criminals. Someone could work with the CEO every day for 20 years and not know the difference, they are that good. This is now a $26 bn per annum scam according to the FBI [107] and usually arrives with an average cost of $5.01 million per breach according to the 2021 IMB Cost of Data Breach Report [108]. Deepfakes erode trust and cause us to question the validity of what we read or are told [109]. From a security perspective that's a good thing most of the time, but in healthcare we rely upon the integrity and accuracy of medical data upon which to make decisions. If there are doubts then that can introduce delays, and delays can result in negative patient outcomes.

AI based integrity attacks pose a significant patient safety risk. But attack tools are stealthy, they can identify and emulate normal application and network activity and change medical data without raising even the slightest alarm. Did an authorized and licensed clinician change a patient's blood type and list of allergies, or did AI? If AI is being used to undermine the integrity of medical records should doctors expect to trust or challenge that data? What happens when a Physician makes a diagnosis using compromised data and who is liable? These are all questions that we need to ask and train for.

AI is already being employed by cybercriminals to strengthen and improve the effectiveness of cyber weapons. We have seen tools used for infiltration, reconnaissance, delivery, and exploitation [110] armed with AI in order to bypass existing signature and heuristics-based security tools used for network and host intrusion detection and anti-malware protection. Attack tools that perfectly emulate normal application and network activity and can therefore avoid the suspicion of defensive security applications. In short, offensive AI attack tools totally bypass healthcare defensive security controls. AI's ability to understand context means AI attacks will be even harder to detect. What's more, AI attacks are fast. Much faster than a human can respond to and thus we need to 'fight fire with fire' by developing AI based defensive security tools. Tools that can respond to cyberattacks in nanoseconds rather than minutes. Tools that recognize AI based attacks and block them automatically. Tools that identify an infection on the network and quarantine infected devices based upon security run books. We can train AI using the vast amounts of transactional data flowing across healthcare systems to automatically identify important features in network traffic, to flag anomalous activity, and to react without human intervention to stop malware in its tracks. According to Forrester's 'Using AI for Evil' report [111], "mainstream AI-powered hacking is just a matter of time". Defensive AI may just provide healthcare the edge it needs to stay ahead of hackers and cybercriminals in what has been till now, a very one-sided battle.

Cybersecurity as an Enabler of New Medical Systems and Services

The unexpected and rapid adoption of telehealth and telemedicine across the United States, is perhaps an example of how NOT to deploy exciting new technologies. In the US, these services were largely born in March 2020 as COVID-19 began to ravage the world and healthcare providers were forced to pivot on the spot. Telehealth adoption was delayed in the United States compared to other countries because payers hadn't figured out just how and what to pay for these services. Remote medical services didn't feature in accepted ICD-10 codes [112] (though they existed) and insurers didn't know how much to pay for a telehealth consult versus an in-person consult at a doctors' office. This applied to both private US healthcare insurance and publicly funded healthcare. The implementation of telehealth was for most US providers a scramble to quickly put something in place so that patients could consult with their care teams without placing everyone concerned at risk by a face-to-face meeting in a clinic or doctors' office. It was also the result of the need to prevent bankrupting small physician practices reliant upon seeing patients. The result was that most US providers were not ready, and nor was the technology approved, forcing the US government to relax the rules.

In other parts of the world, remote patient services like telehealth and telemedicine are a classic example of how cybersecurity can enable new much needed patient services while driving efficiencies. Telehealth can help to increase access for shift workers and those who live in remote locations [113]. It can also be difficult or impossible for those who don't own a computer or smartphone so is a double-edged sword with regard to access. Telehealth can also be much more efficient for doctors and patients. Indeed, it has been suggested that "telehealth is a disruptive technology that appears to threaten traditional health care delivery but has the potential to reform and transform the industry by reducing costs and increasing quality and patient satisfaction." [114] However, to be widely and universally adopted, tele-health needs to be secure.

An earlier example of how security has helped to drive the adoption of innovative patient services is perhaps the simple medical portal or m-health application where patients and their care teams can communicate vital information securely via the Internet and their computer or smartphone. This has helped to drive patient engagement as well as to improve access and patient satisfaction.

In Australia and other countries, it is now even possible for patients to upload their fitness and health data from personal consumer medical wearables including a Fitbit or Apple Watch directly to their electronic patient records (EPRs). This is possible because Australia implemented a national EPR called 'My Health Record', which has been made extensible to communicate with personal health apps and wearables. This would have been unheard of a few years ago but thanks to the building in of acceptable security, this functionality has now been extended to patients. While there are security concerns around the integrity of data especially if mixed with, the EPR, so far at least, no major issues have been reported.

This success perhaps serves as a lesson for entrepreneurs to ensure that their hardware and software systems are properly secured so as to reach the widest possible audience, and to do so without introducing cybersecurity risks to the medical network. Given the constantly evolving threat surface, digital health innovators would be advised to design in the best possible security in order to provide longevity to their healthcare innovations.

Conclusions

Security is now a major consideration for approval or certification of AI and healthcare applications and devices. Thus, good cybersecurity is now a critical success factor of design. Conversely, security risks and concerns about data privacy and access is a major reason why AI adoption in healthcare has trailed other industries. By addressing cybersecurity risks and privacy concerns, the market for healthcare AI appears to be extensive. To date, advanced digital health tools including AI based applications, have barely scratched the surface of what will eventually be possible with the correct security controls in place. This will unlock the exabytes of data that healthcare providers generate, most of which currently remains unavailable to researchers and difficult to extract because of privacy and compliance issues.

References

1. Mark JJ. Health care in ancient Mesopotamia. World Encyclopedia. https://www.worldhistory.org/article/687/health-care-in-ancient-mesopotamia/ Published online 2014. Accessed Nov 2, 2022
2. Cilliers L, Retief FP. The evolution of the hospital from antiquity to the end of the middle ages. National Library of Medicine, National Center for Biotechnology Information; 2002. https://doi.org/10.4102/curationis.v25i4.806.   https://pubmed.ncbi.nlm.nih.gov/14509111/ Accessed 2 Nov 2022
3. The White House. Presidential policy directive—critical infrastructure security and resilience.   https://obamawhitehouse.archives.gov/the-press-office/2013/02/12/presidential-

policy-directive-critical-infrastructure-security-and-resil Published online 2013. Accessed 1 Nov 2022.

4. General Data Protection Regulation (GDPR) https://gdpr.eu/ Published online. Accessed 2 Nov 2022.

5. Australian Privacy Act (APA) 1988 https://www.ag.gov.au/rights-and-protections/privacy Published online. Accessed 2 Nov 2022.

6. Personal Data Protection Act (PDPA) of Singapore 2012 https://www.pdpc.gov.sg/Overview-of-PDPA/The-Legislation/Personal-Data-Protection-Act Accessed 2 Nov 2022.

7. Personal Data Protection Act (PDPA) of Thailand 2019, https://www.trade.gov/market-intelligence/thailand-personal-data-protection-act Accessed 2 Nov 2022.

8. Personal Data Protection Act (PDPA) of Malaysia 2010, https://www.malaysia.gov.my/portal/content/654 Accessed 2 Nov 2022.

9. Personally Identifiable Information (PII) https://www.dol.gov/general/ppii Accessed 2 Nov 2022.

10. Personal Health Information (PHI) https://www.hhs.gov/answers/hipaa/what-is-phi/index.html Accessed 2 Nov 2022.

11. Health Insurance Portability and Accountability Act of 1996 (HIPAA). https://www.cdc.gov/phlp/publications/topic/hipaa.html. Accessed 2 Nov 2022.

12. Health Information Technology for Economic and Clinical Health Act of 2009 (HITECH). https://journalofethics.ama-assn.org/article/hitech-act-overview/2011-03. Accessed 2 Nov 2022.

13. What is the HITECH Act? n.d. HIPAA Journal. https://www.hipaajournal.com/what-is-the-hitech-act/ Accessed 2 Nov 2022.

14. Halock. Chronology of HIPAA, HITECH & the Omnibus Rule. https://www.halock.com/hipaa-hitech-omnibus-definitive-chronology/ Published online 2016. Accessed 2 Nov 2022.

15. The Office of Civil Rights (OCR) is the enforcement arm of the US Department of Health and Human Services (HHS). https://www.hhs.gov/ocr/index.html Published online. Accessed 2 Nov 2022.

16. Resolution Agreements and Civil Money Penalties, https://www.hhs.gov/hipaa/for-professionals/compliance-enforcement/agreements/index.html Published online. Accessed 2 Nov 2022.

17. JDSupra. What is a 'Corrective Action Plan'? https://www.jdsupra.com/legalnews/what-is-a-corrective-action-plan-1938924/ Published online 2021. Accessed 2 Nov 2022.

18. Artificial Intelligence (AI). https://en.wikipedia.org/wiki/Artificial_intelligence Published online. Accessed 2 Nov 2022.

19. Machine Learning (ML). https://en.wikipedia.org/wiki/Machine_learning Published online. Accessed 2 Nov 2022.

20. SwivelSecure. 9 reasons why healthcare is the biggest target for cyberattacks. https://swivelsecure.com/solutions/healthcare/healthcare-is-the-biggest-target-for-cyberattacks/ Published online. Accessed 2 Nov 2022.

21. Landi H. Healthcare data breaches hit all-time high in 2021, impacting 45M people. Fierce Healthcare. https://www.fiercehealthcare.com/health-tech/healthcare-data-breaches-hit-all-time-high-2021-impacting-45m-people Published 2022. Accessed 2 Nov 2022.

22. CDC – The Centers for Disease Control. Health Insurance Portability and Accountability Act of 1996 (HIPAA). https://www.cdc.gov/phlp/publications/topic/hipaa.html Accessed 2 Nov 2022.

23. CSC. The cyber threat to healthcare. White Paper. https://pubs.cyberthoughts.org/The_Cyber_Threat_to_Healthcare.pdf Published 2013. Accessed 2 Nov 2022.

24. The Office of Civil Rights (OCR) of the department of Health and Human Services (HSS) is responsible under HIPAA for enforcing federal laws including the reporting of healthcare breaches. https://www.hhs.gov/ocr/index.html

25. HIPAAJournal. Healthcare data breach statistics. Published 2022. Accessed 2 Nov 2022. https://www.hipaajournal.com/healthcare-data-breach-statistics/

26. IBM. The cost of data breach report. Published 2022. Accessed 2 Nov 2022. https://www.ibm.com/security/data-breach
27. Fierce Healthcare. Published 2022. Accessed 2 Nov 2022. https://www.fiercehealthcare.com/hospitals/may-cyber-attack-cost-scripps-nearly-113m-lost-revenue-more-costs
28. Paul K. Lives are at stake': hacking of US hospitals highlights deadly risk of ransomware. The Guardian. Published 2022. Accessed 2 Nov 2022. https://www.theguardian.com/technology/2022/jul/14/ransomware-attacks-cybersecurity-targeting-us-hospitals.
29. Riggi J. Ransomware attacks on hospitals have changed. The American Hospital Association (AHA). Published online. Accessed 2 Nov 2022. https://www.aha.org/center/cybersecurity-and-risk-advisory-services/ransomware-attacks-hospitals-have-changed
30. Mensik H. Healthcare cyberattacks led to worse patient care, increased mortality, study finds. Healthcare Drive. Published 2022. Accessed 2 Nov 2022. https://www.healthcaredive.com/news/cyberattacks-hospitals-disrupt-operations-patient-care-Ponemon/631439/
31. Cyber@ Ben-Gurion of the Nagev University. Hospital viruses: fake cancerous nodes in CT scans, created by malware, trick radiologists. Published 2019. Accessed 2 Nov 2022. https://cyber.bgu.ac.il/hospital-viruses-fake-cancerous-nodes-in-ct-scans-created-by-malware-trick-radiologists/
32. CylerLabs. Exploiting DICOM flaw to embed Malware in CT/MRI Imagery. Published 2018 Accessed 2 Nov 2022. https://resources.cylera.com/dicom-research-brief-hipaa-protected-malware?hsLang=en
33. Desjardins B, Mirsky Y, Picado M-O, Glozman Z, Tarbox L, Horn R, Horii SC. DICOM images have been hacked! Now what? Am J Roentgenol. 2020;214:727–35. https://doi.org/10.2214/AJR.19.21958. Accessed 1 Nov 2022
34. Dameff C, Tully J, and Corman J. Hacking healthcare live: bits and bytes meet flesh and blood from the 2018 RSA Conference. Published 2018. https://www.cyberthoughts.org/2018/04/hacking-healthcare-live-bits-and-bytes.html. Accessed 2 Nov 2022
35. Jerchich K. Scripps Health slowly coming back online, 3 weeks after attack Healthcare IT News. Published 2021. https://www.healthcareitnews.com/news/scripps-health-slowly-coming-back-online-3-weeks-after-attack. Accessed 2 Nov 2022.
36. HIPAA Journal. Scripps Health Ransomware attack cost increases to almost $113 million Published 2021. https://www.hipaajournal.com/scripps-health-ransomware-attack-cost-113-million/. Accessed 2 Nov 2022
37. Landi H. Scripps Health was attacked by hackers. Now, patients are suing for failing to protect their health data. Fierce Healthcare. Published 2021. https://www.fiercehealthcare.com/tech/following-ransomware-attack-scripps-health-now-facing-class-action-lawsuits-over-data-breach. Accessed 2 Nov 2022.
38. Acronis. The NHS cyber attack. Published 2020. https://www.acronis.com/en-us/blog/posts/nhs-cyber-attack/. Accessed 2 Nov 2022.
39. The Democratic Peoples' Republic of (north) Korea (DPRK). https://en.wikipedia.org/wiki/North_Korea. Accessed 2 November 2022.
40. National Health Executive. Published 2018. https://www.nationalhealthexecutive.com/articles/wannacry-cyber-attack-cost-nhs-ps92m-after-19000-appointments-were-cancelled. Accessed 2 Nov 2022.
41. Dearden L. NHS to spend £150m on cyber security to bolster defences after WannaCry attack. The Independent Sunday 28th April 2018. https://www.independent.co.uk/news/health/cyber-attacks-nhs-wannacry-security-investment-microsoft-a8327091.html. Accessed 2 Nov 2022.
42. Kututak S. Understanding the impact of Ransomware on patient outcomes – do we know enough? NCC Group. Published 2022. https://research.nccgroup.com/2022/06/16/understanding-the-impact-of-ransomware-on-patient-outcomes-do-we-know-enough/. Accessed 2 Nov 2022.
43. Paganini P. France hospital Center Hospitalier Sud Francilien suffered ransomware attack. Security Affairs. Published 2022. https://securityaffairs.co/wordpress/134771/cyber-crime/center-hospitalier-sud-francilien-ransomware.html. Accessed 1 Nov 2022.

44. Catholic Health Services (CHI) was merged with Dignity Health and other providers into Common Spirit Health in 2019. https://www.fiercehealthcare.com/hospitals-health-systems/completion-29b-chi-dignity-health-merger-commonspirit-health-emerges. Accessed 1 Nov 2022.

45. Fierce Healthcare. CommonSpirit Health: Ransomware attack responsible for ongoing IT outages Published 2022. https://www.fiercehealthcare.com/health-tech/commonspirit-health-reported-it-security-incident-affecting-facilities-wash-neb-and. Accessed 2 Nov 2022.

46. CyberTalk. Ransomware attack on CommonSpirit Health could affect 20 million Americans. Published 2022. https://www.cybertalk.org/2022/11/17/ransomware-attack-on-commonspirit-health-could-affect-20-million-americans/. Accessed 2 Nov 2022.

47. Adam S. The State of Ransomware 2022. Sophos. Published 2022. https://news.sophos.com/en-us/2022/04/27/the-state-of-ransomware-2022/. Accessed 2 Nov 2022.

48. Franceschi-Bicchierai L. How cryptocurrency gave birth to the Ransomware epidemic. Motherboard. April 15, 2022. https://www.vice.com/en/article/g5qebq/how-cryptocurrency-gave-birth-to-the-ransomware-epidemic. Accessed 2 Nov 2022.

49. Gracias T. What's the true cost of a Ransomware attack in 2022? Published 2022. https://www.cloudally.com/blog/cost-of-ransomware-attack-2022/. Accessed 2 Nov 2022.

50. Arntaz P. Cyberinsurance companies don't want to pay out for "acts of war". Malwarebytes Lab. Published 2022. https://www.malwarebytes.com/blog/news/2022/01/cyberinsurance-companies-dont-want-to-pay-out-for-acts-of-war. Accessed 2 Nov 2022.

51. Whitley Law Firm. How contributory negligence hurts personal injury claims. Published online. https://whitleylawfirm.com/blog/personal-injury-contributory-negligence-rule/. Accessed 2 Nov 2022.

52. Moore S. When it comes to Ransomware, should your company Pay? Gartner. Published 2021. https://www.gartner.com/en/articles/when-it-comes-to-ransomware-should-your-company-pay. Accessed 2 Nov 2022.

53. Many cyber criminals return after Ransomware payments are made. Insurance Journal November 21, 2022. https://amp.insurancejournal.com/magazines/mag-features/2022/11/21/695627.htm. Accessed 2 Nov 2022.

54. The Hiscox Cyber Readiness Report 2022. https://www.hiscox.com/cybersecurity. Accessed 2 Nov 2022.

55. First Response. Incident Response to Ransomware. Published online. https://first-response.co.uk/articles/incident-response-for-ransomware/. Accessed 2 Nov 2022.

56. CyberLaw Toolkit. Springhill Medical Center ransomware attack (2019). Published 2022. https://cyberlaw.ccdcoe.org/wiki/Springhill_Medical_Center_ransomware_attack_(2019). Accessed 2 Nov 2022.

57. Poulsen K, McMillan R, Evans M. A hospital hit by hackers, a baby in distress: the case of the first alleged ransomware death. Wall Street J. Published 2019. https://www.wsj.com/amp/articles/ransomware-hackers-hospital-first-alleged-death-11633008116. Accessed 2 Nov 2022.

58. Wired. A patient dies after a Ransomware attack hits a hospital. Published 2020. https://www.wired.com/story/a-patient-dies-after-a-ransomware-attack-hits-a-hospital/. Accessed Nov 2, 2022.

59. Akhu-Zaheya L, Al Maaitah MR, Hani B, Hasan S. Quality of nursing documentation: paper-based health records versus electronic-based health records. J Clin Nurs. 2017;27(3–4) https://doi.org/10.1111/jocn.14097. Accessed 1 Nov 2022

60. Committee on Diagnostic Error in Health Care, Board on Health Care Services, Institute of Medicine. The National Academies of Sciences, Engineering, and Medicine, Balogh EP, Miller BT, Ball JR, editors. Improving diagnosis in health care. Washington (DC): National Academies Press (US); 2015. https://www.ncbi.nlm.nih.gov/books/NBK338593/ Accessed 1 Nov 2022

61. CMS. Promoting interoperability programs. Published online. https://www.cms.gov/regulations-and-guidance/legislation/ehrincentiveprograms. Accessed 2 Nov 2022.

62. Srivastava R. Dying at home might sound preferable. But I've seen the reality. The Guardian. 1 May 2017. https://www.theguardian.com/commentisfree/2017/may/01/dying-at-home-terminally-ill-hospital. Accessed Nov 2, 2022.
63. Mercer Capital. Five trends to watch in the medical device industry. Published 2021. https://mercercapital.com/article/five-trends-to-watch-in-the-medical-device-industry/. Accessed 2 Nov 2022.
64. McKinsey. Medical device growth in emerging markets: lessons from other industries. Published 2012. https://www.mckinsey.com/~/media/mckinsey/dotcom/client_service/pharma%20and%20medical%20products/pmp%20new/pdfs/medical_device_growth_in_emerging_markets_invivo_1206.ashx. Accessed 2 Nov 2022.
65. Medinnova. Indian Medical Device Industry—Key Drivers of Growth. Published 2022. https://www.medinnovasystems.com/indian-medical-device-industry-key-drivers-of-growth/. Accessed 2 Nov 2022.
66. FDA. Cybersecurity in medical devices: quality system considerations and content of premarket submissions. Published online. https://www.fda.gov/regulatory-information/search-fda-guidance-documents/cybersecurity-medical-devices-quality-system-considerations-and-content-premarket-submissions. Accessed 1 Nov 2022.
67. McKeon J. FBI warns of patient safety, security risks associated with legacy medical devices. Published 2022. https://healthitsecurity.com/news/fbi-warns-of-patient-safety-security-risks-associated-with-legacy-medical-devices. Accessed 2 Nov 2022.
68. Staynings R. Analysis: What's in an FDA recall? Healthcare IT News. Published 2017. https://www.healthcareitnews.com/news/analysis-whats-fda-recall. Accessed 2 Nov 2022.
69. Florin-Roebig. Top-rated defective medical device Attorneys. Published online. https://florinroebig.com/defective-medical-devices/. Accessed 2 Nov 2022.
70. Miliard M. PATCH Act seeks to shore up security for medical devices, IoT networks. Healthcare IT News. Published 2022. https://www.healthcareitnews.com/news/patch-act-seeks-shore-security-medical-devices-iot-networks. Accessed 2 Nov 2022.
71. CISA. Software bill of materials. Cybersecurity & Infrastructure Security Agency. Published 2022. https://www.cisa.gov/sbom. Accessed 2 Nov 2022.
72. Warner M, Senator. Warner releases policy options paper addressing cybersecurity in the health care sector Published 2022. https://www.warner.senate.gov/public/index.cfm/2022/11/warner-releases-policy-options-paper-addressing-cybersecurity-in-the-health-care-sector. Accessed 1 Nov 2022.
73. HHS 405(d) Aligning Health Care Industry Security Approaches. https://405d.hhs.gov/ Published online. Accessed 2 Nov 2022.
74. Health and public health critical infrastructure working relationship https://lnkd.in/gPyDn9rv Published online. Accessed 2 Nov 2022.
75. Common Vulnerability Exposure (CVE) TechTarget. Published online. https://www.techtarget.com/searchsecurity/definition/Common-Vulnerabilities-and-Exposures-CVE. Accessed 2 Nov 2022.
76. NIST. Security Resource Center. https://csrc.nist.gov/glossary/term/compensating_security_control. Published online. Accessed 2 Nov 2022.
77. Wagner N et al. Towards automated cyber decision support: a case study on network segmentation for security. 2016 IEEE Symposium Series on Computational Intelligence (SSCI), 2016, pp. 1–10, doi: https://doi.org/10.1109/SSCI.2016.7849908. Accessed 2 Nov 2022.
78. Cisco. What is network access control? https://www.cisco.com/c/en/us/products/security/what-is-network-access-control-nac.html Published online. Accessed 2 Nov 2022.
79. Kirkpatric K. Software defined networking. Commun ACM. 2013;56(9):16–9. https://doi.org/10.1145/2500468.2500473. Accessed 2 Nov 2022
80. Raina K. Zero trust security explained: principles of the zero trust model. Crowdstrike. Published 2022. https://www.crowdstrike.com/cybersecurity-101/zero-trust-security/. Accessed 2 Nov 2022.

81. Cisco. What is micro-segmentation? https://www.cisco.com/c/en/us/products/security/what-is-microsegmentation.html. Published online. Accessed 2 Nov 2022.

82. Cylera. Innovation insight for healthcare provider digital twins: a Gartner® Report. Published online. https://resources.cylera.com/innovation-insight-for-healthcare-provider-digital-twins-a-gartner-report. Accessed 2 Nov 2022

83. Khan ZF, Alotaibi SR. Applications of artificial intelligence and big data analytics in m-health: a healthcare system perspective. National Library of Medicine. J Healthc Eng. 2020;2020:8894694. https://doi.org/10.1155/2020/8894694. Published online 2020 Aug 30. Accessed 2 Nov 2022

84. Johnson KB, et al. Precision medicine, AI, and the future of personalized health care. Clin Transl Sci. 2021;14(1):86–93. https://doi.org/10.1111/cts.12884. Published online 2020 Oct 12. Accessed 2 Nov 2022

85. Schork NJ. Artificial intelligence and personalized medicine. Cancer Treat Res. 2019, 178:265–83. https://doi.org/10.1007/978-3-030-16391-4_11. Accessed 2 Nov 2022

86. Skovgaard LL, Hoeyer K. Data authority: public debate about personalized medicine in Denmark. Public Underst Sci. 31(5) https://doi.org/10.1177/09636625221080535. Published online. Accessed 2 Nov 2022

87. Office of the National Coordinator for Health Information Technology (ONC). https://en.wikipedia.org/wiki/Office_of_the_National_Coordinator_for_Health_Information_Technology. Accessed 2 Nov 2022.

88. White House Press Office (2015, Jan 30). Fact sheet: President Obama's Precision Medicine Initiative. https://www.whitehouse.gov/the-press-office/2015/01/30/fact-sheet-president-obama-s-precision-medicine-initiative. Published January 30, 2015. Accessed November 2, 2022.

89. HITRUST. Implementing cybersecurity in precision medicine. Published 2018. https://hitrustalliance.net/content/uploads/PMIFrameworkImplementationGuide.pdf. Accessed 2 Nov 2022.

90. Shen L. The NIST cybersecurity framework: overview and potential impacts. Chicago: Scitech Lawyer; 2014. 10 (4) 16–19. Published online. Accessed 2 Nov 2022

91. Shen K, Tong X, Wu T, Zhang F. The next frontier for AI in China could add $600 billion to its economy. McKinsey. Published 2022. https://www.mckinsey.com/capabilities/quantumblack/our-insights/the-next-frontier-for-ai-in-china-could-add-600-billion-to-its-economy. Accessed 2 Nov 2022.

92. Olecott E. China sets the pace in adoption of AI in healthcare technology. Financial Times. Published 2022. https://www.ft.com/content/c1fe6fbf-8a87-4328-9e75-816009a07a59. Accessed 2 Nov 2022.

93. Imperva. Advanced persistent threat (APT). Published online. https://www.imperva.com/learn/application-security/apt-advanced-persistent-threat/. Accessed 2 Nov 2022.

94. Sharwood S. FBI says more cyber attacks come from China than everywhere else combined. The Register. Published 2022. https://www.theregister.com/2022/02/03/fbi_china_threat_to_usa/. Accessed 2 Nov 2022.

95. Perlroth N. How China transformed into a prime cyber threat to the U.S. New York Times. Published 2021. https://www.nytimes.com/2021/07/19/technology/china-hacking-us.html. Accessed 2 Nov 2022.

96. Future of Life. AI Principles. 2017 Asilomar conference. Published 2017. https://futureoflife.org/open-letter/ai-principles/. Accessed 2 Nov 2022.

97. Babuta A, Oswald M, Janjeva A. Artificial Intelligence and UK National Security Policy Considerations. Royal United Services Institute for Defence and Security Studies, April 2020. Published April, 2020. https://rusi.org/sites/default/files/ai_national_security_final_web_version.pdf. Accessed 2 Nov 2022.

98. Nguyen A, Yosinski J, Clune J. 2015. Deep neural networks are easily fooled: high confidence predictions for unrecognizable images. Proceedings of the IEEE Conference on Computer Vision and Pattern Recognition (CVPR), 2015, pp. 427–436.

99. Nitin Bhagoji A, Chakraborty S, Mittal P, and Calo S. Analyzing federated learning through an adversarial lens. Proceedings of the 36th International Conference on Machine Learning, ICML 2019 (pp. 1012–1021). Published 2019. https://www.princeton.edu/~pmittal/publications/bhagoji-icml19.pdf. Accessed 2 Nov 2022.

100. National Security Commission on Artificial Intelligence. First Quarter Recommendations. Published 2020. https://drive.google.com/file/d/1wkPh8Gb5drBrKBg6OhGu5oNaTEERb Kss/view. Accessed 2 Nov 2022.

101. Allcott H, Gentzkow M. Social media and fake news in the 2016 election. J Econ Perspect. 2017;31(2):211–36. Published online. Accessed 2 Nov 2022

102. Bruno M, Lambiotte R, Saracco F. Brexit and bots: characterizing the behaviour of automated accounts on twitter during the UK election. EPJ Data Sci. 2022;11. Article number: 17 Published online. Accessed 2 Nov 2022

103. Lomas N. Study: Russian twitter bots sent 45k Brexit tweets close to vote. TechCrunch. 2022; https://techcrunch.com/2017/11/15/study-russian-twitter-bots-sent-45k-brexit-tweets-close-to-vote. Accessed 2 Nov 2022.

104. Sample I. What are deepfakes and how can you spot them?. The Guadian Mon 13 Jan 2020. https://www.theguardian.com/technology/2020/jan/13/what-are-deepfakes-and-how-can-you-spot-them. Accessed 2 Nov 2022.

105. Mirsky Y, Lee W. The creation and detection of deepfakes: a survey. ACM Comput Surv. 2022;54(1):1–41. Article No.7, 2 Nov 2022. https://doi.org/10.1145/3425780.

106. Bakarich KM, Baranek D. Something phish-y is going on here: a teaching case on business email compromise. Curr Issues Audit. 2020;14(1):A1–9. https://doi.org/10.2308/ciia-52706. Accessed 2 Nov 2022

107. Intelligent CISO. Counting the cost of the biggest BEC attacks. Published 2022. https://www.intelligentciso.com/2022/06/01/counting-the-cost-of-the-biggest-bec-attacks/#. Accessed 2 Nov 2022.

108. IBM. Cost of a Data Breach Report. https://www.ibm.com/uk-en/security/data-breach. Published 2021. Accessed 2 Nov 2022.

109. Business Insider. Published 2022. https://www.businessinsider.com/guides/tech/what-is-deepfake. Accessed 2 Nov 2022.

110. Lockheed Martin. The Cyber kill chain. Published online. https://www.lockheedmartin.com/en-us/capabilities/cyber/cyber-kill-chain.html. Accessed 2 Nov 2022.

111. Forrester. Using AI for evil. A guide to how cybercriminals will weaponize and exploit AI to attack your business. Published 2018. https://www.forrester.com/report/Using-AI-For-Evil/RES143162. Accessed 2 Nov 2022.

112. AAPC. What is ICD-10? Published online. https://www.aapc.com/icd-10/. Accessed 2 Nov 2022.

113. Marcin J, Shaikh U, Steinhorn R. Addressing health disparities in rural communities using telehealth. Pediatr Res. 2016;79:169–76. https://doi.org/10.1038/pr.2015.192.

114. Schwamm LH. Telehealth: seven strategies to successfully implement disruptive technology and transform health care. Health Aff. 33:2.: Early Evidence, Future Promise Of Connected Health. https://doi.org/10.1377/hlthaff.2013.1021.

Chapter 12
Patent Law at the Collision Point of Artificial Intelligence and Life Science Innovations

Vani Verkhovsky, Logan Bielewicz, and Quan Nguyen

An Overview of Artificial Intelligence (AI) Technology

Artificial Intelligence (AI) is no longer a futuristic notion; rather it is very much at today's forefront. With broad applications in communications, agriculture, education, finance, health care, medicine and beyond, AI technology is deeply embedded into our everyday lives and has been defined as "the science and engineering of making intelligent machines, especially intelligent computer programs. It is related to the similar task of using computers to understand human intelligence, but AI does not have to confine itself to methods that are biologically observable." [1].

Alan Turing, a famed mathematician and computer scientist, is credited with first establishing modern computer science and AI as early as the 1940's [2]. In his seminal work, Turing first proposed the question of "can machines think?" and established a test for determining so, known as the "Turing Test." [3]. The development of AI has gone through multiple phases of highs and lows in conjunction with improvements in computing power. During its early development, AI went through a period of "AI winter" lasting over two decades until the 1990's, indicative of an extended period of time where there was reduced interest in innovating in AI [2]. This period of time was then followed by a stage of rapid development [2].

Traditional AI, developed before 2012, required human input and programming of rule-based algorithms and was limited and used primarily for complex problem solving but often resulted in rigid outputs [2, 4]. More recent "Sophisticated AI," developed in 2012 and later, shifted towards Machine Learning (ML), a statistical-based model that involves providing a system with implicit rules to "learn" originating from a large data set or "problem space" which can then be used to identify

V. Verkhovsky · L. Bielewicz · Q. Nguyen (✉)
Nguyen Tarbet LLC, Tucson, AZ, USA
e-mail: vani@ntiplaw.com; logan@ntiplaw.com; quan@ntiplaw.com

© The Author(s), under exclusive license to Springer Nature Switzerland AG 2023   157
A. Meyers (ed.), *Digital Health Entrepreneurship*, Health Informatics,
https://doi.org/10.1007/978-3-031-33902-8_12

patterns and correlations and make predictions or define behaviors using probability [2, 4].

One particular ML model involves Deep Learning (DL) or Artificial Neural Networks (ANN) which is inspired by the neural communication system of the human brain [2]. Structured similarly to the physiological construction of the brain, ANN uses multiple layers of connections of artificial neurons known as "Perceptrons" which are flexibly weighted and pass inputs through to produce an activation function [2]. Through training, the artificial network adjusts the weight of the perceptrons based on trial and error feedback such that ultimately, the system can be assigned to a new task and utilize its trained network to make accurate predictions [2]. Although capable of great potential within narrow problem spaces, Deep Learning is limited in its broader applications due to the need for significant amounts of quality data and substantial computing power to sufficiently train the system [2].

Although AI technology continues to develop, no AI model is currently capable of understanding cause and effect, and as such, AI continues to lack insight into identifying problems and must be given discrete problem sets that are designed as a task to be solved [2]. Thus, there has been a movement towards the development of Artificial General Intelligence (AGI), or AI technology which can exhibit human-level cognitive, emotional, and creative capabilities [4].

The Application of Artificial Intelligence (AI) Technology in Life Science Innovation

Despite current limitations, AI technology, particularly in the areas of healthcare and medicine, has resulted in the development of powerful tools with profound capabilities. In the context of drug design and development, AI has been used to tackle the most significant limitations in drug discovery and has led to significant advances in rational drug design by facilitating improved efficacy, enhanced specificity, and an overall reduction in the development timeline and costs associated with developing new drugs [5]. DL and ANN technologies are currently being used in biomarker identification, peptide synthesis and small molecule design, structure and ligand-based virtual screening, modeling of pharmacophores, prediction of physicochemical and toxicological profiles, ADMET analysis, and much more [5].

A great boom in AI-healthcare occurred in 2016-2017. A number of biopharmaceutical companies formed partnerships with AI companies, including notably, partnerships between Pfizer and IBM (maker of the well-known IBM Watson) and Sanofi and Exscentia (for drug discovery applications) [6]. Microsoft developed an AI-based machine, known as "Hanover" to analyze massive volumes of data from research publications pertaining to cancer to help predict efficacious drugs based on individual patient diagnoses. Stanford University similarly developed an AI algorithm that could accurately predict skin cancer after "studying" 130,000 images of moles, rashes, and lesions [6].

The COVIDpandemic which began in 2019 was another major impetus for integrating AI in medicine. The COVID pandemic resulted in several AI-healthcare innovations by major corporations including Seegene, Alibaba, and BlueDot [7]. Historically, testing diagnostics can take months of research and development by large groups of scientists. However, with AI applications, Seegene, a Korea-based biotech company, was able to develop a novel coronavirus test at an unprecedented rate, within days of the COVID pandemic outbreak.[1]

Moreover, several partnerships were created including collaborative efforts between the U.S. White House and Microsoft. The Allen Institute of AI issued a challenge to tech enthusiasts and experts to utilize AI to mine COVID-19 data from over 30,000 scientific papers [8]. Importantly, Covid-19 accelerated AI-healthcare development in many areas, including (1) AI in radiology to enhance disease detection and diagnostic capabilities; (2) AI in at-home diagnostic testing and data interpretation facilitated by smartphones; (3) AI in pathology for the analysis of complex samples and for the reduction of misdiagnoses; (4) AI in drug discovery to increase efficiency and facilitate faster development of therapeutics; (5) AI in passive monitoring of biometrics to reduce exposure to viruses and other pathogens, (6) AI in data mining of healthcare information while preserving patient privacy; and (7) AI in hospital process automation to improve healthcare administration and reduce healthcare costs [8] (See Table 12.1).

From 2019 to 2021, venture capitalists (VCs) invested $35 billion in Biotech-AI development [9]. Globally, biotech companies raised more than $34 billion, double the amount raised the year prior in 2020 [9]. After 2021, there was a slight decrease in VC funding; however, significant amounts of money are still being invested in Biotech-AI, particularly in drug discovery and development. Biotech platform technologies that are currently seeing major investment include: cell therapy technology and techniques, next-generation gene therapy, precision medicine, machine-learning-enabled drug discovery and development, improving validation methods for undruggable targets and identifying new delivery methods [9] (See Table 12.1).

Although some reports indicate that the third quarter of 2022 saw a worldwide drop in AI funding as a whole, the integration of AI in Life Sciences continues to advance healthcare and medicine [10]. In October 2022, the San Diego Regional Economic Development Corporation (EDC) based in San Diego, California, a region known as a "Life Science cluster," released a report highlighting San Diego's early adoption and leading role in integrating AI and machine learning into Life Sciences, with applications in medical research, pharmaceutical drug discovery, medical device manufacturing, surgical procedures, and precision medicine, demonstrating AI's continued impact on advancing healthcare innovation [11] (See Table 12.1).

---

[1] [7]; CNN, *Inside the company that used AI to create a coronavirus test*, https://edition.cnn.com/videos/world/2020/03/12/south-korea-seegene-coronavirus-test-kit-watson-vpx.cnn.

Table 12.1 Examples of major trends in Artificial Intelligence (AI) technology in life science innovation

	Area of innovation	Company/Technology examples
1	**Disease Detection & Diagnostics**	**Seegene** [7] (CNN, *Inside the company that used AI to create a coronavirus test*, https://edition.cnn.com/videos/world/2020/03/12/south-korea-seegene-coronavirus-test-kit-watson-vpx.cnn.). *Utilized AI to develop a novel coronavirus testing method within days of the start of the COVID-19 pandemic.* **Alibaba** [7] *Utilized AI to detect coronavirus in CT scans with 96% accuracy.* **Medtronics** (*See* [12]) *Utilized AI to improve accuracy of information received from cardiac monitors reducing false alerts.* *Utilizes AI in the diagnostic imaging analysis for endoscopic procedures to identify pre-cancerous and cancerous colorectal polyps found during colonoscopies.* **MelaFind** (Artificial Intelligence (AI) for Disease Diagnoses, https://thinkml.ai/artificial-intelligence-ai-for-disease-diagnosis/; *See also* [13]) *Utilized advanced AI algorithms trained with skin cancer data to detect cancer (melanoma).* **Case Western University** (Artificial Intelligence (AI) for Disease Diagnoses, https://thinkml.ai/artificial-intelligence-ai-for-disease-diagnosis/; *See also* [14]) *Developed a program utilizing AI technology that can distinguish pathological differences between radiation necrosis and brain cancer recurrence on MRIs.*
2	**Cell Based Therapies**	**Microsoft in collaboration with Oxford BioMedica** (Microsoft Aims to Make Cell Therapies Cheaper with Artificial Intelligence, https://www.labiotech.eu/trends-news/microsoft-oxford-biomedica-synthace/) *Utilized AI to make cell therapy more cost-effective by improving yields and accelerating cost-efficiencies in the manufacturing process of viral vectors used in gene therapies.* **Cystera Cellworks** (How Automation Will Enable the Age of Cell Therapy, https://www.labiotech.eu/interview/cytera-cell-culture-automation/) *Utilized AI to provide cell culture lab automation solutions for large-scale manufacturing of cell products.*
3	**Precision Medicine & Next Generation Gene Therapy**	**MedStar Health & Zephyr AI, Inc.** (AI Precision Medicine Partnership Aims to Improve Chronic Disease Outcomes, https://healthitanalytics.com/news/ai-precision-medicine-partnership-aims-to-improve-chronic-disease-outcomes) *Utilized AI to improve chronic disease outcomes. E.g., for type 2 diabetes, utilized de-identified datasets and patient management expertise to improve timeliness of interventions and decrease adverse outcomes.* **Quantgene** (Quantgene Launches Serenity Complete, the Next Generation Executive Physical, https://www.morningstar.com/news/pr-newswire/20221114la35148/quantgene-launches-serenity-complete-the-next-generation-executive-physical) *Launched Serenity Complete, a precision medicine technology for early detection of chronic illness using AI-analyzed diagnostic data from deep genomics, blood panels and other indicators to provide continuous monitoring of risk factors for cancer, diabetes, stroke, heart attack, etc.* **Genomenon, Inc.** (Genomenon Provides Genomic Data on 450 Diseases to Advance Early Identification of Rare Disease in Newborns, https://www.prweb.com/releases/genomenon_provides_genomic_data_on_450_diseases_to_advance_early_identification_of_rare_disease_in_newborns/prweb19018935.htm) *Utilized AI to develop a newborn screening tool for 450 rare diseases.*

Table 12.1 (continued)

	Area of innovation	Company/Technology examples
4	**Drug Discovery & Development**	**Insilico Medicine** (*See Insilico: linking target discovery and generative chemistry AI platforms for a drug discovery breakthrough*, https://www.nature.com/articles/d43747-021-00039-5; *see also* https://insilico.com/) *Started the world's first Phase 1 clinical trial of a novel drug developed completely using AI. The identification of the drug target and molecule took < 18 months and was only 10% the cost of a traditional drug discovery program.* **Exscientia** (*See* https://investors.exscientia.ai/press-releases/press-release-details/2021/exscientia-announces-first-ai-designed-immuno-oncology-drug-to-enter-clinical-trials/Default.aspx) *Announced the beginning of Phase 1 clinical trials for an AI-designed drug for an established protein target.* **Recursion Pharmaceuticals** (*See* https://www.recursion.com/pipeline) *Utilized AI to repurpose drugs for new indications.* **Sorrento Therapeutics** (*See* Diagnosing the Future: AI and San Diego's Life Sciences Cluster, https://storymaps.arcgis.com/stories/ae5bc95c717f44c8ba95298359570e86; *see also* https://sorrentotherapeutics.com/) *Utilized AI to accelerate drug discovery, the detection and diagnosis of disease, and the selection of therapy.*
5	**Medical Device Manufacturing**	**NuVasive** (*See* Diagnosing the Future: AI and San Diego's Life Sciences Cluster, https://storymaps.arcgis.com/stories/ae5bc95c717f44c8ba95298359570e86; *see also* https://www.nuvasive.com/) *Applied AI to automate techniques used in specialized spinal surgery to create a single platform that advances dexterity and perception beyond current human capabilities.*
6	**Improved Healthcare Administration Efficiency**	**Bluedot** [7] *Utilized AI to predict the coronavirus pandemic. Was utilized for risk assessment through the collection and learning of data from sources including the news, medical databases, health reports and expert statements.* **Medtronics** (*See* [12]) *Utilized AI to support training and education opportunities for healthcare providers using surgical video management and analytics platforms.*

Current Patent Laws Relating to AI

With so much revolutionary potential, protection of current and future AI technologies under governing patent laws is a forefront consideration to foster further development. Key questions have already been raised, such as whether inventions generated by AI ("AI-inventors") can be patented under the existing patent paradigm.[2] This chapter focuses on addressing the current patent policies pertaining to AI in the world's five largest intellectual property (IP) offices (the "IP5") and describing various proposed models for modifying the existing systems to facilitate the patent processes relating to AI technologies and ensure adequate incentivization in AI innovation.

Patent Law Overview

Patent law varies jurisdiction to jurisdiction. For the purposes of this section, US law is discussed as a representative jurisdiction for discussing inventorship and patentability requirements as other jurisdictions are similar. Accordingly, under Article I, Section 8, Clause 8 of the United States Constitution, the legislative branch of government is mandated to "promote the Progress of Science and useful Arts, by securing for limited Times to Authors and Inventors the exclusive Right to their respective Writings and Discoveries."

The US Patent and Trademark Office (USPTO) is the federal agency designated for fulfilling the constitutional mandate of granting US patents and trademarks.[3] Under the Patent Act, "whoever invents or discovers any new and useful process, machine, manufacture, or composition of matter, or any new and useful improvement thereof, may obtain a patent."[4] Designed to foster and incentivize innovation and improve social welfare, the patent system promotes the development of new technologies in exchange for an exclusive, time-limited right to "exclude others from making, using, offering for sale, or selling or importing the invention."[5] Several other rules and regulations govern patent rights, including importantly those related to inventorship. In addition to inventorship, five criteria generally govern patentability including subject-matter eligibility, utility, novelty, nonobviousness and written description/enablement.[6]

---

[2] [18]; *see also Thaler v. Hirshfeld et al.*, No. 1:20-cv-00903-LMB (E.D.Va. September 2, 2021)

[3] *See* About Us, USPTO.gov, https://www.uspto.gov/about-us

[4] 35 U.S.C. § 101.

[5] 35 U.S.C. § 154.

[6] *See* 35 U.S.C. §§ 101 (subject matter eligibility & utility), 102 (novelty), 103 (nonobviousness), and 112 (enablement).

Inventorship The listing of the proper inventor(s) is a critical requirement and without a correct listing a patent application can be rejected and/or an existing patent invalidated [4]. Under 35 U.S.C. §100(f), "inventor" is defined as "the individual or, if a joint invention, the individuals collectively who invented or discovered the subject matter of the invention." An inventor does not include someone who merely assisted the actual inventor after the inventor conceived of the invention or someone who provides well-known principles without having conceived of the invention itself [4].

Subject Matter Eligibility Under 35 U.S.C. §101, four categories of inventions are generally recognized as appropriate subject matter of a patent: process, machine, manufacture or composition of matter. Notably, abstract ideas, laws of nature and natural phenomena are excluded from patent eligibility.[7] A series of U.S. Supreme Court decisions with regard to subject matter eligibility have imposed major hurdles on the patentability of life science innovations. A two-part test has generally been established to determine subject-matter eligibility, known as the "Mayo/Alice Framework."[8] The first step is to determine whether the claims are directed to an ineligible category of invention (e.g. abstract ideas, laws of nature and natural phenomena) and to determine whether additional elements are recited in the claim as to practically apply the judicial exception.[9] If so, a second step is applied where the claims of the invention are analyzed individually and in combination to determine whether the additional elements transform the claim to be patent-eligible (i.e. an "inventive concept").[10] Under this new framework, patents for life science innovations have largely been hindered by falling within a judicial exception without an additional transformation or "inventive step."

Utility Also under 35 U.S.C. §101, inventions are required to be useful or have a specific, substantial and credible utility. Lack of utility may arise where the invention is inoperative (e.g. an invention relating to perpetual motion).[11]

Novelty Pursuant to 35 U.S.C. §102, inventions are required to be "novel" such that it is not identical to what has already been disclosed in the public domain (aka "prior art"). Thus, the invention cannot have been previously patented or "described in a printed publication, or in public use."[12]

---

[7] 35 U.S.C. §§ 101 (2012).

[8] *Mayo v. Prometheus*, 132 S. Ct. 1289 (2012); *Alice Corp. V. CLS Bank International*, 134 Ct. 2347 (2014).

[9] *Ibid.*

[10] *Ibid.*

[11] MPEP 2104, https://www.uspto.gov/web/offices/pac/mpep/s2104.html

[12] 35 U.S.C. §§ 102(a)(1) (2012).

Non-Obviousness Pursuant to 35 U.S.C. §103, inventions must differ from prior art so that "the differences between the claimed invention and the prior art are such that the claimed invention as a whole would [not] have been obvious before the effective filing date of the claimed invention to a person having ordinary skill in the art to which the claimed invention pertains."[13]

Written Description/Enablement Finally, under 35 U.S.C. §112, inventions must be sufficiently described as to satisfactorily disclose the invention and demonstrate that the inventor was in possession of the invention under the written description requirement.[14] Similarly, under the enablement requirement, inventions must be described in sufficient detail such that a "person having ordinary skill in the art"[15] (PHOSITA) would be able to make and use the invention as defined in the patent claims.[16]

Issues with Inventorship and Patentability of AI

In the context of the current US patent law system which currently operates under a "human-centric" paradigm, AI technology has created new challenges for inventorship and patentability, particularly where innovation in AI has begun to replace human efforts. Some challenges with inventorship and patentability of AI technology arise in the context of (1) inventorship of "AI-assisted" Inventions versus Inventions by "AI-Inventors;" (2) the patentability requirement of non-obviousness and the applicable AI-PHOSITA standard, and (3) the patentability requirement of adequate written description and enablement.

Inventorship of "AI-Assisted" Inventions Versus Inventions by "AI-Inventors"

Historically, computing capabilities have permitted the generation of inventions with the assistance of AI. One of the first AI technologies used to generate AI-assisted inventions was the Creativity Machine (CM), patented in 1994 [15] CM consisted of a computer that utilized artificial neural networks to generate novel ideas [15]. Similarly, the IBM Watson computer was developed in 2007 and was capable of generating millions of ideas and ranking the best ones using predictive algorithms [15]. Famously, in 2011 Watson competed on the game show Jeopardy!

---

[13] 35 U.S.C. §§ 103 (2012); MPEP 2141, https://www.uspto.gov/web/offices/pac/mpep/s2141.html

[14] MPEP 2163, https://www.uspto.gov/web/offices/pac/mpep/s2163.html

[15] The "person having ordinary skill in the art" (PHOSITA) is a technical term used to refer to a hypothetical person who would have knowledge in the field of the relevant art at the time the invention was made.

[16] MPEP 2164, https://www.uspto.gov/web/offices/pac/mpep/s2164.html

and beat the top two ranked players using its underlying DeepQA technology [16]. Watson was subsequently modified in 2014 for use in generating recipes based on user input (e.g. ingredients, type of food, style of cuisine, etc.) and more recently has been expanded for use in a wide range of areas including financial planning, in designing health care treatment plans, analyzing genetic profiles for pharmacological treatment and more [17].

For example, drug design and discovery is one area in life science innovation where AI has had a profound impact. Historically, the drug design process has been prohibitively expensive both in monetary investment (costing on average $2.5-3 billion per new marketed drug) and in time (taking on average over a decade) [2]. With nearly 10^{60} potential compounds to search through, the drug discovery process was conducted through a random and repetitive trial-and-error process of "design, make, test, analyze" marred by more failure than success [2]. Through the application of AI, desirable chemical and biological properties can be predicted to reduce the immense time and expense involved in the traditional drug design process, greatly facilitating the drug design and discovery process.

Moreover, recent technical advances have now permitted more sophisticated AI systems capable of more independently generating new inventions. One such advanced AI system was developed by Dr. Stephen Thaler, the first-of-its-kind "AI-inventor," Device Autonomously Bootstrapping Uniform Sensibility (DABUS). Dr. Stephen Thaler asserts that DABUS independently "invented," without human intervention, both an improved travel beverage container equipped for safer handling, as well as a "neural flame" device for search-and-rescue operations [18].

In July 2019, Dr. Thaler filed a patent application with the USPTO listing DABUS AI as the sole "inventor" for the resulting inventions, which has now become a well-known case study in patent policy and law relating to AI.[17] The USPTO denied Dr. Thaler's patent application on the basis that the application was incomplete and failed to list a human as an inventor.[18] Dr. Thaler appealed the USPTO's decision to the U.S. District Court for the Eastern District of Virginia, which upheld the decision.[19] Finally, in August 2022, the US Court of Appeals for the Federal Circuit, the top patent court, upheld the USPTO's finding that "inventors" pursuant to US patent law were required to be "natural persons," i.e., human beings, and rejected AI systems as sole inventors on patents.[20] Importantly, the Federal Circuit noted that its rejection was limited to inventions generated by "AI-inventors" and did not address whether AI-assisted inventions were eligible for patent protection.[21]

---

[17] *See* US Application Nos. 16/524,350 ("Neural Flame") and 16/524,532 ("Fractal Container").

[18] *Thaler v. Hirshfeld*, 558 F. Supp. 3d 238 (E.D. Va. 2021).

[19] *Ibid.*

[20] *Thaler v. Vidal*, No. 21-2347 (Fed. Cir. 2022).

[21] *Ibid.* (holding "[m]oreover, we are not confronted today with the question of whether inventions made by human beings with the assistance of AI are eligible for patent protection.")

The DABUS case is particularly important for AI innovations in the life sciences. In the drug design and discovery context, researchers are utilizing AI by identifying a disease, developing a framework for an "AI problem" for the AI system to "explore," and then evaluating predictions/solutions from the AI with or without researcher input, moderation or direction.[22] The AI predictions/solutions are obtained from massive data sources through which AI systems are able to draw informed correlations.[23] Exscientia, a company that focuses on applying AI to the drug design of small molecules, is one specific example of a company combining AI capabilities with human creativity and expertise.[24] Using Exscientia's AI platform, researchers are able to use AI to sift through millions of small molecule possibilities and narrow them down to 10-20 to be synthesized, tested and optimized as a potential clinical drug at a rate that shortens pre-clinical testing to nearly one-fourth of the typical time frame.[25]

Similarly, in the context of drug repurposing, where existing drugs are used to treat a different disease than originally indicated for, historically, human screening efforts alone have had low efficiency requiring significant cost investment and time due to the large number of potential drugs, drug-target interactions, and potential off-target interactions, among other considerations.[26] Recently, AI technology has been applied to identify unknown drug interactions by again utilizing massive data sources to obtain previously unknown predictions/solutions.[27] BenevolentAI is one example of a large screening library consisting of structured medical and scientific literature. During the initial stages of the COVID pandemic, doctors fed the BenevolentAI platform clues about the virus, which was unidentified at the time. The BenevolentAI platform was then able to utilize AI algorithms to identify baricitinib, a rheumatoid arthritis drug, as a potential treatment.[28] The AI prediction was correct and within two years, baricitinib was validated as an anti-viral and anti-inflammatory COVID treatment that is now recommended by the World Health Organization (WHO).

As illustrated in both of these examples of Life Science-AI innovations, designating inventorship for advanced AI technology within the existing "human-centric" patent regime is problematic. With increasing AI advancements, the creative human contribution behind "AI-inventorship" is minimized or even eliminated as AI technology begins to replace human effort, potentially disqualifying the human from qualifying as an "inventor/co-inventor." [7].

---

[22] *Ibid.*

[23] *Ibid.*

[24] *Ibid.*

[25] *Ibid.*

[26] *Ibid.*

[27] *Ibid.*

[28] *Ibid.*

Patentability Requirement of Non-Obviousness and the Applicable AI-PHOSITA Standard

Under current patent law, when determining whether the elements of non-obviousness, novelty, and enablement have been met, the applicable "person having ordinary skill in the art" (PHOSITA) standard is applied.[29] The PHOSITA standard is applied from the perspective of a hypothetical person with knowledge in the relevant art at the time of the invention.[30] With AI technology, determining the applicable PHOSITA standard can be challenging due to AI's vast capabilities. Many different standards have been proposed that may potentially be applicable including (1) a hypothetical person with expertise about AI systems (e.g. the AI programmer); (2) a hypothetical person equipped with an AI system; or (3) even an AI system itself [7]. Under current "human-centric" patent law, the applicable PHOSITA standard is particularly important when applying tests established by the US Federal Circuit (the "motivation test") and US Supreme Court (the "obvious-to-try" test) which are used to determine whether an invention is "obvious" and therefore unpatentable [7].

As scholars have argued, it is important to recognize that in the context of AI technology, the non-obviousness standard may not even be applicable. While humans have the capability to ask questions and have insight to determine causal effect, AI technology currently lacks this capability and relies instead on mathematical and statistical correlation and statistical predictions which inherently lack purposefulness, creativity and inventiveness for the purposes of determining non-obviousness [2]. As discussed earlier, Life Science-AI platforms utilize predictions and solutions that are obtained by the AI sifting and screening through massive amounts of data. While these predictions and solutions are arguably inherently obvious to a computer, they would not be obvious to human researchers who would require extensive cost investments and effort to reach the same conclusions. Accordingly, under our existing "human-centric" patent law paradigm, the existing obviousness standard would be problematic as applied to AI technology. Arguably, the obviousness inquiry may be irrelevant when AI-inventors are involved.

Patentability Requirement of Adequate Written Description and Enablement

Understanding and predicting how AI technology works is a major challenge, particularly when dealing with complex and sophisticated AI, This challenge is known as the "blackbox conundrum." [7]. Accordingly, insight into AI's innovative processes are limited and cannot be disclosed in detail. This poses a challenge in meeting the written description and enablement requirements under current US patent

---

[29] 35 U.S.C. §103.
[30] *Ibid.*

law. Pursuant to 35 U.S.C. § 112 written description and enablement requirements, inventors have a duty to disclose the technical information underlying their invention.[31] Thus, inventions must be adequately described in the patent application with enough detail that a "person of ordinary skill in the art" could make and use the disclosed invention.[32] Moreover, disclosure is necessary to promote the public policy behind the granting of patents so that the exchange of a time-limited right to exclude others from the invention is balanced with meaningful public disclosure such that there can be progress of the useful arts.[33]

The IP5 Forum

The IP5 was formed in 2007 and consists of the five largest patent offices in the world: the USPTO, the European Patent Office or "EPO," the Japan Patent Office or "JPO," the Korean Intellectual Property Office or "KIPO," and the State Intellectual Property Office of the People's Republic of China or "SIPO."[34] Each sovereign nation has its own patent law system; however, the IP5 work together through cooperative exchange of views to address common challenges in the international patent system, including harmonization of patent practices and procedures, promotion of timely high-quality patent search and examination results, and improvement of cost-efficiency and user-friendliness in an international system.[35]

IP5 AI Policies

As the world's leading patent offices, the IP5 have each taken their own respective positions on the challenges facing the patentability of computer-related inventions and AI. (See Table 12.2).

In the US, the USPTO has taken an active role in engaging with innovators and experts in AI to maintain leadership in AI as an emerging technology and to continue to incentivize further innovation.[36] In early 2019, the USPTO hosted an AI IP policy conference focused on IP issues relating to patent, trademark, copyright, and trade secrets. That same year, the USPTO also issued a request for comments on

---

[31] 35 USC § 112(a) requires that the written description is "in such full, clear, concise and exact terms as to enable one skilled in the art to which it pertains, or with which it is most nearly connected, to make and use" the invention.

[32] 35 USC § 112(a).

[33] *Ibid.*

[34] IP5, https://www.uspto.gov/ip-policy/patent-policy/ip5.

[35] *Ibid.*

[36] USPTO, PUBLIC VIEWS ON ARTIFICIAL INTELLIGENCE AND INTELLECTUAL PROPERTY POLICY (2020).

Table 12.2 Summary of IP5 current AI policies (2022)

IP5 country	Current AI policies	Special AI policy issues
US Patent Office (USPTO)	In 2019, the USPTO requested public comments on patenting AI inventions and copyrighting AI works, but has not issued any new official guidelines. (Request for Comments on Patenting Artificial Intelligence Inventions, 84 Fed. Reg. 44,889, 44,889 (Aug. 27, 2019); *see also* Request for Comments on Intellectual Property Protection for Artificial Intelligence Innovation, 84 Fed. Reg. 58,141, 58,141 (Oct. 30, 2019); USPTO, PUBLIC VIEWS ON ARTIFICIAL INTELLIGENCE AND INTELLECTUAL PROPERTY POLICY (2020)) AI is currently treated similarly to other computer-implemented inventions. Generally, the USPTO has limited AI inventions to those that are narrowly claimed with disclosures for the AI inventions typically requiring descriptions of the computer utilized and the algorithms involved. Future development of Artificial General Intelligence (AGI) with human-like thinking power poses new issues that may change future USPTO AI policy.	**AI Inventorship:** Only natural persons are considered inventors. If AI is used to conceive an invention, the creators of said AI do not need to be listed as inventors. **Enablement:** Difficulties arise when the input and output are known but the logic in-between is unknown. Moreover, enablement of an invention is generally based on how well-known and predictable a field is, but the "predictability" of AI is not yet known. (United States Patent and Trademark Office. Oct. 2020, https://www.uspto.gov/sites/default/files/documents/USPTO_AI-Report_2020-10-07.pdf)
European Patent Office (EPO)	The EPO has made no major changes to its patentability guidelines for AI systems specifically; rather, AI is treated similarly to other computer-implemented inventions. The EPO generally excludes computer software programs from patentability but allows for inventions that involve a cooperation of software and hardware to be patented [19]	**Patentable Subject Matter:** AI is considered *per se* unpatentable because it is of an abstract nature. However, AI can be patentable when it is applied to solve a technical problem or when directed to a specific implementation. **AI Inventorship:** Only natural persons are considered inventors.
Japan Patent Office (JPO)	The JPO has made no major changes to its patentability guidelines for AI systems specifically; rather, AI is treated similarly to other computer-implemented inventions. The JPO generally excludes computer software programs from patentability but allows for inventions that involve a cooperation of software and hardware [20].	**Enablement:** AI systems must be enabled by a correlation between the input and the output supported by the specification and/or general knowledge.

(continued)

Table 12.2 (continued)

IP5 country	Current AI policies	Special AI policy issues
Korean Intellectual Property Office (KIPO)	The KIPO has claimed that it wishes to take the leading role in AI patentability guidelines in the years to come [21] Generally, the KIPO requires patentable computer-related inventions to include information processing performed by a combination of software and hardware. Claims do not involve a human mental activity or offline activities.	**Patentable Subject Matter:** The KIPO acknowledges AI training data inventions, AI modeling inventions, and AI applications. However, "[i]f an invention can be easily made by a POSITA, the invention is not patentable." [22] **Enablement:** AI invention disclosures must have distinguishing technical configurations (training data, data preprocessing, trained model, loss function, etc) and inventors are encouraged to elaborate on the technical effects of the inventive AI [23].
State Intellectual Property Office of the People's Republic of China (SIPO)	The CNIPA allows for "software" as a category of invention and takes algorithm features, business rules and user experience into consideration along with technical features when evaluating an application's contribution [24]	The CNIPA amended their patent examination guidelines as of February 1, 2020 so that claims as a whole must be examined and an Examiner cannot separate out features directed to a business or algorithmic method [24] "[The CNIPA is] looking at improvements to algorithms and big data processing, whether the algorithms have a specific technical relationship with the internal structure of the computer system, and/or improvements to hardware computing efficiency or execution effect. The CNIPA considers improvements to data storage size, data transmission rate and hardware processing speed as evidence of a technical solution required for patentability." [25]

patenting AI inventions including patent policy issues relating to inventorship, ownership, patent subject matter eligibility, enablement, disclosure non-obviousness, and level of ordinary skill in the art.[37] A second request for comments was issued regarding AI policy issues related to other forms of IP, including copyrights, trademarks, trade secrets, and database protections.[38] General public feedback in response to the requests expressed a view that the existing US patent system is adequate for handling AI inventions and that AI-invented technology should be viewed as a subset of computer-implemented inventions.[39] Some issues were identified as potentially posing challenges for the existing patent system, including enablement and the "person having ordinary skill in the art" standard to be applied.[40]

AI Policies in Other Countries

Although the IP5 consists of the world's five largest patent offices, nations outside of the IP5 have also made notable policies in the area of AI in patent law.

South Africa In June 2021, the South Africa's Companies and Intellectual Property Commission granted DABUS the first patent for an invention conceived by an AI inventor.[41] Notably, South African patent laws do not legally define the term "inventor" and patent examination does not involve substantive review.[42]

Australia In July 2021, the Federal Court of Australia reversed a rejection by the Australian patent office finding that Dr. Thaler's patent application listing DABUS as an inventor for DABUS- generated inventions was invalid [26]. In doing so, the Federal Court of Australia held that an AI system can qualify as an "inventor" under Australian patent laws [26]. Importantly, the Court distinguished AI "inventorship" from AI as an "applicant" of an application or "grantee" of a patent, which the Court found to be impermissible [26]. However, in April 2022 the Federal Court's decision in favor of finding AI as an "inventor" was overturned by the Full Court of the Federal Court of Australia which found that an "inventor" was limited to a natural

---

[37] *Ibid.*; *see also* Request for Comments on Patenting Artificial Intelligence Inventions, 84 Fed. Reg. 44,889 (Aug. 27, 2019).

[38] *Ibid.*

[39] USPTO, PUBLIC VIEWS ON ARTIFICIAL INTELLIGENCE AND INTELLECTUAL PROPERTY POLICY (2020).

[40] *Ibid.*

[41] *See* AP7471ZA00, Notice of Issuance, South Africa's Companies and Intellectual Property Commission (dated June 24, 2021); *see also* DABUS Gets Its First Patent In South Africa Under Formalities Examination, https://www.ipwatchdog.com/2021/07/29/dabus-gets-first-patent-south-africa-formalities-examination/id=136116/

[42] DABUS Gets Its First Patent In South Africa Under Formalities Examination, https://www.ipwatchdog.com/2021/07/29/dabus-gets-first-patent-south-africa-formalities-examination/id=136116/

person under Australian patent law.[43] The issue was appealed to the Australian High Court. On November 11, 2022, the Court issued a final, non-appealable denial holding that DABUS could not be named as an inventor for the purposes of an Australian patent application.[44]

Leading Expert's Proposed Changes to Inventorship, Non-Obviousness and Written Description & Enablement Requirements

While AI technology has made significant advances, arguably, AI has not reached a level advanced enough to demonstrate independent thinking and behavior. However, given the investment in AI development and recent rapid advances in AI technology, such advanced level AI may not be far off in the future. Several approaches have been proposed to address the patentability of "AI Inventors."

Inventorship

The USPTO requires that all patent applications include one or more named "inventors." For the purposes of a patent, an "inventor" is a person that contributes to the invention's "conception" or "the formulation in the mind…of a definite and permanent idea of the complete and operative invention as it is thereafter to be applied in practice."[45] Once conceived, an invention should be able to be made and used without undue experimentation by a "person having ordinary skill in the art" (PHOSITA). Moreover, if there are multiple inventors, all must be listed. An inventor must be an "individual" and cannot be a legal entity (e.g., a corporation).[46] When inventorship is not properly included in a patent application, the validity and enforceability of the patent may be undermined.

The Patent Act currently does not address the eligibility of "AI inventors," nor has the USPTO or case law provided direct guidance on the matter. Thus, scholars have made several theoretical arguments both in favor and against "AI inventors." Scholars in favor of "AI inventors" argue that allowing "AI inventors" would be

---

[43] *Comm'r. of Patents v Thaler* [2022] FCAFC 62 (13 April 2022), avail at https://www.judgments.fedcourt.gov.au/judgments/Judgments/fca/full/2022/2022fcafc0062.

[44] DABUS Down- High Court Dashes Hopes of "AI Inventor" Advocates, avail at https://blog.patentology.com.au/2022/11/dabus-down-high-court-dashes-hopes-of.html#:~:text=On%20Friday%2011%20November%202022%2C%20three%20judges%20of,purposes%20of%20applying%20for%20a%20patent%20in%20Australia. (15 Nov 2022).

[45] See Ryan Abbott, I Think, Therefore I Invent: Creative Computers and the Future of Patent Law, 57 B.C. L. REV. 1079, 1080 (2016); 35 U.S.C. § 100(f) (1952); MPEP, supra note 43, § 2137.01(II).

[46] 35 U.S.C. § 100(f).

consistent with the intent and purpose of the Patent Act and encourage and incentivize further development and advancement which would be lacking without AI-invented inventions being eligible for patent protection.[47] Moreover, without patent protection, owners of creative "AI inventors" would be more likely to seek trade secret protections which do not require disclosure; thus, slowing down AI development and advancement.[48] Notwithstanding the above, arguments against "AI inventors" being eligible as "inventors" on patent applications include that software may not require patent protection to incentivize innovation because software innovation is generally less costly and time-consuming than innovation in other technologies.[49] Moreover, scholars argue allowing "AI inventors" might chill human creativity and disincentivize individual human effort due to competition with AI technology, thus favoring large corporations with deep pockets over individual inventorship.[50]

Nevertheless, as Life Science-AI innovations continue to advance, so do the potential applications and profound implications for humanity, particularly in the areas of healthcare and medicine. As discussed earlier in this chapter, we are already seeing significant reductions in the effort, cost, and time required in both drug design and discovery and in drug repurposing, which suggests a need to support the recognition of "AI inventors" to further support innovation in this area.

Non-Obviousness

The non-obviousness guidelines of the USPTO state: "if the differences between the subject matter sought to be patented and the prior art are such that the subject matter as a whole would have been obvious at the time the invention was made to a person having ordinary skill in the art to which said subject matter pertains"… the invention is not patentable.[51] In other words, an invention is not patentable if it is an obvious extension of what already exists and is well-known by an average worker in the scientific field of the invention.

With regard to inventions entirely generated by AI, problems arise when it comes to the term "a person having ordinary skill in the art." Modern computers and advanced AI allow for the definition of a skilled worker to be more lenient than it ever has been before; any average person could potentially use an inventive AI to produce an invention that is patentable in view of the USPTO within a matter of days. This massive influx of inventions would potentially be detrimental to society as a whole, as the amount of patentable subject matter able to be discovered by normal

---

[47] See Ryan Abbott, I Think, Therefore I Invent: Creative Computers and the Future of Patent Law, 57 B.C. L. REV. 1079, 1080 (2016).

[48] *Ibid.*

[49] *Ibid.*

[50] *Ibid.*

[51] United States Patent Trademark Office, *2141 Examination Guidelines for Determining Obviousness Under 35 U.S.C. 103. 2019.*

humans alone without the aid of inventive machines would diminish rapidly. Thus the definition of a person skilled in the art must be updated to prevent such a scenario [27]. Currently, the level of ordinary skill in a given art is determined based on five factors: (1) the types of problems encountered in the art, (2) the prior art solutions to those problems, (3) the rapidity with which innovations are made, (4) the sophistication of the technology, and (5) the educational level of active workers in the field.[52]

Scholars have proposed that a sixth factor should be taken into account in order to update the guidelines for emerging technologies and AI: the technologies used by active workers in the field [27]. This would update the definition of a person having ordinary skill in the art to consider the state and use of inventive machines in the scientific field of the invention, even considering the possibility that a "person" of ordinary skill in the art in some fields might be the inventive machine itself. However, while this new factor at least addresses the influence of technology on ordinary skill in an art, it is still unclear how one could possibly determine what would be *obvious* to an inventive machine. A potential solution to this is determining whether the subject matter generated by AI could be reproduced by a standard machine [27]. The term "standard machine" in this respect may be defined as any machine capable of executing state of the art intelligent AI software at the time of the invention's conception. If the subject matter cannot be generated by this standard machine, then the AI invention would be considered non-obvious.

This standard for non-obviousness will drastically change the landscape of patents as a whole. Inventive machines can potentially access all information and all prior art in any given field in an instant, thus making them far more "skilled" than the current "person of ordinary skill in the art" could ever be. Non-obviousness may eventually require the invention of specialized computers that outperform or think differently from standard machines, and the requirement for what is considered a non-obvious invention will only become more difficult to determine as technology becomes more advanced [27].

Importantly with regard to Life Science-AI, it is becoming increasingly clear that what is "obvious" to an AI platform may not be "obvious" to a human. Thus, Life Science-AI technologies such as those being developed by Exscentia and BenevolentAI have the ability to screen through massive amounts of data to produce predictions and solutions that would be otherwise impossible without extensive human effort, creating a gray area for the application of the obviousness standard in the context of Life Science-AI technology.

Written Description & Enablement

Patent applications submitted to the USPTO are required to comply with a set of guidelines that ensure the specification and claims are sufficiently enabled. The term "enablement" is defined by the USPTO as "the requirement that the specification describes[s] the invention in such terms that one skilled in the art can make and

---

[52] *In re GPAC Inc., 57 F.3d 1573, 1579 (Fed. Cir. 1995).*

use the claimed invention...to ensure that the invention is communicated to the interested public in a meaningful way." [28]. Furthermore, the USPTO requires the written description to clearly describe the invention in question and show that the applicant had the knowledge to conceive said invention.[53] However, issues arise when these guidelines are specifically applied to inventions developed by AI. Inventive AIs tend to act as a "black box," executing a massive number of hidden tasks on an input to generate a new invention as an output. In these prevalent black box models, the calculations and tasks that are carried out between feeding in the input and receiving the output are generally unknown, even to the programmers [29] This presents a clear problem when it comes to the enablement and written description requirements because the "black box" model inherently means that the inventor cannot describe the conception of the invention sufficiently without disclosing the underlying functions of the AI itself. Disclosing this would create issues for the creators of the AI, who may or may not be the same as the owners of the invention in question, since the disclosure would require enough information for others to copy the structure of the AI for their purposes. However, simply describing the "black box" structure of the AI is not considered "full disclosure" by the USPTO for the purposes of written description and enablement (See footnote 53). Thus, a solution is required to reach a middle ground between appeasing inventors of AI/humans who implement inventive machines and patent offices alike.

Scholars have determined four possible scenarios for disclosing AI-generated inventions: (1) undisclosed AI generation of output, where the AI is considered a trade secret and is not disclosed at all; (2) disclosed AI generation of output, where the AI made the invention and the entire AI and invention are disclosed; (3) disclosed AI-based tools, where the AI itself is the invention and the entirety of the AI is disclosed; and (4) undisclosed AI-based tools, where the invention is the AI and the AI technique and reproduction of the invention is not disclosed [30]. For an AI-generated invention, the second of these scenarios must be achieved to comply with USPTO guidelines. A possible solution has been developed to achieve this without fully disclosing the AI structure itself. The AI itself could be described *in its own terms* by extracting a log of transactions that have been automatically generated by the AI over the time of its use. This massive log file can be processed by a separate AI to convert the data into a simplified step-by-step process to be included in a patent application, broad enough to avoid disclosing the AI's internal algorithms, but specific enough to comply with USPTO guidelines of written description and enablement.

Importantly, the "black box" issues with written description would potentially apply to Life Science-AI innovations which also obtain predictions and/or solutions that may not be known and/or describable. However, the important public policy considerations related to the potential advancements in healthcare and medicine arguably outweigh the potential issues with disclosure, particularly where

---

[53] United States Patent Trademark Office, *2163 Guidelines for the Examination of Patent Applications Under the 35 U.S.C. 112(a) or Pre-AIA 35 U.S.C. 112, first paragraph, "Written Description" Requirement. 2019.*

alternatives, such as the proposed partial disclosure of AI structure, may be sufficient to comply with existing USPTO guidelines.

The Future Directions of AI in Life Sciences Innovations

The past decade has borne significant advances in health care and medicine through the interface of AI and life sciences innovation. This progress to date has spurred major VC investments in Life Science-AI technology. Worldwide, VC investment in biotech startups worldwide increased from 2,200 in 2016 to 3,100 companies in 2021 [9]. Moreover, in a single year period between 2020 and 2021, VC investments in biotech more than doubled to nearly $34 billion USD [9]. However, given the uncertainty in patent law worldwide, further future investments in Life Science-AI technology remain unclear. Current lack of guidance with regard to the patentability of AI, particularly in the context of health science innovations, has the potential to reduce investment and slow progress. The public interest strongly encourages patent protection for AI technology in the life sciences and only time will tell if and how the current human-centric patentability criteria will be modified, adapted, and/or re-vamped to continue to support innovation and growth in this field.

References

1. McCarthy J. What is artificial intelligence? Nov 12, 2007.
2. Hao Y. The rise of 'Centaur' inventors: how patent law should adapt to the challenge to inventorship doctrine by human-ai inventing synergies (August 10, 2022).
3. Turing AM. Computing machinery and intelligence. Mind. 1950;49:433–60.
4. Watanabe Y. I, Inventor: patent inventorship for artificial intelligence systems, 57 IDAHO L. REV. 473 (2021).
5. Gupta R, Srivastava D, Sahu M, Tiwari S, Ambasta RK, Kumar P. Artificial intelligence to deep learning: machine intelligence approach for drug discovery. Mol Divers. 2021;25(3):1315–60.
6. Agrawal P. Artificial intelligence in drug discovery and development. J Pharmacovigil. 2018;6:e173.
7. Yanisky-Ravid S, Jin R. Summoning a new artificial intelligence patent model: in the age of pandemic. SSRN [Preprint]. 2020:3619069.
8. CB Insights, Healthcare AI trends to watch. 2020.
9. Leclerc O, et al., What are the biotech investment themes that will shape the industry? McKinsey & Company, Life Sciences Practice, (June 2022), https://www.mckinsey.com/industries/life-sciences/our-insights/what-are-the-biotech-investment-themes-that-will-shape-the-industry.
10. CB Insights, The state of AI: Q3 2022 Report (2022)
11. Diagnosing the Future: AI and San Diego's Life Sciences Cluster, https://storymaps.arcgis.com/stories/ae5bc95c717f44c8ba95298359570e86
12. CB Insights, Healthcare AI trends to watch, 2020; *see also* https://www.medtronic.com/us-en/our-company/artificial-intelligence-healthcare-technology.html?cmpid=PPC_bing_Q1_resp_MOC_INN_Health_System_Leader_061322_071122_FY23&ef_id=:G:s&s_kwcid=AL!5660!3!!p!!o!!AI%20healthcare

13. Monheit G, Cognetta AB, Ferris L, et al. The performance of MelaFind: a prospective multicenter study. Arch Dermatol. 2011;147(2):188–94. https://doi.org/10.1001/archdermatol.2010.302.
14. Tiwari P, Prasanna P, Wolansky L, Pinho M, Cohen M, Nayate AP, Gupta A, Singh G, Hatanpaa KJ, Sloan A, Rogers L, Madabhushi A. Computer-extracted texture features to distinguish cerebral radionecrosis from recurrent brain tumors on multiparametric MRI: a feasibility study. American Journal of Neuroradiology. 2016;37(12):2231–6. https://doi.org/10.3174/ajnr.A4931.
15. Afshar MS. Artificial intelligence and inventorship—does the patent inventor have to be human?, 13 HASTINGS SCI. & TECH. L.J. 55 (2022); *see also* What Is the Ultimate Idea?, IMAGINATION ENGINES INC., https://perma.cc/P877-F33B.
16. Ferrucci D, Levas A, Bagchi S, Gondek D, Mueller ET. Watson: Beyond Jeopardy! Artificial Intelligence. 2013;199:93–105.
17. Abbott R, I Think, Therefore I Invent: creative computers and the future of patent law, 57 B.C. L. REV. 1079, 1080. 2016.
18. Afshar MS. Artificial intelligence and inventorship—does the patent inventor have to be human?, 13 HASTINGS SCI. & TECH. L.J. 55, 2022.
19. "Artificial Intelligence." EPO, 2 May 2022, https://www.epo.org/news-events/in-focus/ict/artificial-intelligence.html.
20. Patent examination case examples pertinent to ai-related technologies. JPO, 12 Nov. 2021, https://www.jpo.go.jp/e/system/laws/rule/guideline/patent/ai_jirei_e.html.
21. So-hyun K. Kipo Vows to Take Lead in Setting International Rules on AI Inventions. The Korea Herald, The Korea Herald, 29 Dec. 2021., https://www.koreaherald.com/view.php?ud=20211229000475.
22. KIPO Publishes Examination Guidelines on Artificial Intelligence. KIPO Publishes Examination Guidelines on Artificial Intelligence – Kim & Chang IP, Kim and Chang IP, 5 Mar. 2021, https://www.ip.kimchang.com/en/insights/detail.kc?sch_section=4&idx=22769.
23. Son M. Patenting AI-related inventions in South Korea. MIP, MIP, 7 Sept. 2022., https://www.managingip.com/article/2a1czl6xdvnfsvilboxs0/sponsored-content/patenting-ai-related-inventions-in-south-korea.
24. Wininger A et al. CNIPA announces amended patent guidelines for patent applications covering AI and blockchain. China IP Law Update, 8 Mar. 2021., https://www.chinaiplawupdate.com/2020/01/cnipa-announces-amended-patent-guidelines-for-patent-applications-covering-ai-and-blockchain/.
25. Xie W. What is AI and how is it treated by the USPTO, EPO and CNIPA? IPWatchdog.com | Patents & Intellectual Property Law, 13 May 2022, https://ipwatchdog.com/2022/05/14/ai-treated-uspto-epo-cnipa/id=149013/.
26. Afshar MS, Artificial intelligence and inventorship—does the patent inventor have to be human?, 13 HASTINGS SCI. & TECH. L.J. 55 (2022); *see also* Thaler v Comm 'r. of Patents, [2021] FCA 879 (30 July 2021) 17-18 (Austl.), available at https://www.judgments.fedcourt.gov.au/judgments/Judgments/fca/single/2021/2021fca0879.
27. Abbott R. *Everything is obvious. SSRN Electronic Journal, 2017,* https://doi.org/10.2139/ssrn.3056915.
28. United States Patent Trademark Office, *2164 The Enablement Requirement. 2013.*
29. *Wigmore I. "What Is Black Box Ai?" WhatIs.com, TechTarget, 31 Aug. 2019,* https://www.techtarget.com/whatis/definition/black-box-AI#:~:text=Black%20box%20AI%20is%20any,sense%2C%20is%20an%20impenetrable%20system.
30. Valinasab O. Big data analytics to automate disclosure of artificial intelligence's inventions. SSRN Electronic Journal. 2022; https://doi.org/10.2139/ssrn.4087752.

Chapter 13
Business Exit Strategy

John Shufeldt

I have started more than thirty businesses over the course of my entrepreneurial life, and it was not until the last decade that I considered how I would exit the business when it was the right time. Frankly, I would start them and not even consider the outcome I anticipated, save for "I hope I can sell it someday." What I finally learned is summarized below. The only thing not included are the sleepless nights, grey hair, and money wasted pursuing businesses from which there was no foreseeable exit—even at the inception.

Business Exit Strategy (BES) BES is a formalized strategic plan (often overlooked) by a business entrepreneur to sell their equity interest in the company, that they helped create as a founder or acquired the business, scaled it, and now wants an *exit* from the business. In short BES outlines the owner's plan to realize their gains in exchange for their skill, lost opportunity cost, capital, and sweat equity. The reasons for wanting to exit are enumerable: the entrepreneur or a venture capitalist wants to move on and profit from the venture, they want to pursue a new opportunity, or for a plethora of personal reasons. It could also be that the business is failing, and they need to mitigate their losses and therefore exit the venture before it loses its entire value.

BES *must* be a strategic part of the initial business plan and not an afterthought. This is necessary in order to secure the entrepreneur's or venture capitalist's financial future. Therefore, BES is a vital consideration in the overall planning of the business. The forms that a solid BES takes are varied and can include the following:

- Total transfer of equity and ownership
- Partial transfer of equity and ownership (liquidating or diluting your interest)

J. Shufeldt (✉)
Xcellerant Ventures, LLC, Scottsdale, AZ, USA
e-mail: Jshufeldt@xcellerantventures.com

© The Author(s), under exclusive license to Springer Nature Switzerland AG 2023
A. Meyers (ed.), *Digital Health Entrepreneurship*, Health Informatics,
https://doi.org/10.1007/978-3-031-33902-8_13

BES plans although formulated at the inception, may not be realized for years to come. But developing a solid BES gives its founders the following advantages:

- It informs investors that the business has a clear vision and goals and will induce a potential buyer.
- It informs potential buyers that the owners have done their due diligence in defining all roles within the company and the transition to the new owner will be smooth. In short there are no surprises with employees and all stakeholders are well informed.
- BES is not just an operational plan of exit. It's a very sophisticated document that requires a detailed analysis of finances of the company - currently, in the near future, and far out in the future. Thus there is also a detailed financial modeling and discounted cash flow "DCF" analysis. As a result, a potential buyer now appreciates the full financial value of the business in her acquisition decision.

Thus, having a detailed BES gives a vision with clear goals and a measurable financial value to a prospective buyer with little room for surprises and even may avert a potential bankruptcy.

There are multiple forms of an exit for a business each with its own advantages and disadvantages. The choice of succession planning is predicated on one's own financial, personal, and business goals. These are:

1. **Mergers and Acquisition (M&A Deals):** An M & A exit plan is ideal for startup companies and entrepreneurs—where the business is sold to a prospective buyer or another company whose goal might be increasing geographic footprint or to eliminate competition or a simple acquisition of your product, intellectual property, or service. The disadvantage with M & As is that they are extremely time consuming and very costly. Defining and analyzing the synergy between the companies is very challenging, resulting in the high rate of M & A failures. The obvious disadvantage of a complete acquisition is that you lose control of your company and may or may not be retained by the acquiror during the transition period. One thing to be cognizant of is whether the acquisition will be an asset or stock sale. Both have pluses and minuses and need to be addressed early in the negotiation.

2. **Selling your equity to a current investor or your own business partner**: This type of BES is also called a "friendly buyer" BES, because you are selling your stake to someone you know and trust. Here the succession and transition tend to be smooth. There is very little disruption in the operations of the business thereby keeping the revenue stream and cash flow stable. Furthermore, the partner/investor already has a vested interest and a stake in the business. The disadvantage of this form of BES is the seller might lack objectivity because they know the buyer. Thus it is not an arm's length transaction, causing the seller to ask for or receive a below market price.

3. **Family Succession or a Legacy Exit**: This type of BES is where the succession is to a family member(s), who have intimate knowledge of the operations and finances of the business and are groomed for transition. This occurs in large

family-owned conglomerates who want to keep the wealth and direction of the business in the family. The issue with this kind of succession is that the successor of the business might lack the business acumen or a blurring of the business and professional boundaries with personal. This can be consequential with significant financial and emotional distress, which can have collateral effects on the operations of the business and make holidays and family gatherings tense.

4. **Management buy outs (MBO) or Employee buy outs (EBO)**: MBOs and EBOs are transactions where the company's management/employees purchases all of the assets of the company and current management transitions into a senior role. The primary reason behind the MBOs is the organization can now go private to increase productivity, operations, and profitability. For most large corporations MBOs are favored when the Board decides to relinquish projects that are detached from its *core* business. MBOs are onerous and there is significant risk involved because the management transition to an owner's role comes with all the attendant risk and responsibility. MBOs must be distinguished from Management Buy-In (MBI) which is where an external management team or individual acquires the current organization and there is substitution of current management. MBIs can be very rocky and difficult because of the dual effect of the acquisition and replacement of the current management. This can jeopardize operations and revenue stream. Leveraged management buy-out (LMBO) is when the company's assets are used by prospective buyers to obtain debt.

Overall MBOs are favored because the buyers are existing managers that are acquiring the company. These managers have been with the company and know the mechanics and operations of the companies and know the stakeholders well. As such there is minimum disruption in the workflow and revenue stream and overall less chaos. The primary incentive for MBOs are financial reward – when they transition from employees to owners.

MBOs are a complex vehicle in business restructuring. One of the disadvantages of an MBO is the *mindset* transition from being a manager to an owner-entrepreneur. This can be a difficult mental exercise because the traits required for an entrepreneur-owner and manager are radically different. Another major concern talked of in the academic literature is that the managers could intentionally buy the company at a deeply discounted price thereby affecting the overall asset value. Although this may not be an intentional sabotage, the unintended consequences might be a drop in the company's value. This analysis bears down on the *conflict-of-interest* issue of the MBOs. Furthermore, the funding vehicle for an MBO (which can be through venture capital or private equity), further clouds the transaction and can impact the revenue stream.

Employees buy outs are more challenging and riskier because the transition from an employee to an owner is profound and employees might lack the sophistication, training, and experience to be owners. However, transferring ownership to an employees is a great way to start a workers cooperative.

5. **Initial Public offering (IPO)**: In the IPO the owners/founders are taking the company public through issuance of shares of stock. An Initial Public Offering sends strong positive market signals to investors about the profitability of the company.

However, the initial regulatory burden and subsequent compliance and reporting requirements are significant in terms of the paperwork, expense, and time that is required. The IPO due diligence is very costly and highly labor intensive requiring multiple professionals including lawyers, financial analysts, and accountants. The good news is that an IPO can lead to a significant profit. The financial crimes of the early 2000s have redefined the regulatory burden of IPOs and the market assesses and values the business on a quarterly basis. The Sarbanes-Oxley Act, which was promulgated in the 2000s, mandates tight reporting and disclosure requirements.

6. **Liquidation**: Over the last few years, the market has seen a surge of liquidations due to the economic downturn created by the pandemic. Liquidation is primarily reserved for a "failing" business. The process of liquidation is less burdensome with generally lower costs. The proceeds from the liquidation are used to pay the debts, taxes, and wages. The remainder goes to the shareholders. After liquidation, the company ceases to exist. A major downfall to the process of liquidation is the severance of ties with all stakeholders (vendors, employees, customers, etc.), which has a negative impact on the reputation of the stakeholders.

7. **Bankruptcy**: Bankruptcy per se is not a part of the BES, but is an unfortunate end strategy for a company that cannot pay its debts. Under Bankruptcy (Chap. 6), the owners will be unburdened of all the pending debts, however there will be a significant impact on their credit and ability to borrow in the future.

   Last year a new form of Bankruptcy was codified under President Trump, called the Chap. 10 Subchapter V, to help small business owners (SBOs) reorganize their business due to the pandemic's significant impact on their revenue stream. The process of Chap. 10 Subchapter V is extremely labor intensive and moves very quickly. The legislative intent behind Chap. 10 Subchapter V was to give businesses a second chance at reorganization.

8. **Leveraged Buyouts (LBOs):** Another form of BES are the Leveraged buyouts (LBO), which is looked upon skeptically by the press and the public because it viewed as predatory and has received a lot of press. A Leveraged buyout is a term used when *leverage(debt)* is used to buy out a company. The buyer in this case can be a venture capitalist, private equity or LBO firm, employees, or management. There are four types of LBOs:

   1. **Savior Plan**: The Savior plan is where employees and management collaborate together and borrow money to save the company that is on a downward trajectory. The potential for success of this plan is low because the company might not be able to pay back the loan with a high borrowing cost and poor return on investment (ROI).
   2. **Portfolio Plan**: The portfolio plan is also called the leveraged-build-up plan because a company can use leverage to buy its competitor or other companies with positive synergies. If successful, the owner's benefit and management can remain. However, the proposition is risky because the ROI might not match the cost of the leverage.
   3. **Repackaging Plan**: The repackaging plan involves a private equity or venture capitalist that uses leverage and then takes a publicly traded company

private by purchasing all the shares and then reorganizes operations and management and finally takes it public. These kind of repackaging plans are common in the health care industry - mostly pharmaceuticals. One of the largest ones in history is when Michael Dell and Silver Lake Partners took Dell private.

4. **Split up Plan**: The split up or break up plan is the most loathed by the press and people. It is also called "slash and burn" or "cut and run". The business likely to fall prey to the split-up plan are big corporations that have moved away from the core business and acquired other businesses, which are on the decline now. The buyer comes in, dismantles the entire conglomerate, and sells the business units to the highest bidder. The process is very disruptive as it involves massive layoffs as part of the reorganization.

In formulating a Business Exit Strategy, the Owners/Founders must be cognizant of the following:

- **Goals, Objectives, and Vision:** What are their goals in the long term? These goals need not be just financial goals, but also personal goals. Do they like to carry on their legacy through a legacy exit? Do they want to divest completely sell their shares and move on to a different project? They should consider what the road ahead would look like.
- **Financial due diligence:** The owners/founders must constantly be vigilant of the company's finances both short term and long term.
- **Operational efficiency:** Monitoring operational efficiency is crucial because this will impact cost and revenue stream.
- **Business valuation:** This is one of the key components of a BES. The owners must know what the business is worth, so that they could negotiate with potential buyers. There are multiple sophisticated tools and methodologies available as well as the utilization of artificial intelligence in business valuation.
- **Arm's length transactions:** An owner-entrepreneur is deeply meshed with the company they help create. However, when it comes to analytics, they must distance themself from the analysis and engage professionals that do conduct an arms-length transaction analysis. The academic literature on entrepreneurship is replete on this matter - most entrepreneurs are good at converting an idea into a business plan, but subsequent governance and leadership requires a different set of skills. My own experiences have taught me that the literature is generally correct in this assessment.
- **Scenario analysis:** A successful BES plan must incorporate a scenario analysis and must incorporate *all* scenarios - not just the best - and worst-case scenarios. The scenario analysis must not only factor in market conditions, but external threats as well - both foreseeable and unforeseeable. A classic example of an unforeseeable external market condition that played out in 2020 was the global pandemic due to COVID, which crippled the global economy with devastating effects on people's lives and livelihoods. A sound scenario analysis must incorporate these variables because, at the end of the day, the scenario analysis is risk management. Controlling or addressing different risks and variables is an indicia

of due diligence and sound strategic planning and most importantly tells the prospective buyer the credibility of the BES.

The BES timeline is another issue that merits discussion. This needs an in-depth analysis as to what the owner's perspective is on *her* timeline for exit and *when* she wants to exit. There are few factors to consider on the timing of exit:

1. **Ideal date for exit:** The ideal date cannot be defined with mathematical precision however, even if the owner finds it difficult to predict this important milestone, they must define a plausible date and then redefine it as the company matures and the dates can be adjusted periodically. The potential for mental or physical incapacitation of the owner/founder is real and must also be addressed – particularly at my age!
2. **Form of exit strategy**: The form of exit strategy chosen will define how long it will take to finalize the exit strategy. For example, a Merger and Acquisition will take longer as opposed to a legacy exit.
3. **Industry Indicators**: Watching the economy and the particular industry trend is also determinative about the timing of exit. It is obvious that when the industry trend is on a positive trajectory it will be more lucrative to prospective buyers and so are the economic trends. A classic example of this was 2020 when the economic downturn due to COVID impacted multiple businesses - both large and small- businesses were less appealing to prospective buyers. Also, consider impending changes in the tax laws and how they may affect both the timing and the form of the exit.
4. **Supply and Demand**: Supply and Demand with the market's appetite for mergers and acquisitions is a very important factor in BES. As an example, when the housing bubble tanked the economy, investors retreated. As the economy continues to recover, investor confidence has again risen. Thus it is crucial for owners to watch the economy. Entrepreneurs should take advantage of low supply and high demand market conditions.

The mindset of a prospective buyer also needs to be addressed for the owner/entrepreneur. Prospective new buyers are more inclined to purchase stable operating business with good fiscal governance and stable cash flows rather than unstable or unsustainable businesses. Thus, the owner entrepreneur must be cognizant of selling his business while it is trending up. The old saying hold up—try not to sell at the peak, but while the business is trending up.

Lastly a discussion on the lessons learned from the pandemic in 2020 on BES is warranted because businesses and individuals have been through much. Lessons include:

- **Prepare for an economic downturn or unforeseeable circumstances**: Very often owners and entrepreneurs are consumed in the day-day operations and growth of the business that they forgot to hit the pause button and look beyond what is immediately in their field of view. This requires the ability to look around the corner and have a backup plan for exigencies you may not appreciate in real time.

- **Cash reserves**: The old wisdom of having a six-month cushion of cash reserves is mandatory, but the pandemic has taught us that even a six-month cash reserve is not sufficient.
- **Succession planning**: During the pandemic most businesses did not have a solid BES and they were scrambling to survive. The media reported on tragic stories of small businesses with no succession planning that simply closed their doors.

Another important consideration is knowing when, if ever, to turn over the reins. In other words, when should the founder-CEO step aside? This came to the forefront last year when Twitter's founder/CEO Jack Dorsey stepped aside and handed over the reigns to Parag Agrawal, Twitter's CTO. Dorsey commented, "There's a lot of talk about the importance of a company being 'founder-led.' Ultimately, I believe that's severely limiting and a single point of failure...I believe it's critical a company can stand on its own, free of its founder's influence or direction."

In the book, The Hard Thing about Hard Things, Ben Horowitz opines founders are often more adapt at early-stage growth then later stage day to day management. Founders are often not suited for the day-to-day operational tempo and have little in common with the leadership traits necessary to start a business. I would concur with his assessment. I have learned over the years that I thrive in the early, start up stage of a business and tend to get bored managing the people and the processes of later stage ventures. Thus, I now start to groom my replacement after the first few years.

Mr. Horowitz and me aside there is evidence that founder as CEO led ventures fare better. A 2021 study [1] of founder/CEOs by Bradley Hendricks and Travis Howell uncovered that founder/CEO led public companies had an approximately 10% higher valuation at IPO; however, after three years this is reduced to zero and then goes negative past the three-year mark.

So where does that leave you? My advice, follow your gut and lose your ego. If the company is better managed by another CEO, step aside, join the board and start your next venture. If you are still excited to come to work every day and the P&Ls reflect that excitement, press on!

Business exits are an exciting, potentially lucrative, and life altering experience. Thus, you always want to enlist the aid of a financial professional whose insights and experiences will prove invaluable on matters such as the business valuation, projected cash flow, revenue streams, risk mitigation, and tax consequences.

Reference

1. Hendricks BE and Howell T. The Founder Premium Revisited (August 1, 2021). Available at SSRN: https://ssrn.com/abstract=3977112 or https://doi.org/10.2139/ssrn.3977112.

Chapter 14
The Why and How of Entrepreneurship Education in Healthcare Training

Owen Berg and Arlen Meyers

Becoming a healthcare professional is an arduous yet well understood and relatively linear process, whether one is pursuing nursing, pharmacy, physical therapy, dentistry, medicine, or another field within healthcare. In all cases, excellent grades in prerequisite coursework, applications to competitive professional schools, and years of professional school including both didactic education and clinical training are the norm. Being or becoming an entrepreneur is another thing entirely; there exists no single definition of entrepreneurship, and some argue that entrepreneurship itself cannot even be taught. In the following chapter, we discuss why entrepreneurship education in healthcare training is vital to the future of healthcare, broad trends in healthcare training that impact entrepreneurship, how entrepreneurship education is taught to current healthcare students, and suggested best practices for entrepreneurship education in healthcare training.

Beginning the Discussion: Defining Healthcare Entrepreneurship

There are many definitions of entrepreneurship. Some are narrow, like creating a company, while others are broader.

O. Berg (✉)
University of Colorado School of Medicine, Aurora, CO, USA
e-mail: Owen.Berg@cuanschutz.edu

A. Meyers
University of Colorado School of Medicine, Aurora, CO, USA

University of Colorado Denver Business School, Denver, CO, USA

President and CEO, Society of Physician Entrepreneurs (SoPE), Norwalk, CT, USA
e-mail: Arlen.Meyers@ucdenver.edu

© The Author(s), under exclusive license to Springer Nature Switzerland AG 2023   187
A. Meyers (ed.), *Digital Health Entrepreneurship*, Health Informatics,
https://doi.org/10.1007/978-3-031-33902-8_14

We define entrepreneurship as the pursuit of opportunity under VUCA (volatile, uncertain, complex, and ambiguous) conditions with the goal of creating and delivering user defined value by deploying innovation using a VAST (valid, automatic, scalable and time sensitive) business model to accomplish the quintuple aims of improving quality, reducing cost, affording equitable access, improving user and healthcare professional experience, and removing waste and unnecessary administrative work.

The pursuit of opportunity requires action and the knowledge, skills, abilities, and competencies necessary to deliver user or stakeholder defined value.

Innovation is something new or "something old done in a new way" that delivers multiples of value when compared to a competitive offering or the status quo.

While this standard definition of entrepreneurship applies to healthcare, it does not fully capture the relevant context. The pursuit of profit is undoubtedly a driver of many individuals, systems, and corporations within healthcare; other aims and goals motivate many of these parties as well. The quintuple aim, a framework that is widely adopted and recognized in the healthcare community, is a set of mutually inclusive common goals that provide a roadmap for healthcare outcomes and process improvement. The five quintuple aims are: (1) improving the patient and clinician experience, (2) improving patient and population outcomes, (3) lowering costs of care, (4) improving health equity and (5) reducing waste [1].

The objective of healthcare entrepreneurship education and training is to provide students with the knowledge, skills, abilities, and competencies to deliver the quintuple aims. Using our broader definition, healthcare entrepreneurship is not just about teaching students how to create companies, but, more broadly, how to create value through medical practice, technology, education, intrapreneurship, and social entrepreneurship as well.

The Argument for Entrepreneurship Education in Healthcare Training

Healthcare professional education and training is remarkably complex. "Fixing" healthcare or higher education in the United States are both wicked problems: a problem that is difficult or impossible to solve due to a host of factors including uniqueness, lack of clarity surrounding characterization or causation, complexity of components, number of interconnected components, relatedness to other problems, and lack of a "true" solution. However, improving specific aspects of higher education or healthcare are complex "sticky problems" that are solvable with the right team, process, and tools.

The healthcare sector is the US's largest employer, and accounts for 19.7% of our GDP as of 2020 [2]. When comparing the US healthcare system with 10 other high incomes countries such as France, Germany, Canada, United Kingdom, New Zealand, and Australia, the US healthcare system ranks last in terms of access to care, administrative efficiency, equity, and healthcare outcomes [3].

Change in the healthcare sector is occurring at an ever-increasing rate. As the market becomes more competitive, innovation is a necessity for employer survival. Parallel to this is a changing medical culture more open to innovation that furthers an organization's pursuit of the quintuple aim. Nearly infinite healthcare demand, finite healthcare supply, an emphasis on improved value of care from both the market and government, overworked healthcare professionals, a projected worsening workforce shortage, and societal demands of improved health equity are all major drivers of innovation towards the goal of providing better healthcare at greater value to more people in a faster and more efficient manner.

Furthermore, the relationships between provider and patient are fundamentally changing as wearables, access to information, and DIY medicine fundamentally alter these interactions, necessitating changes in healthcare delivery to better match current lifestyles and expectations of consumers.

A workforce with increasing technical skills, employees holding multiple positions or careers in a lifetime, healthcare professionals questioning their careers and status quo, and healthcare trainees demanding increased access to education in entrepreneurship are workforce drivers of entrepreneurship. This workforce has increased access to resources for education, entrepreneurship, and capital through the internet, globalization, and local innovation ecosystems, resulting in entrepreneurship being a stronger option than ever before.

Reasons for selecting an entrepreneurial career include pursuing the opportunities for large societal impact, improving health at the local, population, or global levels, changing educational delivery and efficacy, and eliminating environmental waste. Some individuals pursue entrepreneurship for happiness, creativity, autonomy, flexible schedule, or familial reasons. Others may be burned out, wish to change from practicing clinical medicine, which to socialize with patients less, or have a restricted ability to provide clinical medicine for disability or disciplinary reasons. Some want to acquire wealth or security. Others may choose entrepreneurship as a form of self-preservation so that they do not suffer the professional and economic consequences of innovation.

Healthcare trainees, by and large, are an exceptionally bright, motivated, problem-solving, and service oriented group of individuals who eventually have subject matter and domain expertise. As a group, they have the potential to produce many successful entrepreneurs.

The Darkside of Entrepreneurship and Entrepreneurship Education

Entrepreneurship education in healthcare training programs is not an easy, one-size fits all solution that will please all stakeholders. Entrepreneurs, administrators, and educators experience a variety of challenges.

Challenges in family and personal life include pressure and stress from increased responsibility, a demanding work schedule, a lack of time for family, loneliness, and business and financial uncertainty. Business and financial challenges include financial insecurity, legal and financial risk and responsibility for self and others, high operational costs, and potentially unfriendly or hostile environments, policies, and laws locally, nationally or within their institutional ecosystems [4].

Students encounter time constraints within their program, negative attitudes towards innovation or entrepreneurship within their learning environment, pressure or motivation to focus on the test or project at hand, and a lack of resources or knowledge of resources that may make learning, training, and practicing entrepreneurship difficult [5, 6].

The barriers to medical education reform include declining revenues from research grants, clinical reimbursement, and state support (largely due to the Covid-19 pandemic) that limit many institution's resources and/or willingness to allocate resources towards reform. Factors within key stakeholders, departments, and populations such as burnout, stress, mental health, lack of diversity, poor leadership, and fixed mindsets can both necessitate and inhibit change. Fixed mindsets such as a sole/primary focus of graduate programs on publications, grants, and research, an overreliance on the Flexner model of medical education started in 1910 rather than the updated model of integration, and widespread prevalence of outdated sickcare business models are pertinent examples. The challenge of meeting accreditation requirements, teaching to the test, following evidence-based practices, and incorporating cutting edge knowledge or techniques all within a socio-politically complex and logistically challenging environment is no easy task. And after these challenges have been addressed, the difficulty of finding appropriate faculty for encouraging innovation within medical education and teaching entrepreneurship remain [7].

On the individual or organizational level, counterintuitive yet solid advice would be to "embrace the dark side" of entrepreneurship. There are challenges associated with entrepreneurship and entrepreneurship education. Making the best decision individually or organizationally is important. Knowing and accepting these challenges is a vital part of that decision making process. Identifying these challenges, assessing the risk, creating a strategy or plan, and proceeding forward after acknowledging these risks may limit unexpected future trouble and be of help in the process itself.

The skills needed to overcome these challenges are both relevant and inclusive with skills a person, team, or organization might need to succeed in education, medicine, entrepreneurship, and leadership that they likely, at least in part, already exemplify. Strategic thinking and planning, risk assessment, calculated risk-taking, diversification of talent and advisors, collaboration, outsourcing, managing time, utilizing a strengths-based approach, and personally or organizationally developing values, a sustainable approach, and boundaries/policies are pertinent mechanisms for doing this [4].

Broad Trends in Healthcare Training and their Impact on Healthcare Training

Trends in healthcare education and training regarding pedagogy, clinical training, student wellness, and equity provide insights into the opportunities for improvement.

Didactic Education: How Programs Are Teaching and How Students Are Learning

Educational practices at the university and college level are continually evolving to improve the delivery of education, reduce costs for students and institution alike, increase one's ranking in the pecking order, attract the best and brightest students, and ultimately accelerate and increase profits.

The quantity of medical science information that is taught to students is increasing in depth and scope. In addition, many programs are increasing their focus on social skills, social sciences, leadership and entrepreneurship, community service, student participation in research, relevant social and political topics, data and technology literacy, and the organization and financing of our healthcare systems. Because many students have interest in fields adjacent to healthcare, masters and doctoral level programs are offering students the opportunity for dual degrees, most commonly an MPH, MBA, PhD, or JD.

Programs are opting for less class time and optional class attendance. Many lectures are recorded and shared online for asynchronous viewing. Programs are prioritizing cased based learning, small group learning sessions, practice questions, and discussion over traditional lectures.

Advancements in electronic learning management systems and video recording, sharing, and streaming software has allowed for flexible attendance policies, online classes, more efficient studying, and collaborative lessons presented by lecturers in different locations. Massive open online courses (MOOCS) designed by the academies themselves or third parties are more commonly used.

This is by no means a new trend, but a simple look in a lecture hall may shock some: vastly more students are using tablets and laptops for note taking and studying than are using paper notes, textbooks, or notecards, which are becoming more obsolete by the day. Electronic note taking apps, opensource flashcard apps, online messaging board and forums, cloud storage platforms for organizing, sharing, and editing documents, and digital anatomy labs and resources instead of cadavers are major tools used by students.

A host of products that offer a combination of question banks, practice exams, online lecture series, overviews of difficult or commonly tested topics, study plan creation, and flashcards are abundant and widely regarded by students as some of the best primary or supplementary study tools for coursework and licensing exams.

Clinical Training: The Evolution of the Pre-Clinical and Clinical Trainee

With such a vast amount of information available and applicable to clinical practice, having the ability to efficiently access and interpret needed information on command is invaluable; many apps and websites are available to professionals inquiring about just about every clinically relevant topic imaginable. As the quantity of information continues to increase and the tools used to access and apply this information continue to improve, the difference between the caliber of care given by a healthcare worker may become less based upon knowledge and intellect and more on social skills, ability to perform specific procedures or tasks, and the application and clear explanation of information relevant to the patient.

As expectations shift to become slightly less about memorizing information and much more about accessing and applying it, some programs have, and more programs will, start to place greater emphasis on clinical training rather than pre-clinical didactic lectures.

Simulated patients are trained and knowledgeable paid actors that serve as a teacher and guide in the clinical education process. They give students another way to practice communication and clinical based skills. This is a widely used training method that will continue to provide value.

Digital simulations replicate a variety of surgeries, procedures, patient body types, and common anatomical variation. They increase access and flexibility for trainees and minimize potential risks to patients. As simulations improve, they will provide more value and be more widely used.

Student Wellness and Equity: Appropriate Trainee Treatment Improves Public Health

Graduate students, healthcare professionals, and healthcare trainees suffer from poor mental health. Graduate student suicide and depression, understaffed and underappreciated nursing staffs, resident physicians working long hours, and pharmacists taking an ever-expanding stressful healthcare role during covid-19 are pertinent examples.

Worry about academic performance, student loans, inadequate mental health support, high expectations in a highly stressful and competitive environment, long working and studying hours, and a culture that rewards and praises immense sacrifice are responsible for these observed effects. Many programs offer counseling, tutoring, and learning modules regarding wellness to their students, though the systematic factors that cause illness and burnout are in large part unaddressed. Wellness among trainees is a public health issue, among other things. Unwell and overworked healthcare professionals make mistakes, hurt and kill patients, and provide poorer quality care.

Advancements in equity in admissions have been driven by holistic application viewing, nondiscrimination and affirmative action practices, and a greater emphasis on the value of diversity. Yet, a horrifying number of medical students report harassment, discrimination, or inappropriate behavior by educators or classmates and the makeup of students in training programs does not accurately reflect the makeup of the general public [8, 9]. This is a public health issue, among others things, as certain groups tend to receive worse care than others and data suggests that people may receive better treatment from providers that look like them [10–12].

The Lay of the Land: A Snapshot of Entrepreneurship Education in Healthcare Training

Many universities and colleges offering healthcare training programs have fruitful relationships with local business, wealthy philanthropists, and shared resources within their institution. The result is that incubators, accelerators, hack-a-thons, pitch competitions, local mentors, and health specific and non-specific innovation labs and coworking spaces are available and helpful.

In addition, dual degree programs, professional development, social skills training, and other courses, certificates, trainings, continuing education units (CEU), and local organizations focused on development of leadership, communication, business, intrapreneurial, and entrepreneurial skills are available. These reach many people and teach many transferable skills and knowledge that apply to entrepreneurship.

Entrepreneurship Education in STEM Training

Graduate STEM students face a difficult job market and reducing available tenure track positions in academia, so many intend to pursue a career in business or industry [13]. Despite these desires, students perceive many barriers associated with entrepreneurship training: lack of time for additional training outside of their program of focus, higher motivation to focus on tasks that allow them to finish their research and degree, a culture in their lab of insulation from other departments and opportunities, and working in labs that may discourage or be indifferent towards entrepreneurship [5]. Outside of biomedical engineering labs which seem to encourage entrepreneurship more than any other STEM field, healthcare related biological sciences lab such as those in biochemistry, cellular/molecular biology, microbiology, immunology, neuroscience, and genetics have the least encouraging and most discouraging attitudes towards entrepreneurship [6].

National initiatives, often working in tandem with universities, have contributed significantly to entrepreneurship education in STEM. Examples include the National

Science Foundation Innovation Corps (ICorps) program and the Kern Entrepreneurial Engineering Network (KEEN) [14]. Most notably, Icorps, through 2020, has trained more than 5800 innovators and 1900 teams of 3 from 1280 universities, colleges, and other institutions. Half of these teams launched startups that cumulatively raised over $760 million in funding [15].

201 articles were analyzed in a systematic review of entrepreneurship education in STEM in 2021 [14]. 81% of the articles focused on programs for undergraduate students, and only 5.5% and 10.4% focused on graduate students and faculty, respectively. 93.5% of the articles focused on entrepreneurship education in engineering, while only 5% were focused on programs in science. The most common learning objectives, from most to least common, included concepts related to entrepreneurial mindset, teamwork, communication, creativity, value, curiosity, customer-related objectives (i.e., customer discovery and understanding customer needs), and connections (creating, maintaining, utilizing). Pedagogical components consisted of active learning approaches, team-based and project-based learning with a client/customer stakeholder from the community or university, and engineering design.

Elements "outside the classroom" were described in a minority of studies. The most common of these were competitions or challenges focusing on engineering design or creation of a venture. Others included the creation of student clubs or groups with an entrepreneurship focus, creation or use of MOOCs, and faculty development workshops focused on successful implementation of entrepreneurial learning objectives within their course.

43% of the studies utilized KEEN's framework for conceptualizing entrepreneurial mindset, multiple programs used a set of online learning modules developed by KEEN, and KEEN funded 41% of the studies included, though it did appear that many programs described their program with KEEN's framework, rather than courses being entirely driven or developed by KEEN [14].

Widespread shortcoming among studies in the field were: failure to include definitions of the outcomes being measured, limited connection and reference to helpful literature from other fields (such as cognitive neuroscience, social sciences, business, and pedagogy), and limited use of validated assessment instruments (many of which were designed by program faculty). Other limitations included a lack of connection between course learning outcomes, activities performed in class, and assessment measures. Information regarding inclusion, diversity, and demographic information of class participants was severely lacking [14].

Entrepreneurship Education in Pharmacy Training

Applications to Pharmacy schools are decreasing, as programs struggle to ensure graduates obtain conventional roles as pharmacists [16]. Conventional roles as pharmacists are decreasing and in danger as well, as automation promises to do some of a pharmacist's tasks in much less time. Pharmacy education has been tasked with addressing these challenges by improving leadership, addressing shortcomings of syllabi, increasing relevance of pharmacy education, redefining and expanding the roles and knowledge, skills, and attitudes (KSAs) of pharmacists, and instilling a versatile skillset helpful for new challenges in an ever-evolving landscape for both faculty and graduates of their program [17]. Entrepreneurship education is a clear solution.

A systematic review of 27 articles in 2019 described the most commonly identified roles of a pharmacist entrepreneur: innovation, developing and promoting/marketing a service, solving a problem, and benefiting society. Entrepreneurship education in pharmacy training commonly emphasized innovation, included active application of class material, taught basic managerial/operational skills, and focused on problem solving. The most frequently identified KSAs were risk-taking, creativity/innovation, self-starter, proactivity, management, communication, and strategic planning [18].

A follow up of this systematic review consisted of a 29-person expert panel discussing findings and coming to agreement on their meaning. The highest ranked KSAs included communication, business plan development, health system literacy, problem solving, networking, leadership, and strategic principles. Lower in importance but included were a host of specific management and strategic skills and knowledge such as laws and regulations, market analysis, project management, finance, accounting, sales & marketing, human resource management, risk assessment, and managing people [19].

Panelists ranked a mix of didactic and experiential learning as their favored teaching method. The importance of didactic education was stressed for learning foundational knowledge. The panel highlighted active and experiential based methods of teaching such as structured exercises, team-based projects, and competitions as methods of teaching to be used in combination with a didactic approach [19].

No coherent definition or framework for pharmacist entrepreneurship was found in the initial systematic analysis, so the panel constructed a lengthy framework for a pharmacist entrepreneur as one that "identifies, creates, and pursues new opportunities; successfully implements new ideas into practice; is willing to take risks; fills unmet needs; creates new value through innovation; is responsive to change; makes sacrifices; includes social and intrapreneurship; leverages existing knowledge, skills, and resources; goes beyond traditional roles for pharmacists; and improves patient care" [19].

In general, there was a lack of substantial data regarding specific courses in terms of pedagogical approaches, learning objectives or outcome KSAs, demographic information, and assessment measurements.

Entrepreneurship Education in Nursing Training

Most of the research of nursing entrepreneurship focuses on nurse entrepreneurs themselves. Various studies interrogate their characteristics, motivation, roles within healthcare and academia, self-care practices, experience in advanced nursing practices, development of their private practices, perceptions of a definition of nursing entrepreneurship, perceived barriers to entrepreneurship, and the role conflict experienced as a nurse entrepreneur [20].

A literature review focused on the troubling concept of rebel leadership, that highlights not only the need for innovation within healthcare, but lack of representation that nurses have in healthcare innovation and leadership. Nurse rebel leadership occurs when supervisors, regulation, and organizational policy limit a nurse's ability to provide care, and in response a nurse deviates from these rules and supervision to provide improved care [21].

Very few entrepreneurship education resources exist for nursing trainees despite research highlighting perceived educational gaps in nursing leadership skillsets ranging from cognitive to interpersonal to business to self-regulation domains, despite research claiming a need for enhanced marketing, negotiation, and conflict resolution skills to be taught in nursing training, and despite nurses being natural innovators who have a unique understanding of solutions and problems in healthcare delivery due to their close working proximity to patients [22, 23].

Arizona State University offers a PhD focused on nursing and healthcare innovation. University of Minnesota and Arizona State University offer a Doctor of Nursing Practice (DNP) in innovation leadership and University of Pennsylvania offers a DNP in Executive Leadership. The Ohio State University, University of Connecticut, and Arizona State University offer a Master of Healthcare Innovation. Drexel University offers a Master of Science in Nursing in innovation and intra/entrepreneurship in advanced practice nursing. NYU offers a social entrepreneurship course, other universities like Clemson University and Drexel University offer certificates, and many programs offer one or multiple courses without offering a certificate or degree [24, 25]. Particularly successful hack-a-thons are available to nursing trainees, specifically the international twice yearly virtually held NurseHack4Health and the in-person, nurse-only annual hack-a-thon started in 2016 at Northeastern University [26].

No systematic review appraises all or most of these programs. A single systematic review from 2014 analyzes 4 programs, one of which is from the University of Ulster in Ireland. A synthesis of the 2014 systematic review and other recent studies found the expected results: that a variety of programs exist that differ in learning objectives, measured outcomes, and educational approaches [24]. Common themes for learning objectives mirror those in found other healthcare training programs. A focus on active learning approaches and application of theoretical knowledge mirror other findings from other fields. Like in other fields, no precise shared definition of nursing entrepreneurship exists.

Entrepreneurship Education in Public Health Training

The Council on Public Health Education (CEPH), an accreditation agency, made changes to their standards in 2016. These changes included implementing competency based skill training and a focus on developing actionable collaborative sustainable solutions to the well characterized social determinants of health [27, 28]. These changes in accreditation, as well as the increasing need for entrepreneurship in public health, are driven by a prevalence of underinsured and uninsured, changes in healthcare delivery, increased risk of environmental threats and resurgent and emergent infectious disease risk, and shifts in sociodemographic and socioeconomic characteristics of the population [29].

Public health entrepreneurship is an excellent method to improve social determinants of health and address health disparities, with potential impacts in the fields of education, social services, environmental services, fitness, nutrition, holistic health, recreation, tourism, transportation, organizational consulting, urban planning, communications, and more [30, 31]. Furthermore, a sample of public health students widely held the opinion that research must be accompanied by action and that entrepreneurship provides a pathway that gives them a unique skillset to act. Expansion of entrepreneurship education in public health training has been called for [27].

University of North Carolina offers a minor in entrepreneurship with a public health track and a certificate from the Management Academy for public health students [32]. Yale University School of Public Health offers the InnovateHealth program [33]. Harvard University offers a Social Entrepreneurship in Health and the Environment course and an Innovation and Entrepreneurship in Health Care course. The University of Texas offers a Technology, Entrepreneurship, and Applied Innovation in Public Health course [27]. DePaul University offers entrepreneurship education integrated into two public health courses, Public Health Administration and Preparation for Public Health Practice [30].

96 articles were analyzed via a scoping literature review using thematic analysis to create a common framework for characterizing entrepreneurship and intrapreneurship in public health. The components of the framework were design thinking, resource mobilization, financial viability, cross-disciplinary, and systems strengthening [34]. This framework was used to launch a Public Health Entrepreneurship and Intrapreneurship course at Yale University that received an overall rating of 4.3/5 by 55 students. Details regarding this course were not found.

The successful InnovateHealth program at Yale offers programming, mentoring, and venture support to students. As of 2021, over 200 students were coached, over 40 start-ups doing work in 22 countries were funded, over $300,000 in startup funding was awarded, and supported startups received over $10 million in future funding [35]. Specific information regarding pedagogy, services offered, learning objectives, and measures was not found.

The well characterized Management Academy at University of North Carolina has also shown great success. The program ran from 1999–2009 with funding from the CDC. The program trained over 231 teams of 3–6 people from 13 states [36]. From 2000–2002, the program used $2 million to train 490 people comprising 119 teams that generated $6 million in revenue. Almost 40% of the teams expected to generate additional future revenue from the business plan (or a modified version) developed in the course [32]. The program has been replicated in a collaborative effort between the South Carolina Department of Health and Environmental Control and University of South Carolina to great effect [37].

The Management Academy is a 3-phase program lasting approximately 9 months. It includes a 5-day in-person launch, a 3-day in-person session during the course, a final in-person session to end the course that includes business presentations, and 9 months of remote learning. Topics covered include personnel management, business planning, human resources, financial management, civic entrepreneurship, marketing, business communication, partnerships and negotiations, implementation, and team building. Classes use a mix of presentations, case studies, small group exercises, assigned readings, and group discussion. Other core components include extensive evaluation at the beginning of the course followed by a development plan, personal development goals, action steps, and outcome measurements. Teams consist of 3–6 people; a team must include a person from governmental public health and students are encouraged to include community partners and individuals from local public health agencies and organizations. A clearly defined and multi-faceted approach assessing both individual and program outcomes using both internal resources and external agencies was used [38].

Key factors for the program's success were state employed team members and contacts, relevant curriculum, business plan assignment, comprehensive needs assessment for both students and the program, team-based model, active learning, and focus on a combination of abstract concepts and concrete skills [38].

Entrepreneurship education in Public Health training lacks a substantial body of research. Relatively few programs with little research made identifying national trends difficult. Yet, stakeholders clearly view entrepreneurship education in public health training as crucial. Multiple programs exist, with the Management Academy at University of North Carolina being an exceptionally well documented and successful program.

Entrepreneurship Education in Dentistry Training

Substantial peer reviewed research called for increased and improved entrepreneurship education in dentistry. A systematic review of dental student's preparedness to practice identified clinical entrepreneurship and financial solvency skills, communication and interpersonal skills, and social and community orientation as 3 of 6 domains essential for dental student preparedness [39]. Drivers of the need for dentist entrepreneurship specific to dentistry include the number of private practices declining, a decline in private practice profit largely due to decreasing insurance reimbursements relative to overhead costs, and the potential opportunities presented by mobile dental care [40].

No studies focusing on characterizing entrepreneurship courses or programs were found. Only articles highlighting the need for it were available. "True" entrepreneurship was rarely discussed, as most authors solely alluded to dental practice management and associated curricula (PMC) in their discussion of entrepreneurship.

One 2020 study examining recent innovations within PMC from 23 US dental schools is quite relevant to this discussion, due to the similarities between PMC and

BEET and the generalizability and transferability of principles and skills taught in PMC [7]. From 2013 to 2018 dental school graduates' self-assessed preparedness for practice administration rose from 49.5% to 62.5%. This study looked at changes within PMC curricula within that time [7].

All 23 schools had changed their PMC within the last 5 years. Common changes were updating subject matter (100%), enhancing instructional methods (65.2%), and including more technology (52.2%). Regarding instructional methods, 95.7% of courses used a lecture-based format. Many used cased based learning, simulations and video learning labs, and group discussion. Implementation of simulations, video learning labs, and MOOCS were the most common changes when new technology was adopted [7].

Moving forward, respondents endorsed personnel management, marketing, and business plan development as areas for improvement within their curricula. Student interest in practice management was the top motivation for PMC change or expansion, followed by changing accreditation standards and faculty/administration goals. Programs endorsed difficulty finding the faculty with the necessary experience to teach and difficulty finding time in the curriculum to include necessary practice management material [7].

Many other courses with overlapping material in behavioral sciences, ethics, communication, law, finance, and professionalism were offered by the 64 schools that were sent inquiries about their PMC [7]. Other resources identified included student led organizations (SBDO at University of Florida, DICE at University of Pennsylvania), consulting centers offered by dentistry programs (PACE Center at UTHealth Houston), and an entire department of Molecular Pathobiology Innovation and Entrepreneurship at NYU.

Entrepreneurship Education in Occupational Therapy Training

An abundance of researchers and influential leaders in the field recognize that increasing entrepreneurship education would benefit occupational therapist training programs for a variety of general and profession specific reasons. Reasons include increased power and recognition of the profession, the need to meet current market demands, the need to achieve the triple aim, the importance of leadership and business skills for graduates, interdisciplinary opportunities regarding technology, the need to develop hard and soft skills, and recent developments in healthcare delivery [41, 42].

A review of literature found limited research and limited evidence of entrepreneurship being taught to occupational therapist trainees. Of the top 10 programs in the US, a review of their curricula found that only two specifically and explicitly taught entrepreneurship related content and three more taught fundamentals of business that touched on entrepreneurial content [42]. Thomas Jefferson University had the strongest innovation and entrepreneurship curriculum, offering the "Advanced Practice Certificate: Using Design in Healthcare Delivery" certificate and a course where students apply an entrepreneurial framework to nontraditional practice settings [42].

9 educational offerings were identified and reviewed. Topics discussed, with the number of programs discussing each topic in parentheses, included the role of the occupational therapy entrepreneur (6), creation of a business plan (6), potential business models and implications for financing (5), marketing (5), identifying the need for your business (3) starting a home modifications business or private practice (3), product development and design principles and the occupation therapist's role on a design team (2) social entrepreneurship (2), the entrepreneurial mindset (2), history of innovation and entrepreneurship in occupational therapy (1), emerging areas of practice (1), and describing your value proposition (1) [42].

Of all the entrepreneurship educational offerings discussed, only 1 offered documentation for the effectiveness of their program by using a self-developed assessment. This offering was not a course, certificate, or degree, but rather an 8-week learning activity between graduate occupational therapy students and undergraduate management students developing a business plan for a new service to meet an unmet healthcare need [42].

Entrepreneurship Education in Physician Training

A recent 2021 review consisting of a comprehensive search for entrepreneurship programs at American and Canadian allopathic medical schools identified 28 programs from 26 schools. All were taught by faculty with experience in both medicine and business, entrepreneurship, or engineering, and all programs heavily emphasized mentorship and networking. The programs varied significantly. Most programs (75%) used a selection application process. Program length ranged from a five-year (7%) or four-year program (54%) to a one-year course (18%) and a one-week concentration (3.5%), with 36% of programs including a summer component [43].

Guest lecturers (7%) and regular team or individual progress meetings (7%) were implemented rarely and may highlight an area of growth within the field. 27 of the 28 programs used formal lectures/seminars and 25 of the 28 used either problem based or team-based learning. 46% of the programs included simulated workshop experiences where students actively applied skills. Topics taught were business-oriented topics (71%), design and prototyping (68%), and regulation and patent law (36%). 79% of programs used a capstone project as an evaluative metric and only 50% of programs used more than one evaluative metric [43].

A thematic analysis from a similar review of entrepreneurship education programs at allopathic medical schools conducted in 2017 found that innovation, entrepreneurship, technology, leadership, healthcare systems, business of medicine, and enhanced adaptability were themes covered by the majority of programs. Active learning and interdisciplinary teaching were utilized by most of the programs to deliver content [44].

Like in other reviews interrogating entrepreneurship education in other healthcare training fields, the need for improved reporting and study of the curricular design, successes, challenges, demographic data, and outcomes of educational programs, courses, and projects was emphasized [43–45]. An evidence-based guide for effective and high-quality reporting of metrics and markers of innovation within medical education curricula was proposed as a solution [45, 46].

A Note on Entrepreneurship Education in Other Healthcare Training Programs

Information relating entrepreneurship education to Physician Associate/Assistant (PA) training focuses on the expanding and changing role of the PA in practice, innovation within PA educational and training practices, and PAs in private practice. No information regarding specific entrepreneurship education concepts, courses, measures, etc. within PA training programs was found.

Information and resources relating entrepreneurship education to Physical Therapy training highlights the many existing resources for practicing professionals desiring to start or run their private practice or take advantage of the "fitness boom" through coaching, media, marketing, and branding. Some evidence highlights newly practicing physical therapists having a lack of relevant technological and business managerial skills. There are minimal calls to enhance entrepreneurship education within physical therapy curricula, though there are calls to improve knowledge translation into practice across the field and better develop graduates able to meet societal needs. No information regarding specific entrepreneurship education concepts, courses, measures, etc. within PT training programs was found.

Summary and Synthesis

We define entrepreneurship as the pursuit of opportunity under VUCA conditions with the goal of creating and delivering user defined value by deploying innovation using a VAST business model to accomplish the quintuple aims of improving quality, reducing cost, affording equitable access, improving user and healthcare professional experience, and removing waste and unnecessary administrative work. Healthcare entrepreneurship teaches students how to create companies, and more broadly, how to create value through medical practice, technology, education, intrapreneurship, and social entrepreneurship.

There are a host of large scale and individual level positive (opportunity) and negative (avoiding consequence) drivers of healthcare entrepreneurship and BEET programs. Entrepreneurship is, by its very nature, a versatile life school. Entrepreneurship education in healthcare training can improve healthcare professionals, employers, consumers, hospitals, and the US economy.

There are many challenges to implementing entrepreneurship education within a healthcare training program. The challenges are related to finances, faculty, institutional characteristics, logistics, time, and students/trainees. Table 14.1, in the appendix, details common challenges that may be experienced while implementing entrepreneurship education into healthcare training curricula.

Large variety can be found in course structures, pedagogical techniques, and the trainee population. Other factors such as university support, access to local innovation ecosystems, and characteristics of specific educators and administrators greatly impact a program. Table 14.2, in the appendix, summarizes common curricular elements found in entrepreneurship education and highlights useful curricular considerations. Table 14.3, also in the appendix, summarizes common outcome KSAs.

The validity and methodology of assessing outcomes varies widely amongst programs. As there is no consensus on measures used to measure short term or long-term value of these programs and peer reviewed literature on BEET programs is minimal, the value of these programs as currently deployed is relatively unknown and certainly questionable. Table 14.4, in the appendix, summarizes the weaknesses in the body of research for entrepreneurship education in health training programs. Table 14.5, in the appendix, lists suggestions for both teaching entrepreneurship in healthcare training and for publication/reporting of results. Table 14.6, in the appendix, lists recommended resources for learning about entrepreneurship education in healthcare training programs.

Appendix

Table 14.1 Challenges to implementing entrepreneurship education in healthcare training programs

Challenges to implementing entrepreneurship education	
Financial	– Money needed for new courses/programs and faculty – Will a program/course be financially lucrative?
Faculty	– Difficulty finding appropriate faculty to teach – Busy, stressed, disinterested, burnt-out faculty
Characteristics of Institution	– Lack of money & declining revenues – General lack of resources (person-hours, non-collaborative environment, few departments, or professionals able to help) – Socio-politically complex environments can challenge change – Lack of support from key stakeholders – Presence of "outdated/fixed" mindsets – Focus on "teaching to the test" or accreditation criteria – Institutional unwillingness to take risks – Lack of awareness of importance and potential of entrepreneurship education
Logistical	– Implementing changes in a complex system is challenging!
Time	– Building new program/course takes time and effort – Hiring new faculty takes time and effort – Time needed to adequately build, maintain, change, and then assess program/course – "Not enough time in curriculum" to create or integrate new course/content
Students/trainees	– Students needed to take the course/program – Students motivated to focus on degree – Students unwilling to "do extra work"

Table 14.2 Common curricular elements and important curricular considerations

	Common curricular elements	Curricular considerations
Structure of Course	– Structure of course influenced by needs, resources, and constraints of institution, curricula, and students – Lectures and teaching of foundational knowledge generally occurs during pre-clinical years and/or beginning of course – Application of knowledge and final projects generally occurs during clinical years and/or end of course	– Graded vs pass/fail – In-person vs hybrid vs online – Frequency of interaction – Length of course – Summer component – Immersion experience

Pedagogy	– Combination of didactic and experiential learning
	– Active learning methods
	– Learning in teams
	– Community involvement
	  – Community experts as part of team
	  – Working for a client in community
	  – Hack-a-thons
	  – Conferences
	  – Submissions to pitch competitions
	  – Guest lecturers
	– Technology (MOOCs, simulations, online games)
		– Which active learning methods to employ?
		  – Case based
		  – Problem based
		  – Project based
		  – Business plan
		  – Simulations
		  – Discussion
		  – Engineering
		– How will teams be implemented?
		– What degree of community involvement?
		– Which technologies will help the course?

Assessment of Students	– Final Project
	  – Creation of venture
	  – Engineering design
	  – Business plan competition
		– How will skills and competencies be evaluated?
		  – Participation
		  – Written exams
		  – Final project
		  – Self-assessments
		  – Assessed by client
		  – Assessed by team
		– When will assessments occur?

Table 14.3 Knowledge, skills, and aptitudes (KSAs) frequently taught in entrepreneurship courses/programs

Frequently taught knowledge, skills, and aptitudes (KSAs)	
Definitional	– Definition of entrepreneur and entrepreneurship – Role of entrepreneur – Entrepreneurial mindset – Innovation, creativity – Adaptability, resiliency
Thinking Skills	– Problem solving – Strategic thinking
Social Related Skills	– Teamwork – Communication – Networking – Presenting
Systems	– Regulation & patent law – Healthcare systems & business of healthcare
Engineering	– Engineering Design – Prototyping
Leadership	– Leadership Principles – Personnel management – Partnerships & negotiation – Operational management
Business Skills	– Identifying need for business & value proposition – Customer discovery and retention – Business plan development – Business models – Human resource management – Finance & accounting – Risk Assessment – Sales & Marketing

Table 14.4 Weaknesses in body of research for entrepreneurship education in health training programs

Weaknesses in body of research
– Many calls to action but few programs/courses
– Lack of consensus on definition of entrepreneurship
– Lack of consensus on framework for discussing, teaching, evaluating
– Lack of short term and long-term outcome measurements for students
– Lack of short term and long-term outcome measurements for programs
– Limited use of validated and/or widely used assessment measures
– General failure to include definitions and operationalization of outcomes measured
– Lack of connection between desired learning outcomes, activities performed in class, and assessment measures
– Limited connection and reference to helpful literature from other fields
– Limited descriptions of activities performed in class
– Limited data on demographic information of class participants
– Lack of focus on inclusion and diversity
– Heavy focus on private practice application of entrepreneurship

Table 14.5 Recommendations for teaching and reporting entrepreneurship education courses

Recommendations for entrepreneurship education	
Course Recommendations	– Structure course timeline and rigor around curricular considerations and student availability – Employ active learning – Employ team-based learning – Apply foundational and theoretical knowledge – Consider MOOCs, online games, and common tools/concepts (business model canvas, Lean, VAST, etc.) – Incorporate final project – Consider KSAs from Table 14.3 – Collect feedback from participants and other stakeholders to iteratively improve course
Data Recording/Reporting Recommendations	– Collect demographic data on participants – Evaluate participants and program before, during, after course via survey, final project, and/or assessment – Collect long term data on funding, ventures established, entrepreneurial mindset, career direction, etc. if possible – Use validated and/or widely used measures when possible – Connect operationalized learning outcomes to class activities and assessment – Describe learning activities performed in course – Report data even if not publishing in a journal – Consider course/participant evaluation methods from Management Academy from UNC https://doi.org/10.1097/00124784-200609000-00006 – Consider reporting data according to guidelines from https://doi.org/10.1017/cem.2017.28

Table 14.6 Suggestions for further reading

Further Reading	
The Management Academy for Public Health at University of North Carolina	From the *Journal of Public Health Management and Practice* (JPHMP) Special Issue: Management Academy for Public Health Volume 12, Number 5 https://sph.unc.edu/nciph/maph-jphmp/
2021 Systematic Review regarding STEM	Zappe, S. E., Cutler, S. L., & Gase, L. (2021). A Systematic Review of the Impacts of Entrepreneurial Support Programs in Science, Technology, Engineering, and Math Fields. Entrepreneurship Education and Pedagogy. https://doi.org/10.1177/25151274211040422
2019 Systematic Review and Delphi Process regarding Pharmacy	Mattingly, T. J., 2nd, Mullins, C. D., Melendez, D. R., Boyden, K., & Eddington, N. D. (2019). A Systematic Review of entrepreneurship in Pharmacy Practice and Education. *American journal of pharmaceutical education, 83*(3), 7233. https://doi.org/10.5688/ajpe7233 Mattingly, T. J., 2nd, Abdelwadoud, M., Mullins, C. D., & Eddington, N. D. (2019). Pharmapreneur—Defining a Framework for Entrepreneurship in Pharmacy Education. *American journal of pharmaceutical education, 83*(10), 7548. https://doi.org/10.5688/ajpe7548

(continued)

Table 14.6 (continued)

Further Reading	
2017 and 2021 Reviews regarding Medicine	Arias, J., Scott, K. W., Zaldivar, J. R., Trumbull, D. A., Sharma, B., Allen, K., & Gravenstein, N. (2021). Innovation-Oriented Medical School Curricula: Review of the Literature. *Cureus, 13*(10), e18498. https://doi.org/10.7759/cureus.18498 Niccum, B. A., Sarker, A., Wolf, S. J., & Trowbridge, M. J. (2017). Innovation and entrepreneurship programs in US medical education: a landscape review and thematic analysis. *Medical education online, 22*(1), 1,360,722. https://doi.org/10.1080/10872981.2017.1360722
Guidelines for scholarly dissemination of innovative medical education	Hall, A., Hagel, C., Chan, T., Thoma, B., Murnaghan, A., & Bhanji, F. (2018). The writer's guide to education scholarship in emergency medicine: Education innovations (part 3). *CJEM, 20*(3), 463–470. https://doi.org/10.1017/cem.2017.28
Kern Entrepreneurial Engineering Network (KEEN)	https://engineeringunleashed.com/what-is-keen
National Science Foundation's (NSF) Innovation Corps (I-Corps)	https://beta.nsf.gov/funding/initiatives/i-corps
Massachusetts Institute of Technology's (MIT) Hacking Medicine	https://hackingmedicine.mit.edu/
NurseHack4Health	https://nursehack4health.org/
Arlen Meyers, MD, MBA	What entrepreneurship can do to benefit medicine: https://www.linkedin.com/pulse/why-physician-entrepreneurship-arlen-meyers-md-mba/?trk=read_related_article-card_title Trends in medical school innovation and entrepreneurship education: https://www.linkedin.com/pulse/trends-medical-school-innovation-entrepreneurship-meyers-md-mba/ Education business model canvas for designing curriculum: https://www.linkedin.com/pulse/education-business-model-canvas-arlen-meyers-md-mba/ Lessons Learned from teaching entrepreneurship: https://www.linkedin.com/pulse/lessons-learned-teaching-entrepreneurship-1st-year-meyers-md-mba/ Why medical entrepreneurship: https://www.linkedin.com/pulse/why-physician-entrepreneurship-arlen-meyers-md-mba/?trk=read_related_article-card_title What is in the way of medical education reform: https://www.linkedin.com/pulse/what-getting-way-medical-education-reform-arlen-meyers-md-mba/?trackingId=f7vK1PlTRMyCZvp%2BTldHvQ%3D%3D

References

1. Nundy S, Cooper LA, Mate KS. The quintuple aim for health care improvement: a new imperative to advance health equity. JAMA. 2022;327(6):521–2.
2. NHE Fact Sheet | CMS cms.gov: Centers for Medicare & Medicaid Services; 2022 [Available from: https://www.cms.gov/Research-Statistics-Data-and-Systems/Statistics-Trends-and-Reports/NationalHealthExpendData/NHE-Fact-Sheet].
3. Schneider E. Mirror, Mirror 2021: Reflecting Poorly | Commonwealth Fund commonwealthfund.org: Commonwealth Fund; 2021 [Available from: https://www.commonwealthfund.org/publications/fund-reports/2021/aug/mirror-mirror-2021-reflecting-poorly].
4. Ziemianski P, Golik J. Including the dark side of entrepreneurship in the entrepreneurship education. Educ Sci. 2020;10(8):211.
5. Wheadon M, Duval-Couetil N. Student perspectives on developing more relevant Ph.D. Programs in STEM Disciplines through Professional Skills Training. ASEE Annual Conference & Exposition; 2014.
6. Mars MM, Bresonis K, Szelenyi K. Science and engineering doctoral student socialization, logics, and the National Economic Agenda: alignment or disconnect? Minerva. 2014;52(3):351–79.
7. Roberts BS, Roberts EP, Brachvogel W, Stein AB. Practice management curricular changes may lead to enhanced preparedness for practice. J Dent Educ. 2020;84(8):887–94.
8. Medical School Year Two Questionnaire | 2020 All Schools Summary Report. The Association of American Medical Colleges; 2021.
9. Salsberg E, Richwine C, Westergaard S, Portela Martinez M, Oyeyemi T, Vichare A, et al. Estimation and comparison of current and future racial/ethnic representation in the US Health Care Workforce. JAMA Netw Open. 2021;4(3):e213789-e.
10. Fiscella K, Sanders MR. Racial and ethnic disparities in the quality of health care. Annu Rev Public Health. 2016;37:375–94.
11. Takeshita J, Wang S, Loren AW, Mitra N, Shults J, Shin DB, et al. Association of racial/ethnic and gender concordance between patients and physicians with patient experience ratings. JAMA Netw Open. 2020;3(11):e2024583-e.
12. Alsan M, Garrick O, Graziani G. Does diversity matter for health? Experimental evidence from Oakland. Am Econ Rev. 2019;109(12):4071–111.
13. Fuhrmann CN, Halme DG, O'Sullivan PS, Lindstaedt B. Improving graduate education to support a branching career pipeline: recommendations based on a survey of doctoral students in the basic biomedical sciences. CBE—Life Sci Educ. 2011;10(3):239–49.
14. Zappe SE, Cutler SL, Gase L. A systematic review of the impacts of entrepreneurial support programs in science, technology, engineering, and math fields. Entrep Educ Pedagogy. 2021;0(0):25151274211040422.
15. I-Corps Impact | Impact Data: National Science Foundation; 2022. [Available from: https://beta.nsf.gov/funding/initiatives/i-corps/impact-data.]
16. Park SK, Daugherty KK, Kolluru S, Lebovitz L, Gunaseelan S, Janetski BK, et al. Rethinking the pharmacy workforce crisis by exploring unconventional and emerging career pathways and training. Am J Pharm Educ. 2021;8773
17. Nouri A, Hassali M, Hashmi F. Contribution of pharmacy education to pharmaceutical research and development: critical insights from educators. Perspect Public Health. 2020;140(1):62–6.
18. Mattingly TJ 2nd, Mullins CD, Melendez DR, Boyden K, Eddington ND. A systematic review of entrepreneurship in pharmacy practice and education. Am J Pharm Educ. 2019;83(3):7233.
19. Mattingly TJ 2nd, Abdelwadoud M, Mullins CD, Eddington ND. Pharmapreneur—defining a framework for entrepreneurship in pharmacy education. Am J Pharm Educ. 2019;83(10):7548.
20. Neergård G-B. Entrepreneurial nurses in the literature: a systematic literature review. J Nurs Manag. 2021;29(5):905–15.

21. de Kok E, Weggelaar-Jansen AM, Schoonhoven L, Lalleman P. A scoping review of rebel nurse leadership: descriptions, competences and stimulating/hindering factors. J Clin Nurs. 2021;30(17–18):2563–83.
22. Arnaert A, Mills J, Bruno FS, Ponzoni N. The educational gaps of nurses in entrepreneurial roles: an integrative review. J Prof Nurs. 2018;34(6):494–501.
23. Coke LA. Integrating entrepreneurial skills into clinical nurse specialist education: the need for improved marketing, negotiation, and conflict resolution skills. Clin Nurse Spec. 2019;33(3):146–8.
24. Rankinen S, Ryhänen A. Entrepreneurship, Education in Nursing - A Narrative Review. Enterprise Education Conference at Seinäjoki University of Applied Sciences. 2014:2.
25. Leary M, Villarruel AM, Richmond TS. Creating an innovation infrastructure in academic nursing. J Prof Nurs. 2022;38:83–8.
26. Kagan O, Nadel H, Littlejohn J, Leary M. Evolution of nurse-led hackathons, incubators, and accelerators from an innovation ecosystem perspective. Online J Issues Nurs. 2022:26.
27. Becker ERB, Chahine T, Shegog R. Public health entrepreneurship: a novel path for training future public health professionals. Front Public Health. 2019:7.
28. Accreditation Criteria | Schools of Public Health & Public Health Programs. Council on Education for Public Health; 2021.
29. Johnson JHJ, Sabol BJ, Baker ELJ. The crucible of public health practice: major trends shaping the Design of the Management Academy for Public Health. J Public Health Manag Pract. 2006;12(5):419–25.
30. Martin WM, Mazzeo J, Lemon B. Teaching public health professionals entrepreneurship: an integrated approach. J Enterprising Cult. 2016;24(02):193–207.
31. Hernández D, Carrión D, Perotte A, Fullilove R. Public health entrepreneurs: training the next generation of public health innovators. Public Health Rep. 2014;129(6):477–81.
32. Orton S, Umble K, Zelt S, Porter J, Johnson J. Management academy for public health: creating entrepreneurial managers. Am J Public Health. 2007;97(4):601–5.
33. InnovateHealth Social Entrepreneurship | Social Entrepreneurship for Public Health and Education: Yale School of Public Health; 2021. [Available from: https://ysph.yale.edu/innovate-health-yale/.]
34. Chahine T. Toward an understanding of public health entrepreneurship and intrapreneurship. Front Public Health. 2021;9:593553.
35. 2021 InnovateHealth Yale Annual Report. Yale School of Public Health; 2021.
36. North Carolina Institute for Public Health | Training Programs: UNC Gillings School of Global Public Health; 2022 [Available from: https://sph.unc.edu/nciph/programs/].
37. Cumbey DA, Ellison LA. The Management Academy for Public Health: the South Carolina experience. J Public Health Manag Pract. 2006;12(5):468–74.
38. Orton S, Umble KE, Rosen B, McIver J, Menkens AJ. Management academy for public health: program design and critical success factors. J Public Health Manag Pract. 2006;12(5):409–18.
39. Mohan M, Ravindran TKS. Conceptual framework explaining "preparedness for practice" of dental graduates: a systematic review. J Dent Educ. 2018;82(11):1194–202.
40. Mahoney M. The future of entrepreneurship in dentistry. The University of Texas at Austin Plan II Honors Theses-Openly Available; 2020.
41. Anderson KM, Nelson DL. Wanted: entrepreneurs in occupational therapy. Am J Occup Ther. 2011;65(2):221–8.
42. Jordan GH. Embracing entrepreneurship: occupational therapy's introduction to design-thinking for innovation. Boston University Open BU; 2020.
43. Arias J, Scott KW, Zaldivar JR, Trumbull DA, Sharma B, Allen K, et al. Innovation-oriented medical school curricula: review of the literature. Cureus. 2021;13(10):e18498.

44. Niccum BA, Sarker A, Wolf SJ, Trowbridge MJ. Innovation and entrepreneurship programs in US medical education: a landscape review and thematic analysis. Med Educ Online. 2017;22(1):1360722.
45. Suryavanshi T, Lambert S, Lal S, Chin A, Chan TM. Entrepreneurship and innovation in health sciences education: a scoping review. Med Sci Educ. 2020;30(4):1797–809.
46. Hall AK, Hagel C, Chan TM, Thoma B, Murnaghan A, Bhanji F. The writer's guide to education scholarship in emergency medicine: education innovations (part 3). CJEM. 2018;20(3):463–70.

Chapter 15
Pediatric Digital Health Entrepreneurship

Sharief Taraman, Carmela Salomon, and Allen Yiu

Current Pediatric Health Workforce Challenges

A confluence of long-standing and emerging challenges are straining the capacity of the pediatric workforce in the United States. Ongoing workforce challenges have been further exacerbated by the COVID-19 pandemic, rise of chronic childhood diseases, and the rapidly expanding youth mental and behavioral health crisis.

S. Taraman (✉)
Cognoa Inc., Palo Alto, CA, USA

Chapman University, Dale E. and Sarah Ann Fowler School of Engineering, Orange, CA, USA

CHOC (Children's Health of Orange County), Orange, CA, USA

Department of Pediatrics, Irvine School of Medicine, University of California, Irvine, CA, USA
e-mail: sharief@cognoa.com

C. Salomon
Cognoa Inc., Palo Alto, CA, USA
e-mail: Carmela.Salomon@cognoa.com

A. Yiu
CHOC (Children's Health of Orange County), Orange, CA, USA

Department of Pediatrics, Irvine School of Medicine, University of California, Irvine, CA, USA
e-mail: ayiu1@hs.uci.edu

© The Author(s), under exclusive license to Springer Nature Switzerland AG 2023   211
A. Meyers (ed.), *Digital Health Entrepreneurship*, Health Informatics,
https://doi.org/10.1007/978-3-031-33902-8_15

Current and Projected Workforce Shortages

Despite the increasing number of doctors entering pediatric residency programs in the United States, [1] many subspecialties struggle to fill available positions [2]. Resulting workforce shortages contribute to delays in access and care [1, 3, 4] with families sometimes reporting wait times of weeks to months [1]. Pediatric subspecialists with the longest wait times include developmental pediatrics, endocrinology, and neurology [5]. Competing demands placed on pediatric subspecialists and changing workforce expectations further curtail clinical care delivery. Pediatricians associated with academic institutes focused on teaching and research, for example, are seldom incentivized to focus on direct patient care [6]. Approximately 10% of the existing pediatric subspecialist workforce also report working part time, and this number extends beyond 20% in some of the subspecialties with the greatest access challenges [7]. A recent survey [5] of pediatric subspecialist workplace practices found that, on average, respondents report working fewer hours and spending less time in direct patient care than was the case ten years ago. Administrative tasks were reported to take up an average 13.5% of respondents' time, with an additional 19.5% of time spent teaching and researching. Only 60.6% of working time was available for direct clinical care provision.

Variability in growth patterns across subspecialties and uneven workforce distribution create additional access barriers for some families [1]. Growth in the number of first-year pediatric medical subspecialty fellows, for example, is greater in specialties such as emergency medicine and cardiology, and slower in fields such as child abuse and adolescent medicine [1]. The majority of private pediatric subspecialty practices and academic medical centers in the United States are also located in large urban centers [2]. The resulting rural/urban workforce imbalance contributes to inadequate access for children in under-resourced areas [2].

Increasing Case Complexity and Referral Volume

While some pediatric subspecialists report working fewer hours than they did a decade ago, the volume of referrals and complexity of cases managed is growing, [5] placing further strain on workforce capacity. Epidemiologic shifts created by changes in survival of childhood diseases, coupled with rising rates of pediatric obesity, asthma, and mental health conditions, have led to an increase in children with complex chronic conditions requiring care [8]. Over the past 60 years the proportion of children with a chronic health condition serious enough to interfere with usual daily activities has increased by more than 400% [9]. This complexity increases burdens on healthcare resources. For example, a study performed during two discrete time periods (2003–2004 and 2013–2014) reported both a doubling in the percentage of children presenting for emergency psychiatric evaluations between time periods and a significant lengthening in the amount of time children were spending in the pediatric emergency department [10].

COVID-19 and the Worsening Mental and Behavioral Health Crisis

In October of 2021 the American Academy of Pediatrics, American Academy of Child and Adolescent Psychiatry and Children's Hospital Association issued a joint declaration of national emergency [11] due to the worsening crisis in child and youth mental health. The declaration acknowledges the contribution of the COVID-19 pandemic to the current crisis, including loss of employment, loss of life, prolonged school closures, among other impacts [12]. An overview of current childhood mental health statistics highlights the enormity of the task facing the pediatric mental and behavioral health workforce: As of 2018 suicide is the second leading cause of death for young people aged 10–24 [11]. Rates of child-abuse, and child-abuse related injuries rose dramatically since the advent of the pandemic [12]. From April to October of 2020 the number of pediatric emergency department visits for mental health concerns increased by 31%, growing to comprise 69% of total visits [13]. During the first year of the pandemic rates of pediatric hospital presentations for suicide concerns, depression, anxiety, eating disorder and substance use disorders all increased significantly compared to the year prior, and the average length of stay for psychiatric concern more than doubled [2.1 vs 4.6 days, $p < 0.001$] [14]. These figures are particularly alarming in the context of the current national US shortage of child and adolescent psychiatrists with a median of 11 psychiatrists per 100,000 children [15].

Persistent Bias and Inequities in Childhood Healthcare Access and Outcomes

The role of structural racism in disproportionately magnifying the impacts of the pandemic on communities of color, is increasingly being acknowledged [11]. However, gender, racial/ethnic, socio-economic, and geographic inequities in pediatric healthcare access and outcomes are long standing issues of concern in the United States. Key drivers of structural inequities in pediatric care are summarized in Fig. 15.1.

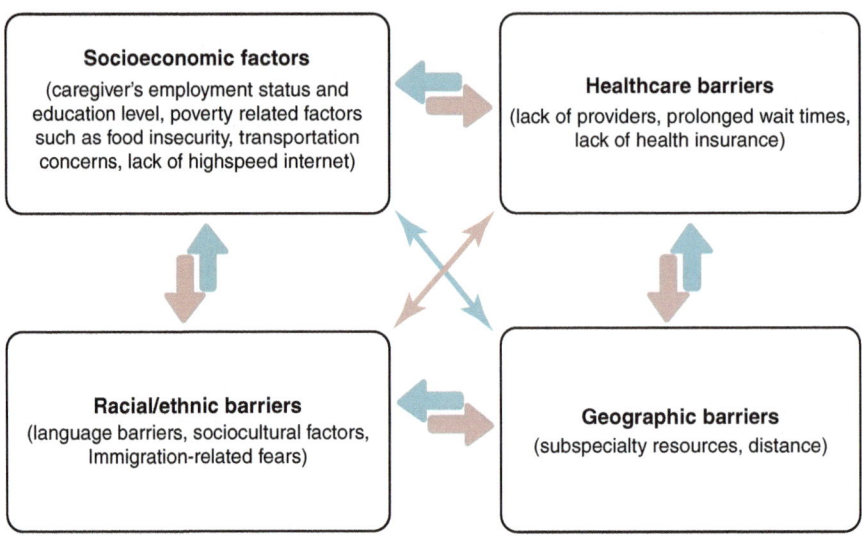

Fig. 15.1 Key drivers of pediatric healthcare inequalities

Digital Health Innovations: Potential Solutions to Key Pediatric Healthcare Challenges

As digital health applications become gradually more ubiquitous and acceptable to patients, the possibility of leveraging them to help address current pediatric healthcare challenges becomes increasingly realistic. A recent census representative survey of U.S. adults found adoption of digital health technologies continues to increase rapidly, with an acceleration of adoption driven by the COVID-19 and the stress it placed on traditional healthcare delivery methods [16]. Technologies such as telemedicine were reported as the healthcare delivery platform of choice by many consumers, *"consumers more than ever expect technology to be part of their healthcare experience … a significant proportion of consumers currently prefer virtual care to in-person visits."* [16] Health-related apps have become one of the most frequently downloaded app-categories [17], with a plethora of pediatric specific health apps being developed to support clinical decision making, deliver family education, and improve disease self-management [18]. The high rates of smartphone ownership among U.S. youth offer growing opportunities for widespread, prospective, real-time health data collection and assessment [19]. As digital natives, it is likely that today's pediatric population will grow into adulthood with both an acceptance and expectation that digital technologies will inform much of their healthcare experience.

Streamlining and Scaling Care, Augmenting Diagnostics and Treatment, and Improving Access

Digital health technologies show potential to ameliorate pediatric healthcare stress in a number of ways. Solutions that streamline care and enhance workplace efficiencies may help to extend pediatric workplace capacity, freeing up time for clinicians to spend in direct patient care. Natural language processing tools, for example, may be leveraged to automate some time-consuming administrative documentation tasks, [20, 21] summarize text, [22] reformulate clinical free text into structured outcomes, [23] and rapidly scan medical reports to identify crucial information to support efficient and accurate diagnoses [24]. Machine learning approaches that excel in detecting subtle non-linear data correlations, may help to augment risk prediction [25–27] and drive discovery of novel clinical insights [28–30] from diverse and ever expanding repositories of pediatric healthcare data. Technologies relying on AI-based nearest-neighbor analysis may support increasingly personalized pediatric medicine [30, 31]. As patients with similar genomic and clinical characteristics are able to be identified and clustered together, treatments will likely become increasingly targeted and efficient, saving time that would have otherwise been spent on delivering less effective generic interventions [32].

Digital innovations may also be leveraged to improve pediatric healthcare access and reduce socio-demographic disparities in health outcomes. Traditionally time-intense pediatric interventions may become more scalable in the future with use of technologies such as AI-based robots capable of autonomously or semi-autonomously delivering therapy to children. A number of published studies describe robot therapy use cases [33]. These include robots aimed at improving social skills, supporting language development, [34, 35] and providing tailored feedback to enhance self-regulation skills [36] in children with a variety of behavioral and mental health conditions. Remote delivery solutions such as tele-health platforms may help to improve access for children in remote and rural areas, offsetting some of the current biases driven by uneven pediatric workforce distribution [31]. Data-driven approaches to product development such as training models on racial, ethnic, socio-economic and gender-concious data-sets, also help to address some of the persistent sociodemographic disparities described in the pediatric literature [37].

Spotlight on Pediatric Innovation

Canvas Dx

Canvas Dx is the first FDA-authorized diagnostic for autism and is intended for use by healthcare providers with children between the ages of 18 and 72 months who are at risk for developmental delay Canvas Dx was developed with the goal of reducing time to autism diagnosis so interventions can start early, during a critical window of high brain neuroplasticity where they can have the greatest impact.

How it works.

The AI-based medical device collects and combines behavioral features predictive of autism. Produces an output of positive, negative or indeterminate for autism to help healthcare providers accurately and efficiently diagnose or rule out autism.

CHADIS

CHADIS is a comprehensive web-based patient engagement and data collection system. It was designed with the goal of assisting in the identification and management of pediatric developmental and behavioral issues.

How it works: Provides a panel of web-based pre-visit screens, linked decision support to provide moment-of-care training, post-visit activities and resources for patients, ongoing education, monitoring, and care coordination.

EndeavorRX

EndeavorRx is an FDA-authorized digital therapeutic indicated to improve attention function as measured by computer-based testing in children ages 8–12 years old with primarily inattentive or combined-type ADHD, who have a demonstrated attention issue.

How it works: Created as a collaboration between neuroscientists and game designers, EndeavorRx uses sensory stimuli and motor challenges to target areas of the brain that play a key role in attention function. Kids are challenged to multitask and ignore distractions by navigating courses, collecting targets, and avoiding obstacles.

GoCheck Kids

GoCheck Kids is an FDA-registered eye screening technology designed to support smooth bidirectional integration of pediatric vision screening technology into primary care networks. Early detection of pediatric vision abnormalities may help to reduce vision impairment and preventable blindness.

How it works: Pediatric cloud-based vision photoscreening conducted via iphones. Leverages machine learning technology and bidirectional electronic health record integration.

HypnoVR
Wearable pediatric medical device leveraging virtual reality technology with the goal of improving the anesthetic experience. Device goals include reduction of postoperative nausea, longer-lasting analgesic effects, reduced opioid use, and faster recovery leading to decreased length of hospital stay and time spent in hospital.

How it works: This multi-sensory immersion headset for pediatric patients enables preoperative, perioperative, and postoperative hypnosedation to patients.

InkSpace Imaging
The InkSpace Imaging Pediatric Body Array device is an FDA cleared product designed for use in the pediatric population. Device goals include improved patient experience, decreased use of general anesthesia and optimized operational costs.

How it works: Lightweight, flexible and low-cost MRI coils tailored for use in pediatric populations.

The Current State of Pediatric Innovation: Roadblocks and Proposed Solutions

While the overall number of digital pediatric start-ups is growing, pediatric innovation has not kept pace with the rapid gains observed in the adult digital health space. A review of FDA approvals and humanitarian device exemptions between 2008–2018, for example, found that only 4% were granted to products indicated for use in 0–2 year olds, and only 10% were indicated for use in patients under 18 years of age [38]. A review of National Institutes of Health (NIH) digital health funding allocation for the 2018 calendar year similarly found that pediatric research comprised only 18.8% of projects and 20.8% of the total funding granted in the digital health research space [19].

Roadblocks to Pediatric Innovation

Physiologic, regulatory and economic factors all contribute to the slower pace of innovation in the pediatric digital health space.

Physiologically, the pediatric population in many ways represents a moving target. Compared to more stable adult populations, children experience significant body changes between the ages of 0 and 18 years. These include alterations in body size, structures and functions, drug metabolism and activity levels [38]. Cognitive capacity, sense of self and emotional maturity also evolves significantly across childhood [39]. The product design implications of these changes are far reaching.

For example, wearable digital device design must account for significant variations in body size and periods of rapid growth. Digital mental and behavioral health innovations require careful tailoring to the cognitive and emotional level of the intended user group. With end-user profiles varying so dramatically across the first 18 years of life, behavioral health companies may need to essentially redesign entirely new products to effectively treat pediatric patients of different ages.

Health and technology literacy also varies dramatically across childhood, meaning pediatric start-ups must potentially account for both the infant who is unlikely to be an autonomous consumer of technology, and the highly competent tech-savvy teenage consumer. Because children are still legally minors, solutions must address, not only end-users, but also their parents and healthcare providers. For teenage users where lines between dependence and autonomy become increasingly blurred, issues of data privacy and information sharing [40] can present pediatric digital health companies with additional challenges.

Pediatric digital health start-ups also face higher levels of regulatory hurdles and institutional review board scrutiny than their adult focused counterparts [38]. Children represent a vulnerable population, both physically and emotionally [41]. From a regulatory and review perspective, this translates to higher levels of surveillance and requirements for clinical research safety monitoring. Protection of vulnerable populations is essential, but at the same time, high levels of regulation can act as a deterrent to innovation [38].

Pediatric innovation challenges described above can translate into lengthier product development timelines and higher costs. Pediatric-specific safety and efficacy testing is expensive. Manufacturing devices in multiple sizes, and robustly accounting for legal and ethical risks can create additional economic burdens. Pediatric care reimbursements are also lower than those in adult care; moreover, variability in state Medicaid coverage and subsequent reimbursements result in unpredictable and shifting payment models [42]. The total size of the pediatric digital health market is also smaller than that of the adult population, leading to concerns about adequacy of return on investment [38]. Perceived poorer return on investment can, in turn, act as a deterrent to future investment in this space [43].

Kickstarting Pediatric Digital Health Innovation: Strategies and Stimulants

While the pediatric digital health space is indeed a niche market, facing diverse challenges from smaller market size and low barriers to entry, to limited economies of scale, it is also a market with huge potential. Advantages of engagement in the pediatric digital health market include lower levels of competition, a loyal customer base, and potential for high profit margins. A number of strategies encouraging future investment and innovation in this space are currently proposed or underway:

- The FDA's 2018 framework for evaluating the potential use of real-world evidence to accelerate medical product development and innovation [44], has clear benefits for pediatric digital health entrepreneurs. This framework has potential to streamline regulatory clearance/approval for pediatric device developers whose target populations may be small (for example- rare disease focused), or otherwise impractical to enroll in randomized controlled trials. Permitting use of real-world evidence in such cases may help to lower costs, thus improving return on investment, and reduce data collection burden and regulatory barriers to innovation. The FDA also grants certain devices intended solely for use in pediatric populations a filing fee charge exemption [38].
- The Eureka Research Resource, supported by the NIH, offers innovators a low cost platform on which to conduct mobile health research. The cloud-based platform includes web interface and iOS application for enrolling, retaining, and conducting studies with large cohorts. While not pediatric specific, use of this resource could potentially support streamlined analysis of mobile health research and accelerated time to clinical deployment.
- Invested parties are calling for the development of clear ethical review guidelines for pediatric research to help standardize review processes across institutions. Additional pediatric specific training for regulatory experts, ethics review committees and government departments, along with inclusion of topic experts on review boards, may help embed evidence-based pediatric specific expertise deeper within product development and regulatory review processes [38].
Regulatory incentives to encourage companies who develop adult focused digital health products to develop pediatric versions in parallel, have also been proposed:

> - *Financial incentives could include reimbursement guarantees, extended patent protection, a vouchers program for pediatric devices, and accepting the results of pediatric clinical testing and post-market experience as a foundation for subsequent adult labeling. Non-financial incentives could include expedited FDA review panels, allowing requests for specific reviewers and recommendations for outside reviewers, additional guidance and support prior to submission, pre-review prior to formal regulatory submission, and expediting the review of resubmissions for devices intended for combined pediatric and adult labeling [38].*

- Other proposed strategies to improve return on investment for pediatric health innovators include: increasing the number of pediatric specific NIH grant programs, incentivizing tax credits, and building pediatric venture philanthropy funding programs [38].
- Additional resources and toolkits for budding pediatric digital health entrepreneurs can be found at the end of the chapter.

Conclusion

As the scope and sophistication of digital innovations expand at a rapid pace, so do the possibilities for leveraging these emerging technologies to address current challenges in the healthcare sector. Within the field of pediatrics challenges include inadequate workforce size and uneven workforce distribution, bias and unequal access to care for some families, and a growing youth mental and behavioral health crisis. In this chapter we have touched upon a variety of digital pediatric innovations with potential to either scale or streamline pediatric diagnostics and therapeutics, reduce bias and inequity, or facilitate delivery of high quality remote care. While physiologic, regulatory and financial barriers to pediatric digital innovation persist, creative strategies for incentivizing investment are growing. As patients become increasingly accustomed to not only *accepting*, but also *expecting* digital technology to form part of their healthcare experience, we are likely to see further exciting innovations in this space.

Resources/toolkits/useful starting points for pediatric digital innovation

- FDA Pediatric Device Consortia Grants Program
  Website: https://www.fda.gov/industry/medical-products-rare-diseases-and-conditions/pediatric-device-consortia-grants-program About: The nonprofit consortia provides a platform of experienced regulatory, business planning, and device development services (such as but not limited to intellectual property advising; prototyping; engineering; laboratory and animal testing; grant-writing; and clinical trial design) to help foster and guide the advancement of medical devices for pediatric patients.
- Institute for Pediatric Innovation Website: https://www.pediatricinnovation.org/
  About: the Institute for Pediatric Innovation focuses on 4 keys to promote IDEA's: Identify, Disseminate, Educate and Advocate. We seek to identify key innovations that are proven and serve our mission. Once identified, we seek to Disseminate new technologies through or network. Education is the importance of engaging both providers and patients in using technology. Finally, Advocacy for public policy that enhances care thru technology for all children
- iSPI – International Society For Pediatric Innovation
  Website: iSPI – International Society For Pediatric Innovation (ispi4kids.org)
  About: iSPI provides a unique forum for pediatric innovation leaders representing hospitals from around the world to come together, exchange ideas, share knowledge, and learn from the collective experience. When it

comes to understanding and adopting new innovations, hospitals everywhere will have the same opportunity to benefit from shared wisdom, as we enter an unheralded era of "exponential convergence".

- National Capital Consortium for Pediatric Device Innovation (NCC-PDI)
  Website: https://innovate4kids.org/.
  About: Provides expert advice, support services, and fund management of pediatric device innovation. Brings together individuals and institutions that can support pediatric medical device progression through all stages of development – ideation, concept formation, prototyping, preclinical, clinical, manufacturing, marketing, and commercialization.
- Southwest National Pediatric Device Innovation Consortium
  Website: https://swpdc.org
  About: The Southwest National Pediatric Device Innovation Consortium, based at Texas Children's Hospital and Baylor College of Medicine, is a "free and no-strings-attached" virtual accelerator that supports pediatric device innovators throughout the pediatric device life cycle. We provide direct device and seed funding, consulting assistance, engineering and design assistance, potential clinical collaborators, and connections to local programs and resources.
- The West Coast Consortium for Technology and Innovation in Pediatrics
  Website: https://www.westcoastctip.org
  About: The West Coast Consortium for Technology & Innovation in Pediatrics (CTIP) is an FDA-funded pediatric medical device accelerator centered at Children's Hospital Los Angeles (CHLA) and the University of Southern California (USC). CTIP addresses the most important components necessary for pediatric device innovation: simultaneously engaging clinicians, engineers, designers, regulators, hospital administrators, patients and the business and investment community in the process of assessment and development of technology. UCSF-Stanford Pediatric Device Consortium
  Website: https://pediatricdeviceconsortium.org
  About: The UCSF-Stanford PDC aims to improve the health, safety, and quality of life of pediatric patients by accelerating high-value, high impact pediatric device solutions at all stages of the total product lifecycle towards commercialization.

References

1. Macy ML, Leslie LK, Turner A, Freed GL. Growth and changes in the pediatric medical sub-specialty workforce pipeline. Pediatr Res. 2021;89(5):1297–303.
2. Keller DM, Davis MM, Freed GL. Access to pediatric subspecialty care for children and youth: possible shortages and potential solutions. Pediatr Res. 2020;87(7):1151–2.
3. Bohnhoff JC, Taormina JM, Ferrante L, Wolfson D, Ray KN. Unscheduled referrals and unat-tended appointments after pediatric subspecialty referral. Pediatrics. 2019;144:6.
4. Primack WA, Meyers KE, Kirkwood SJ, Ruch-Ross HS, Radabaugh CL, Greenbaum LA. The US pediatric nephrology workforce: a report commissioned by the American Academy of Pediatrics. Am J Kidney Dis. 2015;66(1):33–9.
5. Rimsza ME, Ruch-Ross HS, Clemens CJ, Moskowitz WB, Mulvey HJ. Workforce trends and analysis of selected pediatric subspecialties in the United States. Acad Pediatr. 2018;18(7):805–12.
6. Macy ML, Van KD, Leslie LK, Freed GL. Engagement in research among pediatric subspe-cialists at the time of enrollment in maintenance of certification, 2009– 2016. Pediatr Res. 2020;87(6):1128–34.
7. Freed GL, Moran LM, Van KD LLK, Pediatrics RAC of the AB of. Current workforce of pediatric subspecialists in the United States. Pediatrics. 2017;139:5.
8. Cohen E, Berry JG, Sanders L, Schor EL, Wise PH. Status complexicus? The emergence of pediatric complex care. Pediatrics. 2018;141(Supplement_3):S202–11.
9. Perrin JM, Anderson LE, Van Cleave J. The rise in chronic conditions among infants, chil-dren, and youth can be met with continued health system innovations. Health Aff (Millwood). 2014;33(12):2099–105.
10. Nadler A, Avner D, Khine H, Avner JR, Fein DM. Rising clinical burden of psychiatric visits on the pediatric emergency department. Pediatr Emerg Care. 2021;37(1):1–3.
11. American Academy of Pediatrics. AAP-AACAP-CHA Declaration of a National Emergency in Child and Adolescent Mental Health. 2021 Oct.
12. Abrams EM, Greenhawt M, Shaker M, Pinto AD, Sinha I, Singer A. The COVID-19 pan-demic: adverse effects on the social determinants of health in children and families. Ann Allergy Asthma Immunol. 2022;128(1):19–25.
13. Leeb RT, Bitsko RH, Radhakrishnan L, Martinez P, Njai R, Holland KM. Mental health–related emergency department visits among children aged< 18 years during the COVID-19 pandemic—United States, January 1–October 17, 2020. Morb Mortal Wkly Rep. 2020;69(45):1675.
14. Ibeziako P, Kaufman K, Scheer KN, Sideridis G. Pediatric mental health presentations and boarding: first year of the COVID-19 pandemic. Hosp Pediatr. 2022;
15. American Academy of Child & Adolescent Psychiatry. AACAP Releases Workforce Maps Illustrating Severe Shortage of Child and Adolescent Psychiatrists. 2018 [cited 2021 Nov 19]; Available from: https://www.aacap.org/AACAP/Press/Press_Releases/2018/Severe_Shortage_of_Child_and_Adolescent_Psychiatrists_Illustrated_in_AAACP_Workforce_maps.aspx
16. DeSilva J. Digital Health Consumer Adoption report 2020 [Internet]. Rock Health; 2021. Available from: https://rockhealth.com/insights/digital-health-consumer-adoption-report-2020/
17. Krebs P, Duncan DT. Health app use among US mobile phone owners: a national survey. JMIR Mhealth Uhealth. 2015;3(4):e4924.
18. Nievas Soriano BJ, Uribe-Toril J, Ruiz-Real JL, Parron-Carreno T. Pediatric apps: what are they for? A scoping review. Eur J Pediatr. 2022:1–7.
19. Riley WT, Oh A, Aklin WM, Sherrill JT, Wolff-Hughes DL, Diana A, et al. Commentary: pediatric digital health supported by the National Institutes of Health. J Pediatr Psychol. 2019;44(3):263–8.

20. Greenfield D. Artificial Intelligence in Medicine: Applications, implications, and limitations [Internet]. 2019 [cited 2021 Nov 11]. Available from: https://sitn.hms.harvard.edu/flash/2019/artificial-intelligence-in-medicine-applications-implications-and-limitations/
21. Coiera E, Kocaballi B, Halamka J, Laranjo L. The digital scribe. NPJ Digit Med. 2018;1(1):1–5.
22. Goldstein A, Shahar Y. An automated knowledge-based textual summarization system for longitudinal, multivariate clinical data. J Biomed Inform. 2016;61:159–75.
23. Kreimeyer K, Foster M, Pandey A, Arya N, Halford G, Jones SF, et al. Natural language processing systems for capturing and standardizing unstructured clinical information: a systematic review. J Biomed Inform. 2017;73:14–29.
24. Bressem KK, Adams LC, Gaudin RA, Tröltzsch D, Hamm B, Makowski MR, et al. Highly accurate classification of chest radiographic reports using a deep learning natural language model pre-trained on 3.8 million text reports. Bioinformatics. 2020;36(21):5255–61.
25. Movaghar A, Page D, Scholze D, Hong J, DaWalt LS, Kuusisto F, et al. Artificial intelligence–assisted phenotype discovery of fragile X syndrome in a population-based sample. Genet Med. 2021;1–8
26. Lingren T, Chen P, Bochenek J, Doshi-Velez F, Manning-Courtney P, Bickel J, et al. Electronic health record based algorithm to identify patients with autism spectrum disorder. PLoS One. 2016;11(7):e0159621.
27. Bedi G, Carrillo F, Cecchi GA, Slezak DF, Sigman M, Mota NB, et al. Automated analysis of free speech predicts psychosis onset in high-risk youths. NPJ Schizophr. 2015;1(1):15030.
28. Le S, Hoffman J, Barton C, Fitzgerald JC, Allen A, Pellegrini E, et al. Pediatric severe sepsis prediction using machine learning. Front Pediatr. 2019;7:413.
29. Chahal D, Byrne MF. A primer on artificial intelligence and its application to endoscopy. Gastrointest Endosc. 2020;92(4):813–20.e4
30. Topol EJ. High-performance medicine: the convergence of human and artificial intelligence. Nat Med. 2019;25(1):44–56.
31. Buch VH, Ahmed I, Maruthappu M. Artificial intelligence in medicine: current trends and future possibilities. Br J Gen Pract. 2018;68(668):143–4.
32. Shu LQ, Sun YK, Tan LH, Shu Q, Chang AC. Application of artificial intelligence in pediatrics: past, present and future. World J Pediatr. 2019;15(2):105–8.
33. Rabbitt SM, Kazdin AE, Scassellati B. Integrating socially assistive robotics into mental healthcare interventions: applications and recommendations for expanded use. Clin Psychol Rev. 2015;35:35–46.
34. Fiske A, Henningsen P, Buyx A. Your robot therapist will see you now: ethical implications of embodied artificial intelligence in psychiatry, psychology, and psychotherapy. J Med Internet Res. 2019;21(5):e13216.
35. Pennisi P, Tonacci A, Tartarisco G, Billeci L, Ruta L, Gangemi S, et al. Autism and social robotics: a systematic review. Autism Res. 2016;9(2):165–83.
36. Cibrian FL, Lakes KD, Schuck S, Hayes GR. The potential for emerging technologies to support self-regulation in children with ADHD: a literature review. Int J Child-Comput Interact. 2021:100421.
37. Aylward BS, Gal-Szabo DE, Taraman S. Racial, ethnic, and sociodemographic disparities in diagnosis of children with autism Spectrum disorder. J Dev Behav Pediatr JDBP. 2021;
38. Sanger T, Chang A, Feaster W, Taraman S, Afari N, Beauregard D, et al. Opportunities for regulatory changes to promote pediatric device innovation in the United States: joint recommendations from pediatric innovator roundtables. IEEE J Transl Eng Health Med. 2021;9:1–5.
39. Zanolie K, Crone EA. Development of cognitive control across childhood and adolescence. Stevens Handb Exp Psychol Cogn Neurosci. 2018;4:1–24.
40. Hiriscau IE, Stingelin-Giles N, Stadler C, Schmeck K, Reiter-Theil S. A right to confidentiality or a duty to disclose? Ethical guidance for conducting prevention research with children and adolescents. Eur Child Adolesc Psychiatry. 2014;23(6):409–16.

41. Oates J. Research ethics, children, and young people. Handb Res Ethics Sci Integr. 2020:623–35.
42. Espinoza J, Shah P, Nagendra G, Bar-Cohen Y, Richmond F. Pediatric medical device development and regulation: current state, barriers, and opportunities. Pediatrics. 2022;149:5.
43. Peiris V. CDRH: Building a national ecosystem for pediatric innovation (PowerPoint style). In New Orleans; 2019.
44. U.S. Food and Drug Administration. Framework for FDA's Real-World Evidence Program. [Online]. [Internet]. 2018 Dec [cited 2022 Aug 17]. Available from: https://www.fda.gov/media/120060/download#:~:text=Real%2DWorld%20Evidence%20(RWE)%20is%20the%20clinical%20evidence%20about,derived%20from%20analysis%20of%20RWD.

Chapter 16
Artificial Intelligence and Ethics

**Doreen Rosenstrauch, Utpal Mangla, Atul Gupta,
and Costansia Taikwa Masau**

"The computer is only as smart as the person in front of it," postulates the bright-eyed kindergartner with a sincere tone in his voice echoing through the majestic auditorium resembling Harry Potter's Hogwarts Hall. During an iD-Tech computer summer program at the Rice University the instructor gently challenges the children with the question "Do you think that a computer knows the difference between good or bad?" To which a witty kid responds swiftly without losing a beat: "My mom always says that consequences will teach you if you did something right or wrong".

It begs the question: Will computers ever know the difference between good or bad? "...maybe an intelligent computer...," a child might respond. If so, would Artificial intelligence (AI) be able to do the right thing and be considered an ethical AI?

The original version of the chapter has been revised. A correction to this chapter can be found at
https://doi.org/10.1007/978-3-031-33902-8_17

D. Rosenstrauch (✉) · C. T. Masau
DrDoRo®Institute, Healthcare Consultancy and Advisory Services, Houston, TX, USA
e-mail: info@DrDoRo.com

U. Mangla
Industry EDGE Cloud at IBM Cloud Platform, Toronto, ON, Canada
e-mail: utpal.mangla@ca.ibm.com

A. Gupta
Enterprise Data Architecture, Sun Life, Toronto, ON, Canada

Lead Data Architect, Merative, Toronto, ON, Canada
e-mail: atul.gupta@sunlife.com

© The Author(s), under exclusive license to Springer Nature Switzerland AG 2023,
corrected publication 2023
A. Meyers (ed.), *Digital Health Entrepreneurship*, Health Informatics,
https://doi.org/10.1007/978-3-031-33902-8_16

What Are Ethics?

To make sure humans are doing the right thing, humans have the law and guidelines that they live by.

The law is defined as the system of rule which a particular country or community recognizes as regulating the actions of its members and which they may enforce by the imposition of penalties.

The guidelines that humans live by are called moral principles. Moral principles include things like honesty, fairness, and equality.

A moral philosophy or code of morals practiced by humans is called **ethics***.*

Moral choice is committing to act for what one believes is right and good [1].

In general, humans consider love, honesty, kindness as good while hate, lying, cruelty are considered bad. Simply put, ethics is a system of moral principles.

What Is Artificial Intelligence?

In 1955, John McCarthy defined AI as "the science and engineering of making intelligent machines" [2]. In 2022, Fedorko et al. admit that it "is not easy to find a uniform and correct definition for AI" [3]. In an attempt to provide evidence-based scientific support to the policymaking process, the Joint Research Centre, European Commission's science and knowledge service, proposed an operational definition of AI. This definition is composed of a concise taxonomy characterizing the core domains of the AI research field and transversal topics, as well as a list of keywords representative of such taxonomy. Recognizing that AI is a dynamic field, an iterative definition that can be updated over time to capture its evolution was proposed.

AI systems are software (and possibly also hardware) systems designed by humans that given a complex goal, act in the physical or digital dimension by perceiving their environment through data acquisition, interpreting the collected structured or unstructured data, reasoning on the knowledge or processing of information derived from this data, and decide the best action(s) to take to achieve the given goal.

AI systems can either use symbolic rules or learn a numeric model, and they can also adapt their behavior by analyzing how the environment is affected by their previous actions [4].

Elements of AI Are Architecture, Algorithm, and Data

1. Architecture

    AI relies on the following architectural structures:

    * Artificial Neural Networks (ANN)
    * Deep Neural Networks (DNN)

  * Convolutional Neural Networks (CNN)
  * Recurrent Neural Networks (RNN)
  * Random Tree Forests (RF)
  * Support Vector Machines (SVM)

2. Algorithms

Algorithms are the learning and training methods. The basis of AI autonomy demonstrated during training are:

  * Supervised machine learning
  * Semi-supervised machine learning
  * Unsupervised machine learning
  * Reinforcement machine learning

3. Data

AI depends on the following data, which are fed to AI, also called input data:
  * Training data, Unclassified (unlabeled) training data, Classified (labeled) training data
  * Test data
  * Unstructured data, Semi-structured data, Structured data
  * Personal data, Non-personal data
  * Raw data, Real-time data, Secondary data, Synthetic data, Metadata

A trained AI system can be called Machine Learning (ML) Model (MLM). At its core, MLM has a Classifier, a mathematical function that assigns an output to any given input. The Classifier is the essence of the MLM. It allows a trained AI to classify new data or predict outcomes for new data [5].

Applications of AI include expert systems, natural language processing, speech recognition and machine vision [6].

What Is Not AI?

AI is not robots and robots are not all AI [7]. While AI systems can capture real-time data, process data in real-time, and make a human independent decision based on the processed data, non-AI systems can perform automated processes but cannot adjust themselves based on real-time data input. While AI systems are trained with data and algorithms and can learn, non-AI systems cannot. While AI systems learn from mistakes and experiences and try to improvise on their next iteration, non-AI systems work on fixed algorithms, which always work with the same level of efficiency that is programmed into them. While AI systems can analyze the situation and make decisions accordingly, non-AI systems cannot make decisions on their own.

What Are AI Ethics?

The United Nations Educational, Scientific and Cultural Organization (UNESCO) approaches AI ethics as a systematic normative reflection, based on a holistic, comprehensive, multicultural, and evolving framework of interdependent values, principles and actions that can guide societies in dealing responsibly with the known and unknown impacts of AI technologies on human beings, societies and the environment and ecosystems, and offers them a basis to accept or reject AI technologies [8].

AI can simulate human intelligence processes. With that, challenges arise for humanity, which different nations and entities around the globe have begun to address.

The following potential AI risks and challenges have been of concern.

- Autonomy loss

As AI becomes more autonomous and increasingly supersedes humans and human decision-making, there is the risk that humans might lose the ability to make their own life rules, decisions, or shape their lives.

- Bias

AI bias, also called Machine Learning bias, or sometimes called algorithm bias, is a phenomenon that occurs when an algorithm produces results that are systemically prejudiced due to erroneous assumptions in the machine learning process.

- Deception

AI might have the ability to learn to deceive and therefore to lie without having a true understanding of what deception actually is [9]. Deceptive behavior of hiding resources or information, or providing false information might be unintentionally just to achieve the setout goal and an unwanted side effect of an algorithm.

- Deep Fakes

AI could be used to create convincing false images or audios and video hoaxes called deep fakes.

- Discrimination

AI might treat people unjust, especially on the grounds of race, age, or sex, or treat different categories of things unjust or with prejudice.

- Erosion of society

Some fear that AI could lead to the erosion of traditional sociopolitical structures and the possibility of great loss of lives due to accelerated growth of autonomous military applications and the use of weaponized information, lies and propaganda to dangerously destabilize human groups. Others also fear that cybercriminals will reach into economic systems [10]..

- Exclusion

If AI is only available to a few, then there is a risk that only the few will control AI and or that AI may only be exposed to data from a selected entity or group leading to foregoing the inclusion of the majority of people and or data and missing out on their representation.

- Humane treatment of AI

AI would need to be able to think, perceive and feel, not only be able to pass a version of a Turing test to be considered sentient. With the recent claim of a sentient AI [11], it stands to reason the possibility of a need to treat AI humanely.

- Incompetence

AI can neither understand ("grasp") causality nor can AI – qua computation – understand anything at all [12]. This might be an alternative explanation for AI errors.

* Inequality
AI might worsen the lack of equality; Social disparity income inequality measured using the distribution of income and wealth inequality measured using the distribution of wealth.

* Lethal Autonomous Weapons
Autonomous AI weapons that would harm humans are a possibility. Nations will need to continue the dialogue around this topic. The UN is the prime forum for such a discussion [13].

* Malicious use
AI use with the intent to do harm could threaten digital security and is an increasing risk while moving from analog to digital.

* Privacy violations or loss
The General Data Protection Regulation (GDPR) regulates the use of personal data in Europe. The CCPA (California Consumer Privacy Act) is the US equivalent of GDPR. The Health Insurance Portability and Accountability Act of 1996 (HIPAA) is a federal law that requires the creation of national standards to protect sensitive patient health information from being disclosed without the patient's consent or knowledge. Not following compliance requirements for *AI* systems that stem from *privacy* regulations poses risks for individuals, organizations, and nations alike.

* Safety
If AI is not implemented with the dogma "Safety first!" then AI could cause harm, endanger, or injure humans. UpToDate risk mitigation strategies will improve the safety of AI systems.

* Security
Freedom from danger or threat might be jeopardized by un-secure AI systems. AI systems themselves are vulnerable to a new type of cybersecurity attack called an "artificial intelligence" attack as well. Public policy creating AI Security Compliance programs might reduce the risk of attacks on AI systems [14].

* Transparency loss
There is the notion that AI is considered a "black box" without offering insights or explanations on the process of how AI arrives at a particular decision. The lack of transparency might jeopardize the ability to build trust. This lack of transparency might violate regulatory standards with the inability to audit AI systems.

* Unintended consequences
AI may overfit predictions, responding to patterns specific to one dataset that does not accurately reflect the trends in the real world. This may lead to inflated accuracy or inaccuracy, which in turn could lead to unintended outcomes.

Global Community and Ethical AI

To assure AI is utilized for the good of humanity, the global community must continue the ongoing dialogue on ethical AI. In 2019 investigators analyzed and mapped principles and guidelines on ethical AI in the global landscape of AI ethics guidelines. Results revealed a global convergence emerging around the following five ethical principles, transparency, justice and fairness [15], non-maleficence, responsibility, and privacy [16]. As the field of ethical AI is evolving developments have been taken into consideration since then. However, a universal global standard on ethical AI is still outstanding. Nations, organizations, and entities around the globe continue to provide perspectives on ethical AI.

United Nations Perspective on Ethical Concerns in AI

The United Nations (UN) with the development of the Sustainable Development Goals (SDGs) considers the ecological, social, and economic dimensions as interdependent for sustainable development. To tackle societal problems and to improve public welfare, AI for social good (AI4SG) is explored [17]. Recognizing potential risks, the UN provided an overview of the ethical concerns in AI and a framework to mitigate risks [18]. The ethical AI framework includes:

- **Human-centered AI** places humans in the center of it all ensuring that human values are central to all actions and non-actions of AI.
- **Safe AI** ensures the well-being and safety of humans.
- **Trustworthy AI** ensures that AI can be trusted and that AI can be relied on to be honest, truthful and law abiding.
- **Beneficial AI** ensures that AI is fair and will be favorable or advantageous for humans.
- **Transparent AI** ensures that AI can be easily perceived, accessed, and detected.
- **Responsible AI** ensures the accountability for AI and that humans are in control and in charge of AI.
- **Explainable AI** ensures that AI can be understood.
- **Interpretable AI** ensures that AI can be comprehended.
- **Meaningful AI** ensures that AI makes logical sense for humans and adds value.

World Health Organization's Perspective on Ethical Concerns in AI

The creation of ethical AI is a socio-technological challenge for the global community and calls for collaborations of all cultures and nations around the world to develop and maintain policies on how AI should be governed. In 2021, the World Health Organization (WHO) issued a guidance on Ethics and governance of artificial intelligence for health. The WHO identified six core principles:

1. **Protect human autonomy**
   The principle of autonomy requires that the use of AI will respect human autonomy. In the context of healthcare, this means that humans should remain in control of healthcare systems and medical decisions. Respect for human autonomy also entails related duties to ensure that healthcare professionals have the information necessary to make safe, effective use of AI and that people understand the role that such systems play in their care. It also requires protection of privacy and confidentiality and obtaining valid informed consent through appropriate legal frameworks for data protection.
2. **Promote human well-being and safety and the public interest**

AI should not harm people. The designers of AI should satisfy regulatory requirements for safety, accuracy, and efficacy for well-defined use cases or indications. Measures of quality control in practice and quality improvement in the use of AI over time should be available. Preventing harm requires that AI not result in mental or physical harm that could be avoided by use of an alternative practice or approach.

3. **Ensure Transparency, Explainability and Intelligibility**

AI should be intelligible or understandable to all alike; developers, healthcare professionals, patients, users, and regulators. Two broad approaches to intelligibility are to improve the transparency of AI and to make AI explainable. Transparency requires that sufficient information be published or documented before the design or deployment of an AI and that such information facilitate meaningful public consultation and debate on how AI is designed and how AI should or should not be used. AI should be explainable according to the capacity of those to whom they are explained.

4. **Foster Responsibility and Accountability**

Humans require clear, transparent specification of the tasks that AI can perform and the conditions under which they can achieve the desired performance. Although AI performs specific tasks, it is the responsibility of stakeholders to ensure that they can perform those tasks and that AI is used under appropriate conditions and by appropriately trained people. Responsibility can be assured by application of "human warranty," which implies evaluation by patients and healthcare professionals in the development and deployment of AI. Human warranty requires application of regulatory principles upstream and downstream of the algorithm by establishing points of human supervision. If something goes wrong with an AI, then there should be accountability. Appropriate mechanisms should be available for questioning and for redress for individuals and groups that are adversely affected by decisions based on AI.

5. **Ensure inclusiveness and equity**

Inclusiveness requires that AI for health be designed to encourage the widest possible appropriate, equitable use and access, irrespective of age, sex, gender, income, race, ethnicity, sexual orientation, ability or other characteristics protected under human rights codes. AI, like any other technology, should be shared as widely as possible. AI should be available for use not only in contexts and for needs in high-income settings but also in the contexts and for the capacity and diversity of low- and middle-income countries. AI should not encode biases to the disadvantage of identifiable groups, especially groups that are already marginalized. Bias is a threat to inclusiveness and equity as it can result in a departure, often arbitrary, from equal treatment. AI should minimize inevitable disparities in power that arise between providers and patients, between policymakers and people and between companies and governments that create and deploy AI and those that use or rely on them. AI should be monitored and evaluated to identify disproportionate effects on specific groups of people. No technology, AI or otherwise, should sustain or worsen existing forms of bias and discrimination.

6. **Promote AI that is responsive and sustainable**

Responsiveness requires that designers, developers, and users continuously, systematically, and transparently assess AI during actual use. Humans should determine whether AI responds adequately and appropriately and according to communicated, legitimate expectations and requirements. Responsiveness also requires that AI be consistent with wider promotion of the sustainability of health systems, environments, and workplaces. AI should be designed to minimize their environmental consequences and increase energy efficiency. That is, use of AI should be consistent with global efforts to reduce the impact of human beings on the Earth's environment, ecosystems, and climate. Sustainability requires governments and companies to address anticipated disruptions in the workplace, including training for healthcare professionals to adapt to the use of AI, and potential job losses due to use of automated systems [19].

Practitioners View on AI and Ethics

AI practitioners are constantly challenged with achieving balance across AI data gathering, Ethics and delivering AI guidance and solutions. This three-prong challenge makes them accountable, risk-prone and may limit the expansion of AI solutions. The synthetic data even though sounds promising, has not been able to deliver the results needed from AI algorithms. In a reference paper from Harvard on Principled Artificial Intelligence [20], eight key themes were recognized as:

- Privacy
- Accountability
- Safety and Security
- Transparency and Explainability
- Fairness and Non-discrimination
- Human control of technology
- Professional Responsibility
- Promotion of Human Values

The practitioner's viewpoint and consideration of these themes and principles will make it '*deployment ready*.' The questions that need answers:

- Are consumers ready to share the data to organizations?
- Are commercial businesses, non-profit or research organizations ready to risk ethical boundaries to achieve their AI goals?

As an example, any data from people less than 18 or 19 years of age depending on legal jurisdictions, when collected with consent from parents or legal guardian's may be used for AI purposes only until the person reaches the age of majority and is capable of providing their own consent for use of such data. *The ethical layer here is time-bound* and needs to be revisited after the expiration of such timeline or when the person attains majority age and is capable of consenting on their own. The operational AI aspect in this example needs governance established, monitored, detected, and reported to consumers, businesses, and all involved parties. The additional costs and delays to implement governance layer will either stop the organizations to use of such data for AI algorithms or question the economic feasibility of AI solutions. The unethical use of such data may cause permanent injury to person's data collected ethically but used beyond the ethical expiry of the collected data. This extends to next question—can the AI inferences and guidance deduced and delivered from such person's data be continued to be used even after the timeline expiry?

In another macro example with data inputs from tribal regions for economic, environmental, or human sustainability AI solutions. This may occur as data from a newly or recently discovered tribal areas in remote locales may get collected and used for but may cause AI and ethical concerns of different nature. Firstly, the tribes may not be aware of such data being collected from their areas by more sophisticated human societies for commercial or research purposes or secondly the tribes may have their own customs and traditions to govern such data exposure to outside communities which the modern-day society is unaware of and data get collected and used for AI as *'data usage in ignorance'*.

Examining aforementioned two examples through the lens of Ethical AI principles of **fairness, accountability, transparency, safety and human values**—the AI practitioners will need to gain maturity to make sure the ethical use of the data is *manageable, explainable, and attainable.*

In the context of AI and Ethics, *manageable* will mean the deployment scale of AI solutions and still managing the intended policies, guidelines, and procedures. This is not limited to governance but also operational aspects with all the embedded logic in monitoring all tool and techniques used for AI solutions. As the AI solutions are deployed and used by consumers, implementors should be able to make it *explainable* to average consumer and population at-large. This also means that data inputs, algorithms used, and inferences deduced should all make sense in understanding the reasoning and logic used to generate results. Once the AI solutions surpass research and are used for first-generation success, the *attainable* aspect is important in making sure the growth trajectory attains the success with ethical considerations, global policies and thereafter sustains the trajectory for those achieved and future targets.

The AI and Ethics together poses challenges and many opportunities which need carefully drafted and implemented policies, frameworks as well as mature tools, procedures and governance. The tools, techniques, algorithms are only as effective as diverse data is ingested into AI systems and applications. The ethical challenges should not paralyze or prohibit AI practitioners to explore the opportunities.

The AI trustworthiness and adoption mature together. If consumers don't trust the AI solutions, the ethical layer might be questioned for algorithmic techniques or improper data collection and scrubbing. The legitimacy and transparency of the AI data needs very careful governance before wide adoption of AI solutions can be achieved globally. If not governed properly, it may trigger investment risks and market failures while raising long term risks and consequences.

In one of the perspectives in medical AI, Responsibility Beyond Design: Physicians requirements for ethical medical AI [21], beyond the forward-looking responsibilities, an emphasis was put on duty to report uncertainty to patients, understanding and critically assessing the AI outputs, knowing and understanding the input data, assessing and monitoring of outputs, etc. These considerations are starting point for governance of AI and Ethics. Unless we see wide adoption of these starting points in the mind-sets of AI practitioners, the risk of crossing the ethical boundaries will evolve and will deaccelerate AI solution delivery roadmaps.

In another perspective of AI solutions in research, production, and testing of healthcare medications—potentially serious lethal autonomous weapons can emerge if data is not protected and governed ethically. In this example, healthcare AI models, injected with malicious alteration to medication dosages at research labs, or testing facilities may downstream into operations. It may impact the medication dosages consumed with serious risks to patients as it can expand very fast since it is deeply embedded in AI models and algorithms that before being detected, the patient and healthcare facilities impact will already be wide-spread. It is a different kind of lethal weapon targeting humans from malicious and unethical handling of data.

The AI principles and themes at democratic global levels can be the driving force in the right direction only if the tools, techniques, and business adoption match the quality and constraints of such principles. AI is known to be enhancing and augmenting human intelligence and the AI guidance is still in its infancy. If first-generation implementation of AI solutions succeeds using unethical data inputs, then it can potentially cause catastrophic consequences and may put a stop on the future of AI.

An additional consideration was put forward by the AI visionary and cardiologist, Dr. Anthony Chang and his team at AI-Med, sharing thoughts on a potential situation: If a safe, validated and approved AI system is available, but a practitioner selected not to utilize it for the benefit of a patient, what would be the ethical considerations? Mitigating the risks involved in the application of AI brings with it the need for a clear standard of accountability and ethical behavior with the consideration of human rights, democracy, and the rule of law [22]. The study by the European Parliamentary Research Service on applications, risks, and ethical and societal impacts proposes mitigation measures and policy options to minimize potential risks and maximize the benefits of medical AI, including multi-stakeholder engagement through the AI production lifetime, increased transparency and traceability, in-depth clinical validation of AI tools, and AI training and education for both clinicians and citizens [23]. Specifically, the following policy options are proposed:

- Extend AI regulatory frameworks and codes of practice to address healthcare-specific risks and requirements
- Promote multi-stakeholder engagement and co-creation throughout the whole lifecycle of medical AI algorithms
- Create an AI passport and traceability mechanisms for enhanced transparency and trust in medical AI

- Develop frameworks to improve the definition of accountability and monitoring of responsibilities in medical AI
- Introduce education programs and campaigns to enhance the skills of healthcare professionals and the literacy of the general public in medical AI
- Promote further research on clinical, ethical, and technical robustness in medical AI
- Implement a strategy for reducing the European divide in medical AI

Furthermore, the deployment of AI applications into healthcare management has the potential to make a significantly positive impact on the quintuple aim in healthcare by enhancing the patient care experience, improving population health, improving the satisfaction and well-being of the healthcare team, advancing health equity, and reducing healthcare costs—while improving overall productivity [24]. Employing AI to gain clinical and operational efficiencies can put AI on a path to transform how healthcare organizations operate. This is an investment that has the potential to be a game changer for society and for the economy.

The Future of AI with Ethics

The future of AI with ethical considerations is more sustainable in data input, selection of algorithms and eliminating machine learning bias. This will be helpful in gaining the consumer confidence, trust, reliability, explainability and make it more reliable for future expansion. The publication "Experts Doubt Ethical AI Design Will Be Broadly Adopted as the Norm Within the Next Decade" addressing AI design considerations mentioned that AI is more capable than humans of delivering unemotional ethical judgment [25]. Marcel Fafchamps, professor of economics and senior fellow at the Center on Democracy, Development and the Rule of Law at Stanford University, commented, *"AI is just a small cog in a big system. The main danger currently associated with AI is that machine learning reproduces past discrimination..."*

The discrimination risk stems from unethical use of data in the context that it will limit the data inputs from preferred sources and will undermine the AI inferences. During Design, the aim should be to reduce the past mistakes in the data collection scope and use of such data for AI solutions. AI future needs wide variety of data and should have fair representation from population at-large.

The future of AI and ethics has human element to it as well. All AI solutions eventually will be used to operationalize AI in multiple industry sectors, and they need to consider all human values as part of it. If the AI model lacks the data representation from population at-large, it starts creating machine learning bias. There are bias mitigation techniques and algorithms which may be helpful in certain situations in lab but may not pass the real-life tests. Unless the human element is built into AI solutions, the AI and ethical challenges will continue to show in various aspects.

Conclusion

The AI and ethics journey has started to gain traction and its maturity needs careful considerations from research institutions, collaborations of commercial organizations and government around the world to yield the collective effectiveness and efficiency.

AI must pass the ethics layer to grow and solve the business and industry problems before gaining human AI adoption. The ethical layer will determine the pace of AI adoptability in the future, and will revolve around it being *manageable, explainable, and attainable.*

The ethical challenge needs governance in design and needs constant monitoring and maturity during operationalization of AI tools and techniques. In as much as the need of ethics in bringing in input data to AI, it is as much for the refinement of AI algorithms, elimination of machine learning bias. The wide adoption of AI guidance can be achieved by getting human trust and making sure it is explainable to them. The fairness and transparency will make sure humans understand the flow of steps taken to yield the AI inferences.

The global policies need to be aligned for AI and Ethics to work at a global level across all nations without discrimination and should not be limited to developed countries. AI needs wholesome data with ethical standards and best practices in place. It is as much important to engage UN, WHO and other global organizations as much of the country leads for all policy making and governance purposes. The procedures should be laid out in a way that it respects all human populations and data inputs are seamlessly monitored and governed to generate AI inferences and guidance. The design, development, and deployment of ethical AI is multidisciplinary, ranging across industries, the branches of science, and philosophy, ethics, economics. As AI evolves, learns, and adapts, so must humans by continuously revisiting and revising policies, best practices, standards, and the law collaboratively by a diversity of stakeholders on a global level. Ethical AI should be inclusive and be reflective of the diversity of all humans on earth with focus on their well-being. Next generations might have to deal increasingly with ethical issues than with technological issues. Therefore, solving the Tech Industry's Ethics problem must start in the classroom [26]. Shall the words of a child hold true:

> *"The computer is only as smart as the person in front of it."* Duke oTTo R.O., 6 years old, youngest computer technology student at iD Tech in Texas, USA, in 2015.

Appendix

Growing List of AI Regulations around World

Americas

- United States of America (USA), State-by-State Artificial Intelligence Legislation Tracker, the Chamber of Commerce, 2022, https://www.uschamber.com/technology/state-by-state-artificial-intelligence-legislation-tracker

USA, State of State Legislation on Artificial Intelligence, Centers of inclusive Change, 2022, https://www.inclusivechange.org/ai-governance-solutions

USA, Trends in biometric information regulation in the USA, 2022, https://www.adalovelaceinstitute.org/blog/biometrics-regulation-usa/

USA, Recent Developments in Artificial Intelligence Cases, American Bar Association, 2021, https://businesslawtoday.org/2021/06/recent-developments-in-artificial-intelligence-cases/

Canada, Canada introduces new federal privacy and AI legislation, IAPP, 2022, https://iapp.org/news/a/canada-introduces-new-federal-privacy-and-ai-legislation/

Asia

- China's AI regulation, Blankrome, 2022, https://www.blankrome.com/publications/chinas-regulation-internet-recommender-systems-what-us-companies-should-know

Europe

- European Union (EU), The AI Act, the proposed bill to regulate AI in the EU, 2022, https://artificialintelligenceact.eu/

EU, Risto Uuk, The EU AI Act Newsletter, Future of Life Institute, https://artificialintelligenceact.substack.com/

United Kingdom (UK), AI, machine learning & big data laws and regulations, 2022, https://www.cms-lawnow.com/ealerts/2022/05/ai-machine-learning-big-data-laws-and-regulations-2022

UK, UK rejects EU approach to artificial intelligence in favour of 'pro-innovation' policy, Science Business, 2022, https://sciencebusiness.net/news/uk-rejects-eu-approach-artificial-intelligence-favour-pro-innovation-policy

Global

- Mapping AI governance, a database of national AI governance efforts around the world by Nesta, https://www.nesta.org.uk/data-visualisation-and-interactive/mapping-ai-governance/

A review of AI policies and practices in 50 countries, Center for AI and Digital Policy, 2020, https://www.caidp.org/reports/aidv-2020/

Ignacio González Royo, privacy and AI laws in the US and the EU, Meitar Law Offices, https://cdn-media.web-view.net/i/axteeushww/IP.pdf

References

1. Chambers DW. How to make moral choices. J Am Coll Dent. 2011;78(4):56–63. PMID: 22416620.
2. McCarthy J. What is artificial intelligence? Stanford University. 2007. http://wwwformal.stanford.edu/jmc/whatisai.pdf.
3. Fedorko R, Kráľ Š, Bačík R. Artificial intelligence in E-commerce: a literature review. In: Saraswat M, Sharma H, Balachandran K, Kim JH, Bansal JC, editors. Congress on intelligent systems. Lecture notes on data engineering and communications technologies, vol 111. Singapore: Springer; 2022. https://doi.org/10.1007/978-981-16-9113-3_50.
4. Samoili S, Lopez Cobo M, Gomez Gutierrez E, De Prato G, Martinez-Plumed F, Delipetrev B. AI WATCH. Defining artificial intelligence. Luxembourg: EUR 30117 EN, Publications Office of the European Union; 2020. ISBN 978-92-76-17045-7 (online). https://doi.org/10.2760/382730 (online), JRC118163.
5. Früh A, Haux D. Foundations of artificial intelligence and machine learning. (Weizenbaum Series, 29). Berlin: Weizenbaum Institute for the Networked Society—The German Internet Institute; 2022. https://doi.org/10.34669/WI.WS/29.
6. Simply Learn (SL). AI applications: Top 14 artificial intelligence applications in 2023. 2022. https://www.simplilearn.com/tutorials/artificial-intelligence-tutorial/artificial-intelligence-applications.
7. Smith W. AI is not robots, but it can make us smarter than we might otherwise be, Data Driven Investor, May 15, 2019. https://medium.datadriveninvestor.com/ai-is-not-robots-3228f27e1f84.
8. UNESCO, draft text of recommendation on the ethics of AI, SHS/IGM-AIETHICS/2021/JUN/3 Rev.225 June 2021. https://unesdoc.unesco.org/ark:/48223/pf0000377897.
9. Choudhury S, Deb AK, Mukherjee J. Designing deception in adversarial reinforcement learning. 2011. https://citeseerx.ist.psu.edu/document?repid=rep1&type=pdf&doi=b6bd550d5e8859e34fa55460d32015e9847c22e5.
10. Anderson J, Rainie L, Cohn S. Pew Research Center, December, 2018. Artificial intelligence and the future of humans. https://www.pewresearch.org/internet/2018/12/10/artificial-intelligence-and-the-future-of-humans/.
11. DeCosmo L, Google Engineer claims AI Chatbot is sentient: Why that matters, is it possible for an artificial intelligence to be sentient?, Artificial Intelligence, Scientific American, July 12, 2022. https://www.scientificamerican.com/article/google-engineer-claims-ai-chatbot-is-sentient-why-that-matters/.
12. Bishop JM. Artificial intelligence is stupid and causal reasoning will not fix it. Front Psychol. 2021;11:513474. https://doi.org/10.3389/fpsyg.2020.513474.
13. Gill. The role of the United Nations in addressing emerging technologies in the area of Lethal Autonomous Weapons Systems. 2020. https://www.un.org/en/un-chronicle/role-united-nations-addressing-emerging-technologies-area-lethal-autonomous-weapons.
14. Comiter M. Attacking artificial intelligence AI's security vulnerability and what policymakers can do about it. Harvard Kennedy School, Belfer Center for Science and International Affairs. 2019. https://www.belfercenter.org/sites/default/files/2019-08/AttackingAI/AttackingAI.pdf.
15. Mangla U, et al. What you cannot miss in any AI implementation: fairness, May 2021. https://lfaidata.foundation/blog/2021/05/19/what-you-cannot-miss-in-any-ai-implementation-fairness/.
16. Jobin A, Ienca M, Vayena E. The global landscape of AI ethics guidelines. Nat Mach Intell. 2019;1:389–99. https://doi.org/10.1038/s42256-019-0088-2.
17. Astobiza AM, et al. AI ethics for sustainable development goals. IEEE Technol Soc Mag. 2021;40(2):66–71. https://doi.org/10.1109/MTS.2021.3056294.
18. Hogenhout L. A framework for ethical AI at the United Nations, Unite Paper 2021(1). https://unite.un.org/news/unitepaper-framework-ethical-ai-united-nations.
19. WHO (World Health Organization). Ethics and governance of artificial intelligence for health: WHO guidance. Geneva: World Health Organization; 2021. License: CC BY-NC-SA 3.0 IGO. https://www.who.int/publications/i/item/9789240029200.

20. Fjeld J, Achten N, Hilligoss H, Nagy A, Srikumar M. Principled artificial intelligence: mapping consensus in ethical and rights-based approaches to principles for AI (January 15, 2020). Berkman Klein Center Research Publication No. 2020-1. https://doi.org/10.2139/ssrn.3518482.
21. Sand M, et al. Responsibility beyond design: physicians requirements for ethical medical AI. 2021. https://onlinelibrary.wiley.com/doi/full/10.1111/bioe.12887.
22. Leslie D, Burr C, Aitken M, Cowls J, Katell M, Briggs M. Artificial intelligence, human rights, democracy, and the rule of law: a primer. The Council of Europe, The Alan Turing Institute; 2021. https://www.turing.ac.uk/sites/default/files/2021-03/cahai_feasibility_study_primer_final.pdf
23. European Parliamentary Research Service (EPRS). STUDY Panel for the future of science and technology, artificial intelligence in healthcare, Jun 2022. PE 729.512 ISBN: 978-92-846-9456-3. https://doi.org/10.2861/568473. QA-07-22-328-EN-N. https://www.europarl.europa.eu/RegData/etudes/STUD/2022/729512/EPRS_STU(2022)729512_EN.pdf.
24. Rosenstrauch D, Mangla U, Gupta A. Edge how AI can transform healthcare management. American College of Healthcare Executives; 2022. https://www.ache.org/blog/2022/how-ai-can-transform-healthcare-management
25. Raine L, et al. Experts doubt ethical AI design will be broadly adopted as the norm within the next decade. Pew Research Center, June 16, 2021. Experts Doubt Ethical AI Design Will Be Broadly Adopted as the Norm Within the Next Decade | Pew Research Center.
26. Durmus M. The AI thought book. 2021. https://www.amazon.com/dp/B08Z4BWN1X?asin=B08Z4BWN1X&revisionId=f771d9c8&format=1&depth=1.

Correction to: Artificial Intelligence and Ethics

Doreen Rosenstrauch, Utpal Mangla, Atul Gupta, and Costansia Taikwa Masau

**Correction to: Chapter 16 in: Arlen Meyers (ed.),
Digital Health Entrepreneurship,
https://doi.org/10.1007/978-3-031-33902-8_16**

The previous version of Chapter 16 was inadvertently published with the editor's name included as one of the authors. Chapter 16 has now been corrected with correct authors as follows: Doreen Rosenstrauch, Utpal Mangla, Atul Gupta and Costansia Taikwa Masau.

The updated version of this chapter can be found at https://doi.org/10.1007/978-3-031-33902-8_16

Index